Transportation Management

A Practical Handbook

Jim Hendrickson

Heartland Professional Services
3830 Saddlebrook Court Suite 1570
Columbus, Ohio, USA

ISBN 978-0-578-51394-2

Dedication

I want to start by thanking my parents, Jim and Judy who have always encouraged me to live my dreams. To my sisters and brother, Laura, Susan, and Scott for all your support, encouragement, and camaraderie. You all make me so proud to be a part of our family.

To Sam Starr, a dear friend, mentor, and "big brother" who I lost way too soon. You pushed me further than anyone else ever had but never let me break. You were pivotal in helping me to be the professional I am, and I miss you every day.

To our three children, James, Joseph, and Emma, thank you for your support, your encouragement, and you're never ending reminder that I'm never too old to try new things. It's an amazing experience to see your children grow into adults and have the chance to develop an new dimension of relationship with them and we have done that. Thanks for the advice and counsel!

To Walter Zinn, my friend, mentor, and first Department Chair. You me not only helped figure out how to transition to an academic environment, you paved the way. Making you proud of my work has always driven me.

To Tom Goldsby willing to be the mentor of a new member of the faculty and then became my boss. Your support, advice and counsel, and understanding allowed me to continue my dream. Likewise, To Michelle Anderson who has always been there and kept my feet to the fire to finish this book. You are a great partner and support!

None of this, however, could have been remotely possible without the love, support, and encouragement of my wife, Leann. For the last 35 years you have been my muse, my best friend and my confidant. None of it would matter without you, my "My Heart".

TABLE OF CONTENTS

Table of Contents

This page is intentionally left blank.

Preface

I never desired to write a book until I spent time at the university. I am generally skeptical about books, especially the ones who tout "the next big thing". I don't believe that anything in supply chain can be called "definitive" today because of the pace of change, the ongoing need for new processes, new metrics, and new technology and the global extent to which companies have both needs and opportunities.

As a Senior Lecturer, my job is to teach and help build the next generation and take that mission seriously. Over the last five years I have tried to build a course where students, upon completion of it, could hit the ground running with their career in logistics. I've tried to create a "this is really how it's done" kind with high practicality and a good dose of reality.

Each year, I found I hadn't yet accomplished my mission to the level I wanted, so I would find more to add, more to do. About three years ago, I changed the format of the course and spent half the course in lecture and the other half in very practical exercises that teach students how to build transportation networks, evaluate and build loads, rather them, and create orders for transportation carriers. The exercises are not simple or intuitive but through doing them, the students learn and excel. I got feedback from both students and employers this made a difference, so I have continued to work to perfect it.

The lectures have got faster and faster even with more complex material so we can keep the second half of the class intact. In the 2018-2019 school year, many of my students asked if a book went with the course material because the pace was so fast, they thought that having a book would help. I thought about this for a few months and then decided they were right. I needed to provide a book on transportation from the real-world perspective.

And so, I have created this work based on industry standards, conversations with hundreds of companies over the last decade, ongoing research and conversations with logistics and commercial manufacturers and retailers, and my experience both in industry and in my consultancy.

It has become a work of passion for me and I hope it does the job I intend it to do. It will be my core academic book, but this is also very relevant to people who work with transportation but have no real experience. This can help start you on the road to knowledge.

INTRODUCTION

Transportation has become the key link the in the supply chain over the last 30 years. Before 1990, transportation was an important part of the supply chain that linked manufacturing to distribution and to customers. Using transportation during this period differed greatly from today. Transportation back then was typically done by moving masses amounts of goods between storage sites, warehousing and distribution, using a production method built for mass markets and mass consumption. Back then, inventory was king. Inventory is an asset in business and therefore has balance sheet value. Transportation is a necessary expense to generate revenue.

During the 1990s, companies realized that having a large of amount of inventory on their balance sheet wasn't very efficient due to the concept of carrying costs. Carrying costs are the costs associated with holding and managing inventory to ensure it is correctly counted, not damaged, not stolen or lost, and not unusable (obsolete). Industry experts then and today compute the average carrying cost of inventory to be around 20 – 25% of the value of the inventory itself.

To understand this better, let's make a comparison. Let's say you were home shopping and found the deal of a lifetime. Someone had a 5,000 square foot home next to the ocean available for sale for $300,000 while other homes had an average price of $600,000. You research the home and realize it has the same insurance and liability costs of the more expensive homes. You inspect the home and find nothing wrong that would account for the value difference. You compute your monthly mortgage and realize it is only $1,600 compared to the over $3,200 the others would pay. Then, in looking at the deed, you find there is an arbitrary 25% payment per year based on the value of the principal of the home and this 25% payment goes through the entire life of the loan. The other homes do not have this and when you compute the additional cost you discover the monthly cost for that is $6,250 per month! Then, when you compute the cost for the $300,000 house it comes to about $7,850 per month over double what the $600,000 homes would cost.

In the very strange example above, we find that paying 25% per year for the 'privilege' of owning an asset doesn't make sense. That is what most global businesses figured out in the 1990's. They were paying a very large cost for the privilege of holding much more inventory than they needed at any point in their business cycle.

Coincident to this realization was the release of an advanced automation capability referred to as the Enterprise Resource planning, or ERP system. The ERP system was one of the most comprehensive pieces of technology ever built to manage a business. Its core function was helping manufacturing companies determine inventory, production, and finished goods levels that helped drive efficiency in the business. It also included critical functions like the company's financials, fixed asset management, inventory management and production management. Later it would add human resources management and more.

These systems were complex and expensive but through the 1990's and into the turn of the century, consulting companies, education programs, and others helped people to learn how to effectively plan, implement and operate these systems. One of the principal results of these systems was the ability to classify inventory based on criticality and usage and to manage the sourcing and delivery more aggressively.

During this time companies sought to reduce their inventory levels dramatically by embracing new concepts in manufacturing based on the studies and principals of W. Edwards Deming used to help build the Japanese manufacturing economy after World War II. Deming's principles of quality and statistical analysis gave birth to what we think of as lean, or "just-in-time" manufacturing today.

The hallmark of just-in-time manufacturing is a dramatically reduced inventory base that arrives "just-in-time" to be transformed from a raw material into a finished good. Companies that have embraced this approach have found they produce higher quality products at a much lower cost. This had had been considered almost impossible before the development of lean principles.

The key to this new way of operating was transportation. In lean principles, we replace high inventory levels that are static, i.e. stored, to rolling inventory on trucks, rail cars, ships and shipping containers and on airplanes. Companies order just what they need for a much shorter production schedule, typically 2 – 5 days, and rely on transportation to be the conduit to ensuring supply is available constantly.

Because of this, business dramatically reduced the number of warehouses and distribution centers and the resulting held inventory with transportation under constant movement.

Today, transportation drives the supply chain; no pun intended. Every element of the supply chain is critical to successful business operations and consumer satisfaction.

Transportation's role has evolved since 1990 to where today, transportation is part of customer satisfaction for customer direct delivery using parcel or Less Than Truckload (LTL) shipment methods. It is a critical link in the movement of raw material to the factory especially in lean manufacturing where the average factory is carrying just a few days of inventory rather than months like it did.

In this book, we walk through all the major aspects of modern transportation management to give the reader a keen understanding of what transportation is, why it works the way it does, and how it affects businesses locally and globally. In addition, we provide the language of transportation throughout as we explore modern transportation. Understanding the language is almost as important as understanding how transportation works because much of the language is built to connote very specific meaning. For instance, in business and the supply chain, we revenue producing event is the 'order'. An order is customer's commitment to buy a specific product in a specific quantity and at a specific price. It also includes an element of delivery which defines exactly when the product is supposed to be provided.

The core role of transportation is taking completed orders and sending them to buyer. When we "order" transportation, we do so by exciting a transportation "tender", which is often called tendering a load. If we order transportation using such a strange word, why not just call it a transportation order. We call the transportation order a tender to ensure we do not confuse it with the customer order. By doing this we create more purposeful communication. Take for example the following question:

"Do you have an order status"? If we did not differentiate the two, we might be talking about the customer's order or someone might be inquiring whether we've received confirmation of transportation order. Here, "Do you have an order status" means the customer order because if it was transportation related, we would ask "Do you have the tender status?"

While this is a small example, transportation's role, influence, and impact in the global supply chain is critical to the success of the supply chain. In this book, you'll learn the keys to why it is so critical and how it embraces that role.

CHAPTER 1: HISTORY AND OVERIVEW

INTRODUCTION

In this chapter, we will begin our study of transportation by understanding how transportation has evolved globally and specifically in the US to create the transportation environment we have today. We will then look at some foundations of transportation and shipping. The first will an examination of landed cost. Landed Cost is a critical element of any shipping situation in terms of the impact of cost on the product and the ultimate consumer. From there, we'll move to a brief discussion of the modes of transportation which will be covered extensively in PART II of this book. We will then discuss the trade-off decisions we make in transportation based on the freight, the specific situation and the need to satisfy customers while keeping overall costs down. This section will highlight why we choose one mode of transportation over another. We'll complete this chapter with an analysis of a specific transportation problem along with two examples that show these trade-offs.

MILESTONES IN US TRANSPORTATION

Transportation is not new. The wheel, the first boats and the first domesticated animals for used in transportation were invented and developed over 5,500 year ago. The first road networks were believed to have been created by the Roman Empire around the first century A.D. The steam boat came on the scene around 1780 and was quickly followed by the steam engine that would launch the rail industry around 1800. The internal combustion engine would follow about 100 years later giving birth to the basics of modern transportation. Similarly, flight came on the scene about the same time. The eras of the 1700's to today have seen exponential invention of ideas and capabilities that have yielded the transportation capabilities in this modern world.

There are several milestones we experienced in the United States of America's (USA) transportation infrastructure that specifically affected the development of infrastructure and use of transportation including:

- **1825:** The opening of the Eerie Canal that enabled trade through the St. Lawrence Seaway and the US and Canadian Great Lakes.

- **1866:** The Intercontinental Railway is complete enabling rail to move virtually anything across the entire US.

- **1887:** The government determines that, based on the practices of the rail industry, it must create <u>regulations</u> that create legal and illegal practices and rules that ensure transportation does not take advantage of the country's citizens and businesses.

- **1903:** The first <u>airplane flight</u> in the US opens the door to what will become the airline industry a part of which is the air freight industry.

- **1904:** The <u>Panama Canal</u> opens dramatically reducing the time and potential dangers of moving goods from the Asian and Australian regions to ports in the Gulf of Mexico and the eastern ports in the US.

- **1941:** <u>US enters World War II</u> and focuses its economic power to training soldiers, creating weapons and materials to fight the war and in shipping the soldiers, material and ongoing replenishment of suppliers to the European and Asian theatres. Doing so required dramatic changes, innovations, and inventions in transportation.

- **1956:** President Eisenhower signs the Federal-Aid Highway Act of 1956 creating the first <u>Interstate Highways</u> to ensure the country could defend all of its borders rapidly if invasion occurs. The impact of the infrastructure was wide ranging from dramatically improving the abilities of truck transportation to changing the fabric of society.

- **1980:** The government <u>deregulates transportation</u> in the US by eliminating their practices of controlling prices, establishing an oligopoly of five rail companies and freeing all modes (air, ship, rail, truck, and pipeline) to pricing based on the competitive free markets.

- **2003:** Creation of the <u>Department of Homeland Security (DHS)</u>. After the tragedy called 9/11 which occurred on September 9, 2001, the government created the Department of Homeland Security initiating the Transportation Security Administration (TSA) to focus on protecting and securing commercial air transit from terrorism. Today, besides the TSA, Immigration and Naturalization Services (INS), Federal Emergency Management Agency (FEMA) and the US Secret Service, DHS also includes important agencies involved in trade, trade security and global transportation including the US Customs and the Coast Guard. The Coast Guard is attached to DHS during times of peace but move back to the Department of Defense (DOD) in times of war against US borders.

The US is not that different from the rest of the world when thinking about the development and evolution of transportation. An entire book could be written just on the key milestones in transportation of the countries around the world. Regardless of the milestones, history has provided virtually the same set of foundational capabilities to all countries over time fundamental to global shipping.

THE CONCEPT OF LANDED COST

At the heart of any physical supply chain is the products created and sold to create revenue and profit. Many costs go into a product from its design, the bill of material that describes every component part of the product, the manufacturing cost, packing cost, warehousing, and distribution costs, corporate overhead costs and transportation costs. Mostly, companies can calculate and allocate these costs into the cost of the product. In most systems, the revenue, or the aggregate of the company's sales, is immediately offset by the cost of goods sold, an accounting term that describes all the direct costs of the product. Transportation is an allocated cost that takes the total cost of transportation and applies it to the cost of goods sold. At a macro level this is fine. However, it's critical to understand that transportation costs are variable costs related to each load of goods shipped and delivered. Unlike material costs or production and warehousing costs, the cost of transportation as a unit cost varies greatly based on the point of origin and delivery, the distance from that point of pick up to the destination and any costs charged to the shipment based on factors like taxes, import and export fees and others. The understanding of the actual cost impact of transportation to the consumer is called landed cost.

As defined, landed cost is the final cost to the consumer and includes the price of the product itself plus the cost of transportation to get it to that consumer and any additional fees incurred in that transportation process; most typically taxes and other fees.

On a domestic (intra-country) basis, this is a relatively straight forward proposition, especially when taken at a true consumer level. Take an eCommerce buyer as an example. The online buy chooses a product and then sees any taxes charged along with any transportation cost associated with the shipment of the product to them. They have high transparency in the buying process and are certain they know what the total cost will be when they pay at the end of the buying transaction. If the consumer is paying for transportation, that cost will be immediately apparent and part of the purchase price; hence the landed cost is easy to see. If the shipping is free to the consumer, the landed cost does not include a specific transportation cost, but it included in the overall cost to the consumer either in the product cost or as a reduction in gross profit to the company.

In an international environment, this is very different today. For instance, let's assume someone in Columbus, Ohio wanted to ship a guitar in a case to Salzburg, Austria. To do so requires understanding the two locations and a tariff code, which, after finding a site, looking it up and making several mistakes, is 920209. When complete, I find a shipping cost of $821.37 and a three-day shipping time by air. The cost is high due to the unusual size of the package. If it were 12 inches by 12 inches by 12 inches tall parcel weighing ten points (kind of the standard for parcel shipping) it would only cost $321.00. I know these numbers seem outrageous and they are. It underscores the complexities of shipping internationally along with the cost primarily based on inefficiency based on lack of infrastructure, visibility, and coordination.

When considering shipments between international locations, it's important to understand that not all customs charges are known and included in the basic shipping costs. We stated earlier that the <u>landed cost equals the cost of the product, the transportation cost and other fees.</u> It's in these "other" fees we get obscured from the true cost. Let's look at a few international shipping examples to understand this well. At the heart of landed cost for international shipping is customs entry process. When shipping internationally, especially from the US, there will be several carriers involved in the transaction and they might include national carriers US citizens understand like UPS or Fedex. Regardless of the approach, when it gets to the country of destination, on its way to the consumer who lives in that country, it must pass through customs. We'll deal specifically with customs later on I, but for now, let's recognize that once a product enters customs it will go through evaluations to determine whether the goods are allowed in the country, what additional duties and taxes may apply to the cost and what other fees may be associated with it. Up to this point, the landed cost has included:

1. The cost of the product at the retail price to the consumer

2. The transportation cost to ship the product to the customs destination and the expected cost of domestic shipment to the customer

3. Any fees we will incur in Customs.

Customs will determine which fees may be incurred by using the <u>Harmonized Tariff Code.</u> These codes are 8 to 10 number in length and defines the product category for the good being received, the first characters are universal but the last few characters are specific between the shipping and receiving countries and represent any tariff costs associated with the trade policies between these two countries. Fees will be charged for duties if they exceed the *de minimis* value of the receiving country which vary widely. In the US, the de minimis value is $800 but it can be much lower like in Canada where the value is $20 CAD.

Besides the customs duties there are also international tax rates that may apply and the customs office may charge a flat processing fee to clear and enter their country.

Companies that ship internationally regularly work with third parties to understand the various fees and duties to ensure their shipping cost to the consumer covers everything needed. International eCommerce buyers are wary of these additional fees and if they encounter a site that doesn't provide a good, transparent view of these, they abandon the transaction. Research done by PayPal has revealed that Canadian buyers will abandon the transaction 42% of the time if the other fees like taxes and duties are not clear. This is most likely learned behavior from previous buying experiences where the buy was surprised by fees they had to pay out of pocket because Canada's *de minimis* values are so low.

The good news about landed cost is there are third party software and service providers that help business to stay on top of and ensure their landed cost to the consumer is correct. For most large B2B shipments in manufacturing and retail, the process is more transparent and it's easier to know the costs because these companies are constantly shipping and have both in-house and third party support and expertise in these critical shipments.

TRANSPORTATION SERVICES MARKET

What Functions provide transportation services and who does them? This is an important question to answer at the outset of understanding transportation. For our purposes, we will look at the broad transportation services market to understand the key functions, types of companies, and roles that people play in management and executing transportation worldwide. There are two broad categories of companies that make up the transportation services market.

The first are <u>transportation carriers</u>. Transportation carriers are companies whose sole purpose of business is to move freight between origination and destination points. They are the meat of the industry and the reason everything else happens. Shippers often work directly with transportation carriers to coordinate their shipments of freight all over the world. There are different ways we look at transportation carrier and we'll explore those more when we get into the transportation modes section. We'll discuss these transportation modes and some of their characteristics in this chapter and much more as we explore each mode separately.

The second category we will discuss are <u>Transportation Service Providers (TSPs)</u>. TSPs are a set of companies and services used to support the planning, operations, and execution of transportation as part of day to day business. The roles of these companies may overlap or be very different from each other. They are specialized because of the support work needed will be covered in depth later in the book.

These two categories make up the entire market. Figure 1 provides a snapshot of the market. Carriers, which are the most common form of an outsourced service in transportation make up about 55% of the entire market with the other TSPs making up the rest (45%). One will notice that some transportation roles are much more specialized and have

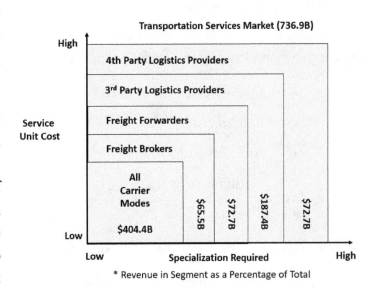

Figure 1. Transportation Services Market

a much higher cost per unit of service than others. Part of this related to the advanced specialization needed to provide non-carrier-based transportation services.

WHAT DOES LOGISTICS COST?

The cost for logistics of any company is directly related to amount of goods they produce and hold in inventory, the approach to distribution and warehousing, the modes use, and the transportation required, and the management of the payment of transportation through capabilities like freight audits and other means to ensure carrier compliance. Generally, companies spend between 8 and 15% of their revenue on logistics costs. Of this, the bulk of the spending will either be related to inventory, warehouse, and distribution management, or transportation management. Companies that use a traditional "Make-to-Stock" method of production will carry large amounts of raw and finished goods inventory and can often use cheaper, bulk transportation modes like rail rather than requiring other more flexible modes, like trucking. Because of this, companies very efficient at this production model will find that 55-70% of the logistics spend of these companies will be related to inventory and distribution with 30-45% being related to transportation.

For companies in a "just-in-time" production model will be having low raw material inventory costs and faster distribution of finished goods in the just-in-time model. Because of this, companies very effective at this production model will find that 75-80% of their costs will be transportation related where 20-25% will be related to inventory and distribution costs.

TRANSPORTATION MODES

There are many ways we transport goods domestically and internationally. When we think of the different transportation carriers, we define them in "modes":

- Motor Carriers, or Truck Transport
- Rail Carriers
- Airlines and Air Carriers
- Maritime Shipping
- Pipelines

There are a few immediate notes to make about these modes:

- Pipelines are the most specialized mode. As we will see when we cover modes in more depth, the pipeline mode is not a mode available to move goods to the general public. Because of this, I look at the pipeline mode as a private mode of transportation and while its value is high as a mode for those who use it, most cannot use it

- The two modes used for continental to continental transportation are air and maritime. Interesting, air is the most expensive mode and maritime is one of the cheapest suggesting that goods going internationally can be very expensive, but shipped quickly, or slow, and cheaply

- Maritime, as a mode, has the most diversity of shipping styles. Maritime includes river shippers, lake shippers, coastal shippers and intercontinental shippers

- Motor Carriers, or trucking, has the most flexibility of any mode of transportation and is involved, at some point, in over 80% of all shipments

- Rail, as a mode, has limited competition from other railroads but has very strong completion from other modes

The goal of understanding modes of transportation lies in understanding their role in transportation along with the individual mode characteristics that drive differentiation and competition.

Every mode of transportation has something that it is good at. For some, carrying extreme amounts of volume and weight at one time at a low price creates a competitive advantage. For others, unparalleled speed makes the difference. Flexibility, too, plays a key role in the trade-off decisions of modes.

Table 1 shows a brief depiction of the transportation modes and their key areas of differentiation. In it, we evaluate the characteristics of weight (the more a mode can carry at one time, the higher the score), time (the faster the delivery the higher the score), flexibility (the greater the ability to deliver to many locations with different solutions the higher the score), and value, the more value the mode carries, the higher the score).

Transportation Mode	Weight Moved	Time in Transit	Flexibility	Goods Value
Truck	5	7	9	8
Rail	10	4	5	6
Air	4	10	9	10
Maritime	10	3	5	6
Pipeline	5	2	1	2

Table 1. Comparing Various Modes of Transportation

In looking at Table 1, one might assume the pipeline mode is not that effective. Remember the lower scores are directly related to its limitations in the customers the pipeline mode serves. For oil, gas, and chemicals, the pipeline is a superior solution, but it is so highly specialized, it does not do well against those with more common carrier capabilities.

It should be clear that air and truck are favored in areas like time, flexibility and value. This makes sense for air as it is the fastest mode of transportation, it has reasonable flexibility, to the airport, and it carries high value, low weight goods. Maritime and rail, by far, can carry the most weight. This is a key differentiator. With rail, however, it also has flexibility in that it can provide straight rail that can move 1,000's of tons at a time or intermodal rail which uses shipping containers to move higher value goods; like consumer goods. While maritime can do this, it does so with less flexibility.

Finally, notice that the truck mode has relatively high scores across all characteristics. This is one reason trucks are considered 'work horse' in transportation. It can quickly adapt its mission to many situations and only high movement of mass weight limits its abilities.

THE CONCEPT OF SORTATION AND "BREAK-BULK"

Throughout the book we will discuss operations wherein freight loads arrive in bulk, are sorted, and then re-configured into new freight loads bound for different destinations. We will see some example of this in almost every mode of transportation especially when dealing with many points of origin and many points of destination. While we'll cover this in more detail in the book, a simple analogy hopefully will provide the reader a conceptual idea of the value and need in moving goods through transportation. Every day there are about 2.6 million passengers that board airplanes bound for another location. Let's say 40% of these are direct flights where the passenger boards the plan at their home airport and travels directly to their destination. That leaves, 1,560,000 passengers that must have at least one connecting flight before they reach their destination.

Aunt Mary is travelling from San Antonio Texas to Spokane Washington to see her sister's newborn baby. To do this, she leaves the San Antonio airport with about ninety-six people and flies to Dallas. She is so excited that to keep her occupied she memorizes the faces of everyone on board. She has a gift for remembering faces. When she gets to Dallas, she lands in Concourse A at gate 27. She must now finder her way to Concourse B, gate 12. She notices the airport in Dallas is crowded with thousands of passengers. As she finds her way to the tram and then travels to the B Concourse, she notices about twenty people on the tram on her flight. "How interesting", she thinks, "I wonder where they are all going". As she gets to Concourse B, she then gates 12. This flight is taking her from Dallas to Seattle Washington. The gate has over 250 people waiting for their flight. She looks around and even though she saw twenty people on the tram, she only sees four apparently going to Seattle. "I guess the other fifteen are going somewhere", she thinks as she looks around and sees over 30 gates in the Concourse. Shortly, the flight boards and she has a relaxing trip to Seattle enjoying both the snack and beverage provided. Like always, she memorizes all 250 people on the flight. It helps pass the time on the flight.

When she arrives in Seattle, she still has one more flight to get to Spokane Washington. She sees she landed in Concourse A gate thirty-two and needs to get to Concourse B gate 3. She moves quickly because it's a tight connection. This time she walks to the gate and notices hundreds of people passing her. When she arrives at her gate, she notices there is also a passenger from the Dallas flight that must be going to Spokane too because she sees her sitting at the gate. She sees no one from San Antonio. She sits next to the woman and says, "Didn't I see you on the Dallas flight I just came in on?" The woman replies she had been on the flight and they make introductions and have a nice chat and sat together on the Seattle to Spokane flight. They arrive safely in Spokane and both women walk together to baggage claim where Aunt Mary sees her sister waiting for her with the newborn girl in her arms. She's glad she took the flight even if it did mean two connections and four airports!

What you just read happens millions of times a day, although not so much the face recognition but the part about connecting flights. This is sortation and break-bulk. Often freight that starts together of original has many ultimate destinations. Like passengers coming in on an inbound flight, freight comes into a facility to be sorted and combined with like freight going to the NEXT destination and then is loaded for that destination. When it arrives, it is again sorted and combined with like freight going to the NEXT destination and so on until the freight arrives at its ultimate destination. This is a core principal in transportation logistics. There are some freight loads that will have one point of origin and one destination in most modes. There is also freight that will come from many origins to many destinations. Regardless of location and methods, freight transportation develops transportation networks that serve both approaches and often uses different kind of freight handling terminals to enable the sortation and break-bulk needed to keep the movement efficient.

THE CONCEPT OF PRIVATE VERSUS COMMON CARRIER

Private or Common Carrier

A final area of understanding that will apply to all modes is whether the carrier in the mode is a private or public, e.g. common carrier. Private carriers are typically fleets owned by a private company who use these vehicles as part of their company operations exclusively and are not available to move goods for others. This may include larger or grocery retailers that operate their own trucks for delivery within their own network. It can include route-based trucks for soda, bread, and other perishables. It also includes all the service trucks operated by telecommunications and utility companies as part of doing their job. The difference here is that no carriers will accept loads from the general public. This is an important distinction to regulators and once a company defines itself as public or private, it must operate in that mode and cannot cross over between private and common.

Common carriers are commercial vehicles available to move anyone's freight. Like private carriers, this is an important distinction. Common carriers have Operating Authority by the US Department of Transportation to carry commercial freight and receive compensation for it. Carriers have areas of service in which they operate and, generally, must provide rates and haul freight, when the rate is accepted by the customer, if the freight is in or going into a service area. Common carriers must rate and carry commercial freight and their general rates must be consistent across similar customer segments and situations. If they are not, they could be subject to antitrust violations due to price discrimination.

SUMMARY

Transportation is not a new industry but many ways we use transportation today is very new compared to 20 years ago. Domestic transportation is considered predictable, stable, and very effective in most global economies. International transportation has elements of stability and predictability, especially when considering the movement of goods through intercontinental shipping, but the cross-border processes, including those that involve landed cost, are still relatively new and brittle. In the next chapter, we will pull back the layers of transportation by looking at the regulatory environments that govern transportation.

CHAPTER 2: TRANSPORTATION REGULATION

INTRODUCTION

Regulation is a part of many businesses. Transportation, as an industry, is a heavily regulated industry in the US. The Mercatus Center at George Mason University characterizes the number of regulatory restrictions various industries by capturing regulation by NAICS codes. In Table 2[1], we find the following core industries and their related scores for the five most regulated industries:

Industry	"Score"	Rank
Agriculture, Fishing, Hunting NAICS 11	26,314	5
Manufacturing – oil, gas, coal NAICS 324 / 325	56,580	2
Transportation Equipment NAICS 336	34,370	4
Transportation NAICS 48/49	**59,244**	**1**
Financial Services NAIC 52	44,490	3

Table 2. Regulation by NAICS Codes

From the table we see that the transportation industry is one of the most regulated industries in the US closely behind oil, gas, and coal. Regulating transportation began in the late 1800's and went through several eras before becoming what today. One might wonder why the transportation industry is so heavily regulated. As we'll see in this chapter, the answer to that question is based on the government's view of their need to influence the transportation industry in the areas of economic, social, and antitrust behavior. There is little in this world that transportation doesn't touch. Because of this the need for public trust and fairness in transportation is critical to economic growth, safety, and security.

This begs the question, what gives a government the authority to regulate? There are many ongoing debates as to whether the government has this right, but it doesn't stop it from creating regulation over industries, so we accept the governments right to regulate as part of our daily life. Governments regulate an industry to ensure it operates in the best interests of the public. This typically involves scrutiny related to how the industry charges and the rates it charges to different groups, safety issues, issues of security and control of the industry's output, and environmental needs. The government also recognizes that creating monopolies (one company controlling an industry) is never in the public interest.

---

[1] https://www.mercatus.org/tags/regulation

A more substantial question is the regulatory rights between the federal US Government and the State US governments. With over three million truck drivers in the US, one can imagine focused interest in the potential value of taxation and other federal and state revenue producing activities like inspections, permits, licensure, and more. Similarly, some states are more "truck-friendly" than others. For instance, the Department of Transportation of each state sets the rules for time a patron can park and whether the rest area allows overnight parking. Only twelve states allow overnight parking at rest areas creating challenges for truck drivers when trying to find parking spaces. Truck stops help but are a limited solution. State troopers also vary by state in terms of their level of monitoring of trucks on highways and the severity of fines.

The Federal Government has precedence over all regulation for interpreting regulations between the US Department of Transportation (and other agencies) and the state's departments of transportation and public safety law enforcement. It's important to note there are certain checks and balances in place, more formal than others, which provide some interpretive license. For one, states may not make a federal regulation stricter. For instance, a federal hours of service regulation defines eleven hours as the maximum time a truck driver can operate their vehicle in any twenty-four hour period. A state could not adjust that to eight hours, for instance, because that would be making the regulation stricter. They also wouldn't likely increase the eleven hours because, as a single state, it wouldn't make much sense or have much value.

Another way the Federal Government has leverage over states is through budget funding. One of the protected funding sources in transportation is the Department of Transportation (DOT) funds that come from the gasoline taxes and other taxes imposed in the interstate Highway System. The bulk of these funds are protected to maintain and improve roads. This includes interstates and also can be used for state roads. The government may, when it wants to exert pressure, withhold funds from states it deems in non-compliance with regulations.

If a federal regulation is passed it becomes law and that law applies to all fifty states and the District of Columbia. If a state law expressly conflicts with the federal law, the states must change or remove the law. Most often, regulation is written with this in mind, and the Federal Government covers what it believes to be the most critical compliance items and allow states some flexibility in interpreting it within its boundaries. The checks and balances help to allow states to tailor their regulations based on the circumstance in the state while still complying with federal law. An example of this checks and balances is found in the 1970's maximum speed limit laws (see inset).

Transportation regulations cover every kind, or mode, of transportation that exists: Truck, rail, ship, rail, and pipeline. Each mode has the potential for having unique needs or issues that drive the regulatory approach. Regardless of approach, governments will typically regulate three areas:

- Economic Regulation: Regulation that may be as restrictive as setting the maximum and minimum rates that a mode can charge (this is done in a regulated, versus deregulated government environment). It also covers taxation and usage fees which we'll discuss later in this chapter.

- Social Regulation: Social regulation is a catch-all for three specific areas: Safety, Security, and Environmental.

- Antitrust Regulation: This area of regulation seeks to ensure a fair competitive market and outlaws' monopolies and other non-competitive practices.

Besides restrictions on business and other practices through regulation, governments also provide public promotion. Public promotion is a process related to government investment and support to aid in development and ongoing needs of specific modes. We'll cover this in more detail later in the chapter.

DEVELOPMENT OF TRANSPORTATION REGULATION IN THE US

If we looked back a century to 1918, the US transportation regulatory environment would be unrecognizable from today. The biggest area of regulation developed was related antitrust and the rail industry and the government had thought little beyond that. The last century was the period in which the government went from controlling and regulating the industry to deregulating the industry. The journey from the first transportation regulation to today has created the issues, lessons, learnings, and philosophies that have led us to our situation of a deregulated industry. That journey from the first regulations to total deregulation took about one hundred years and spanned four key "eras" that shaped our transportation world today.

The Era of Initiation (1887 – 1920)

After the Civil War ended in 1865, the country busied itself with the reconstruction of the south and expansion west. By this time, railroads were the most modern and had the most carrying capacity of any other land based transportation approach. Rail was used extensively in the reconstruction and expansion, especially in tying together the west (now called the Midwest and including states like Iowa, Illinois, Indiana, and Ohio and more) with the eastern region of the US. This was time of great opportunity and saw some of the purest forms of capitalism in the US's history. From this era roses a few capitalists considered both "Captains of Industry" and "Robber Barons".

Is it possible that both terms would be applicable? To a degree, yes, but generally not like we would think. If we look at these men, given their accomplishments, it's difficult to not consider them some of the greatest entrepreneurs. Most came not from wealthy families and worked their way to the level of success they enjoyed. Most have left lasting legacies that include, among others, Stanford and Vanderbilt Universities, the Carnegie Mellon University and the many charitable foundations that last to today.

There was also another side of these that involved leveraging the lack regulation, or weak regulation, to exploit people through low wages, child labor, and unsafe conditions. They openly created monopolies and worked together, through collusion, to build themselves up while eliminating the competition. These practices were unethical, and some were even legal, kind of, but as there was a paucity of regulation much of what was done was, strictly speaking, legal. It was through the impact of the practices of these entrepreneurs that the Federal Government began to more aggressively drive industry regulations and transportation regulation than had been done.

As the railroads gained power, they used it to drive their interests. Westerners and rural areas were victims of rate discrimination, e.g. price discrimination. Two farms could be part of the same community and look almost identical, yet one would get rates to move their goods to market that allowed them to thrive while the other paid exorbitant fees and was often put out of business. A farmer's collective, called the Grange Movement, and brought their case to president, Glover Cleveland, and congress. The result was the Interstate Commerce Commission (ICC) which was found in 1887 and the Sherman Act of 1890 that made it illegal to own and operate a monopoly or to create one.

The ICC helped curb the unfair practices of the railroad. Shortly after its creation, the ICC published the first maximum rates that railroads could charge creating economic regulation that would curtail the abusive practices. By the late 1890's the major railroads sued and, due to their influence over state governments, won cases that severely limited the power of the ICC. Then congress stepped in with additional legislation that would ultimately giver the ICC the right and control over rate setting, safety standards, and extended the concept of transportation beyond railroads to include ships, bridges, ferries, and pipelines.

By 1920, the ICC oversaw a forced consolidation of railroads in the country to twenty-one regional railroads to help manage competition and rail business practices. The Transportation Act of 1920 would never get passed. The timing of the act and the work to create the regional railroads would come under fire due to the great depression and the subsequent world war. While this act never became law, it did create the concept ultimately used during deregulation to create five "class I" railroads for the country. The ICC would continue to be the primary regulator of transportation until after deregulation.

Besides basic regulations for economic and safety issues, the government also passed its first antitrust regulation. In the late 1800's the larger railroads consolidated smaller railroads into their system and used the size to drive more out of business. Similarly, other industries like oil and steel that had virtually become monopolies during this period. The Sherman Antitrust law was passed in 1890 to ensure that companies could not restrain trade or form a monopoly.

1914 the Clayton Act was passed which created the Federal Trade Commission (FTC) and gave it the power to oversee and approve mergers and acquisitions, along with price discrimination and tying contracts (see inset).

Era of Positive Regulation (1920 – 1935)

The Era of Positive Regulation continued the support of antitrust measures, especially for consumers and smaller businesses. It is also the era where we see significant government investment in creating a national infrastructure for transportation.

In 1936, the US Congress passed the Robinson-Patman Act which further strengthened price discrimination including protecting smaller businesses from large businesses providing discounts on prices that would cause the small business to be non-competitive. The most common issue was a product manufacturer providing a deep discount to a national chain store but not to a local merchant. Today, most corporations have very detailed policies on discounting, discount authority, and discount levels to ensure they comply.

During this era, the US road system expanded and the government put significant investment (public promotion) into building road infrastructure. In addition, the telecommunications industry would begin with radio broadcasts that could reach throughout the country. Early radio stations were often owned by large corporations who used the radio to promote products.

In addition to railroads, the government added roads and telecommunications to the ICC's areas of authority. With the 1927 stock market crash, the country fell into the worst depression in its history. With unemployment almost 25% by 1932, Franklin Delano Roosevelt (FDR) instituted his New Deal plan that dramatically increased government spending and debt while also growing the economy and reducing unemployment. Transportation was a major benefactor of the new deal through the public works projects. Over 11,000 road projects were completed during this period as were several major airports including New York's LaGuardia airport.

This was an era where investment in transportation as public promotion became a trend. <u>Public Promotion</u> is a policy whereby the government actively invests in segments of an industry. For transportation, public promotion flows from the country's DOT transportation Strategic Plan. The current plan covers the years 2018 – 2022 and lays out the strategic goals and objects for the nation's transportation systems and infrastructure. The four key themes of the plan are safety, infrastructure, innovation, and accountability. From this plan, we learn the country's key priorities for change and growth in transportation. The need for investment is provided through public promotion based on the plan and the ongoing needs identified and part of the national budget.

Public promotion, as a concept, is not intended to be fair across all potential modes or elements of transportation. Investment is provided based on what the government believes is needed to manage transportation efficiency. And not all modes are subject to getting public promotion. Table 3, below, shows that two modes, railroads and pipelines do not receive public promotion. The primary reason

Mode	Receives Promotion?	Impact of Promotion	Examples of Promotion	Special Situations
Air	Yes	Lower Costs	Airport Building / Expansion	ATC Operations
Water	Yes	Port Infrastructure; advocacy	Port construction Management of Locks and Dams in inland waterways Coast Guard Safety support Maritime Academy	Maritime Academy Reserve Fleet Cabotage / Cargo Preference Laws
Truck	Yes	No Infrastructure costs; significant market advantage	Road maintenance Infrastructure investment	Accident Research, Efficiency Research
Rail	No	Must maintain own infrastructure (15% of annual revenue)	N/A	Low cost loans for major projects if determined to be part of the national need
Pipeline	No	Pipelines are considered private carriers	N/A	Eminent Domain

Table 3. Public Promotion Opportunities by Mode

is related to how the railroads were formed during deregulation and that pipelines are considered a specialized and not a public carrier like other modes.

When the government provides public promotion, it does so based on an expected value experienced based on the investment. The government, however, is different than the private sector and the approach to defining value is different due to restrictions in how the government allocates and obligates money in the national budget.

The government operates under a twelve-month budget cycle that runs from October 1 to September 30 of each year. Budgets are developed by congress and approved by the president. When a budget is approved, money is allocated per congressional rules, but it is not until the money is spent through contracts, purchase orders, etc. that we consider the budget to be obligated. Obligated is an important term because before obligation, the budget could change. Regardless, once money is obligated it is spent.

The government has an unusual constraint compared to the private sector. For the government's budget, if any money is not obligated before September 30, that budget will be lost and not available for the next fiscal year. Further, an obligated budget is only for this year meaning that if there is an ongoing cost to a project or activity, money must be allocated into the next fiscal year or that project or activity cannot continue.

Because of this restriction, the government uses a Benefit Cost Ratio (BCR)[2] to determine value rather than a more traditional Return on Investment (ROI) or Internal Rate of Return (IRR) done in the private sector. To compute the BCR, the following formula is calculated:

$$BCR = \frac{\text{Net Benefit over the Life of the Project}}{\text{Sum of the Initial Project Costs}}$$ A BCR > 1 means a project has value.

What is the difference from the above to a more traditional ROI? The primary difference is in the denominator. The government looks at the benefits of a project over a longer while but can only use the initial investment costs as its denominator. The BCR does not consider maintenance or operating costs unless it is part of the initial investment.

The era of positive regulation was a time when the government's influence was felt more directly as regulation expanded to enforce issues that affected citizens and business and as an investor in the growth of the country's broader transportation industry.

The Era of Intermodal Regulation (1935 – 1975)

In some ways, perhaps the Era of Intermodal Regulation was the most important era in the timeline of transportation. The challenge of that statement is this era, like the others simply built upon what came before and responded to the historical and economic situation of the time and the needs of the country's citizens and businesses. As a steppingstone, however, it is an era of great expansion and change and an era of crisis and issues that drove regulations, investment and new practices in transportation.

---

[2] https://en.wikipedia.org/wiki/Benefit%E2%80%93cost_ratio

This era begins with the country coming out of the depression through the new deal. The world had been hit by the hardest economic downturn in history. Countries throughout the world saw their trade with the US go down significantly as the US pulled in its borders to focus on domestic issues and jobs. Through these crisis, new political ideas and parties came into being to displace governments seen as ineffective. The infamous of these was the rise of Adolf Hitler in Germany that ultimately lead to World War II.

Initially, the US did not get involved in the war effort seeing it as a "European" conflict. The US entered the war after the attack on Pearl Harbor, Hawaii, on December 7, 1941. Within a few days the Germans declared war on the US and the US began its historical build up to support the war effort.

In 1935, which marked the start of the second new deal, the national unemployment rate had dropped from about 25% to 20% because of the great drought, also known as the "dust bowl" which resulted in droughts and regular dust storms in parts of Kansas, Nebraska, Colorado, New Mexico, Oklahoma and Texas. This had a crippling effect on agriculture and the newly felt western expansion. The drought ultimately ended around 1939.

The Dustbowl in 1935

World War II, however, changed the US economy and many approaches to transportation. The war came on unexpectedly just as the US was getting back in swing. Because of the criticality of victory, the US put almost its entire economic power to the war effort. By 1943, unemployment was down to less than 2% as the conscription of soldiers for the war to almost every able man to the war effort. Similarly, the defense budget tripled as the government- built machines and weapon systems for the Army and the Navy (the Marines were part of the Navy as they are today, and the Air Force was part of the Army as the Army air Corps). The buildup over a short time, created a very complex and demanding logistical operations to manage the movement of everything from tanks and soldiers to food, medicine, and ammunition.

Complexities abounded during this period. Imagine the procurement and purchasing of material to build 1,216 ships, over 324,000 aircraft, over 100,000 tanks, over 250,000 artillery pieces, about Million machine guns and 10,000,000 soldiers. The logistics and transportation just to move the material between raw material suppliers and factors stretched the country's transportation beyond its limits let alone the massive movement of these troops and equipment overseas to be delivered in active war zones.

At the beginning of this period, the movement of goods across the world was done primarily through transportation ships and freighters. Freighters would take on cargo in any form and most goods and material was shipped in individual pallets or as individual items. This was an inadequate way to move so much equipment and people in such a short time that several innovations took place to simply meet the needs of the war. Below are some of the most critical innovations of this era which should help to understand the reason we call this the intermodal Era:

Logistics Influences Strategy and Execution

A military truism says, "Amateurs talk strategy while professionals study logistics". World War II was recognized as a war of logistics in a document provided to congress in 1993 called World War II Logistics: Final Report of the Army Service Forces[3]. This is not an understatement. While the movement of goods has always be a consideration in execution, World War II propelled logistics planning to a strategic activity. The government had to make difficult decisions on the uses of its natural resources to create a military war power capable of winning the war. At every turn, logistics considerations were critical, if not dictated due to constraints that would affect strategic planning. Strategic military plans had to be broken down into procurement activities, production activities, and ultimately transportation activities. The plans could be brilliant but if they couldn't be executed, they were equally useless.

For the first time, the country faced a dramatic scarcity of logistics assets and capabilities needed to execute their plans. Logistics studies used to help define the requirements and capabilities of mobilizations often showed the weakness of the strategic plans being developed because of issues of practicality. Each time, teams defined the bottlenecks and determine the most efficient way to solve them. More times than not, the problems could not be solved feasibly due to lack of resources or a prohibitive cost. The collaboration process itself, however, aided in developing new methods and approaches to solving these bottlenecks which ultimately became new practices in domestic and global logistics.

<u>Roll-on / Roll-off Ships (RO/RO) -</u> moving tanks and other tracked or wheeled equipment was very difficult during the early 1940s. The general freighter was the only real means one could ship items. As the Allies in Europe developed the plan for the Landing in Normandy, also known as D- Day which occurred in June of 1944 one of the biggest challenges they faced was how to rapidly move heavy equipment from ships to landing zones.

An LST at Work at Normandy Beach

---

[3] https://archive.org/details/LogisticsInWorldWarII

There was no effective way to do this on a mass scale. To solve this problem the US Bureau of Ships created a new class of vessel called the LST, or Landing Ship, Tank. These vehicles were used extensively during the D-Day to rapidly move tanks from their ships to the beaches. Similar ships were used to liberate the Suez Canal and during the battle of Malta. The typical LST could carry about 20 – 25 battle tanks depending on size and the crew needed to operate them. It was considered a significant feat and was a big part of the reason the invasion worked. Today, a dedicated auto/truck carrier RO/RO can carry over 6,500 vehicles in a single shipment!

The US Army Transportation Corps – One might not think of developing a new branch in a military service but developing the Transportation Corps in the US Army was milestone event. Created in 1942 in response to the need for a mass mobilization never attempted in the world prior, the Army Transportation Corps was given the mission to move man, material, and equipment into active war zones in four continents. To do this, the Army Transportation Corps had to create new approaches, processes, and methods that changed the way our country thought of transportation. Initially, its primary mission involved deep water ships, harbor craft, ports, and railroads so it could focus on its sole mission of mobilization and ongoing support. During the war, the transportation corps moved over 30 million soldiers in the US and over 7 million into foreign zones along with 126 million tons of cargo. This ability, to so rapidly move man and material into the fight, ultimately overwhelmed the Axis powers in Europe and Asia. Many lessons learned during the war especially related to intermodal transportation (transportation that uses multiple modes in moving goods and people), laid the foundation for how transportation would evolve in the US both in the military and in the commercial sector.

Airplanes as a core of the US Transportation System – The airline industry was still in its infancy but had evolved to provide global transportation by the time of WWII. During the war, the commercial airlines industry generally stopped functioning as all US commercial airlines served the mobilization effort to move man and material rapidly from the US to the theatres of battle. Using air assets for transportation throughout the war reinforced the value of air travel and the airlines themselves leading the development of larger aircraft, the jet engine, and helped to user in the modern era of air travel. It would still take about 30 – 40 years after the war for air travel to be affordable to the general population but the efforts used in WWII solidified air's role in the US transportation system.

The Shipping Container – during the early part of WWII for the US, shipments were done primarily through general freighters. As virtually all mobilization transportation was intermodal this created an environment where items would be loaded in truck trailers or rail cars and then shipped to ports.

At the port, the entire load would have to be unloaded manually and then hoisted on board the freighter using a crane system. This method was generally called break-bulk shipping and was very labor intensive and expensive. During the mobilization efforts in World War II, the military loaded freighters piece by piece. There were no shipping containers to support the effort. During the Korean War, the US military developed the "Connex" which was a small shipping container. But Malcom Mclean, a trucking company executive ultimately created the first shipping container. He observed that the Port of New Jersey always had long wait times because of the time to load ships. He developed a single container that could have as many pallets as a tractor trailer, have a single manifest and packing slip, be loaded just before transportation and then moved through the system as a single unit. The time savings alone helped reinvent transportation. But it was the ability to move a container across truck, rail, and ship that ultimately drove the growth and flexibility of intermodal shipping.

Perhaps the Greatest Innovation in Transportation from WWII

While World War II created many innovations in shipping beyond the few mentioned above, but the one that changed the country most dramatically didn't occur until almost a decade after the war. To set the stage:

> The Allied forces had landed in Normandy in July 1944 and in Southern France in August. After working through the initial resistance, the Allies moved quicker than expected the France and into Germany. They experienced logistics issues as they crossed into the Ardennes valley of Germany. Since the area had favorable ground for defense, General Dwight D. Eisenhower held the Army there and allow his supply lines to catch up. It was a good decision given that military intelligence indicated the area had German troops but was generally an area for German troops to rest and re-fit. As Germany's forces were focused more on the mounting threats in the eastern front with Russia. His hope in splitting the Allies was that he could negotiate a piece with the US and England separate from the Russians.

In this context in September, 1944, Adolf Hitler, devised a counter-offensive plan that would attempt to split the Allies in half and form a breakout with his armored divisions that would require the Allies to retreat and regroup buying him some much needed time to resolve the eastern front conflict so he could then focus on the approaching Allies. Over the next two months, the German Army would quietly accomplish a massive build up on the western front that included the movement of about 200,000 German troops along with their 400 tanks and 1,900 artillery pieces. In addition, the Germans moved over 2,200 newly built armored vehicles before the start of the battle. From an intelligence perspective, the Allies had a few pieces of intelligence that suggested a buildup, but the most trusted sources did not corroborate this until it was too late.

On December 16, 1944, the Germans bombed the Allied front with artillery and then made a focused and massed attack on the Allied lines in the Ardennes forest. Initially the Germany forces almost broke through the line. Four weeks later, on January 18, 1945, the battle was over and the Allies moved into Germany and by May of 1945, the European portion of WWII was over.

While the Germans had several infrastructure issues, roads were not one of them. The Germans had built a super-highway called the "Autobahn" in the 1930's and in the early part of the war used it extensively to rapidly move troops around the country. The buildup of the Battle of the Bulge also used the Autobahn to create the front of the counter-offensive. After Germany's defeat in the Battle of the Bulge, the Allied took advantage of the Autobahn as part of their offensive. After the war was won, General Eisenhower became the military head of occupied Germany. Through this, he debriefed many German officers and did careful studies of the use and effectiveness of the Autobahn.

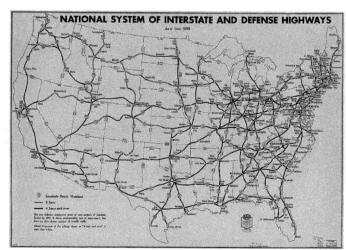

Early Map of the Eisenhower Interstate System

When General Eisenhower became President Eisenhower in 1953, one of his first tasks was getting approval for a US highway system like the Autobahn. The cold war had begun and the stated concern for the highway system was like Germany's use in WWII: He wanted to move man, material, and equipment quickly across the country from the military bases in the event of an attack on American soil. In 1956, President Eisenhower signed the Federal-Aid Highway Act of 1956 which authorized the development of a national "interstate" transportation system. This was considered one of the greatest public works projects in the country's history and was largest public promotion project approved to date. The initial allocation (remember the previous discussion on how the government budgeting works for transportation) was $1.1B for states to begin the infrastructure. The total cost expected for the project would be around $33 billion. In today's dollars, the initial allocation would be worth over $10 billion dollars with the total project cost being over $303 billion. Today, this is roughly the cost of the US interest on its debt annually.

While the military rationale was sound, most Americans and virtually all US business was strongly behind the plan. Before the Eisenhower Interstate System, it was generally a slow process to get across country. A trip from New York to Los Angeles typically took up to two – three weeks for motorists and a good two weeks for trucks. This time was cut by over 65% by the time the system was operational allowing a truck with freight to go from New York to Los Angeles in just about five days. The impact on commerce in the US was very significant. For one, it created new competition for the rail industry which had been the most common way to move industrial goods. With the trucking industry gaining the value of the interstate system, trucks could be developed with greater capacity giving birth to what we think of today as our modern system of truck transportation. Manufacturers and distributors located among key arteries of the system allowing trucks to use the interstates extensively with minimal use of other roads.

The Federal-Aid Highway Act of 1956 also created the first standards for trucks related to weight. The Motor Carrier Act of 1935 put the trucking industry as part of the ICC and the ICC had very strict rules for "certifying" who could be a trucking company and who could not. It also set rates and tariffs and had economic and licensing barriers in place to limit the number of trucking companies in the US. With the interstate system, this approached seemed ineffective. For one, the country had just added about 47,000 miles of four lane continuous roads the infrastructure of the country. Second, the standard for total weight of a truck cab, trailer, and full load of freight was set to 73,280 pounds which opened the door to much freight possibilities for trucks. Over the next twenty years this would be to be a continuing challenge until the reality of deregulation was achieved opening the market to full competition and a free market approach.

Before the 1970's, it was very normal for a person to be born, raised and employed in the same basic area as that person's parents and grandparents. Mobility was limited due to lack of infrastructure to support easy movement across the country and the costs of transportation. The Eisenhower Interstate System changed that forever. Beginning in the mid-1970's it was easy for virtually every American to take their vehicle anywhere in the country. Vacations to destinations like Disney in California and Florida became much more affordable. Hotel chains grew making it easier to travel and US citizens explored the country of their birth. The outcome of this has been a significant shift in the country's demographics and even the definition of "family". While it's a matter of opinion as to whether this was ultimately a good thing or not, the impact has been profound and continually shapes the psyche and culture of America.

The Era of Economic Deregulation (1976 – Present)

Through the first three eras we see a transportation system and regulatory environment based on transportation as a regulated industry. In this last era, we will change all this through the creation of a transportation system deregulated. This begs an important question as to the distinction of regulated versus deregulated industries. Are regulated industries bad because they create too many restrictions? Does a deregulated industry have no regulations? Before we get into the specifics of the US transportation deregulation process, we need to unpack these two questions further.

To the first question of "Are regulated industries bad because they create too many restrictions?" We answer, like many other questions in logistics and transportation, "It depends". This is said not to dodge having a specific answer but because of the many factors that may affect the answer. Assigning good or bad can be difficult because these decisions are often evaluated based on the governmental system in place, the culture of the country, its ability to embrace and take advantage of free markets, the integrity of its business culture and more. We should pause for a moment and understand just what it means to have a regulated industry.

To be clear, there is a strong difference in an industry having regulations and being a regulated industry. Those differences lie in the way the government approaches the industry to ensure fair practices and safe operations. In a <u>Regulated Industry</u>, the government has two major characteristics we do not have in a deregulated industry:

- <u>Ownership</u> – In most regulated industries, the government itself is an active owner in the industry. These are typically called State-Owned Enterprises (SOEs). In the transportation industry, we estimate about 40% of land and pipeline transportation globally are done through SEOs. Air transport is about 13% and commercial maritime shipping and rail are below 10% although it is not uncommon for rail to have SEOs, especially in China.

- <u>Price controls and Barriers to Entry</u> – The second area of a regulated industry is pricing controls. In regulated industries the government will, most often, set the minimum and maximum rates that can be offered for commercial services. If the government has an SEO along with other competitors, it will often use its rate to manage competition if it doesn't set rates. In addition, the government will put in unilateral controls that create significant barriers to entry if there is any ability to enter the industry. These barriers to entry may still exist in a deregulated environment but are much more stringent and harsher in a regulated industry.

Some countries have a strongly regulated system whether it's in financial services, oil and gas, transportation, or some other industry can be beneficial. There is a general belief in the US that having a government run something versus the private sector is always bad because the government doesn't run industries well. Globally, there many examples that support this notion and just as many as do not. While many factors play into the decision to regulate an industry or not, we cannot just assume it is a bad thing to have a regulated industry. In the US, regulation is something that citizens want to avoid and instead prefer the actions of free markets. The challenge of this, like issues in the Era of Initiation is that free markets can be corrupted just like a regulated market. Regulations should come from the government's desire to ensure all citizens have free access and opportunities to the same things. Because of that a government will create regulations and, in some instance, own assets in the industry and control certain aspects of it.

Our Second question easily flows from the first: "Does a deregulated industry have no regulations?". Oh, that it would be true, but it is not! The biggest difference between the two is that the government does not own and operate businesses in the industry and allows the market, rather than itself, to set the prices. It does not mean that the government does not issue regulations. Sometimes after a government deregulates a regulated industry we end up with many more regulations and restrictions than before. This may be surprising but there is logic to this. When a government regulates an industry, any regulations created regulate itself. So, when a government deregulates an industry it almost guaranteed that it will put more regulations in place than it did when it owned and controlled the industry to ensure the commercial companies know the standards and expectations that regulations bring.

In the US transportation environment, we see a period of about 100 years where the government regulates the industry due to specific practices it wants to extinguish which then leads it to create various levels of regulated industry through price setting and controls and ultimately to eliminating these controls and creating a framework for deregulation. As we've discussed, the journey from initiation of regulation to deregulation is full of lessons on how to create the best transportation infrastructure, processes and controls to ensure the industry can operate and service its customers and flourish. Most will agree that the system we have today, while not perfect, is more expanded and more capable than the system we experienced as a regulated industry.

In 1976, after the government had been regulating transportation in some form or fashion, a decision was made to move to deregulation. What drove this decision? How was it accomplished? How successful have we been? There are all important questions to understand well as we approach the modern global transportation market. In the US deregulation of the transportation industry began with the Railroad Revitalization and Regulatory Reform Act of 1976. While the act was central to the rail industry, it was the first salvo in deregulating an industry. The current regulatory environment in 1976 was detrimental to the public good and law makers and others in the Federal Government recognized it and were committed to changing it.

Let's look at contemporary examples of the time for each area:

- Overly Bureaucratic – As part of the regulated environment, the Interstate Commerce Committee (ICC) established in 1890, the Civil Aeronautics Board (CAB) established in 1938, along with the Federal Maritime Commission (FMC), established in 1961 were the major regulators for the segments of the transportation industry. Each agency had definitive authority over applications for new entrants in the market and the process for entering the market. The ICC had established a system that virtually ensured no new entrants to the system. When a new application was received, if any other existing company, i.e. competitor, complained, the application would either be terminated or would not be acted upon creating the same result. Similarly, the CAB operated using a constraint system by defining an acceptable capacity for air travel that resulted in low demand and higher supply ensuring no new entrants in the market and likely consolidation of those within the industry.

This led to limited demand and high competition with maximum rates set for the industry. The result was long bankruptcies that hurt the industry and its ability to serve the public. The FMC was relatively new but had a legacy dating to the shipping act of 1916. By the early 1970's it found itself burdened with regulation become more and more obsolete due to global changes in shipping needs and intermodal transport and containerization.

- <u>Capacity Constrained</u> – Primarily because of the significant barriers to entry into the transportation industry, between around 1940 and 1980, there were very few new trucking companies, railroads were capacity constrained to lead to too much supply for the demand which lead to a large wave of bankruptcies, which also occurred in the airlines industry. If we look at the airline industry in 1938, there were sixteen "trunk line" carriers. A trunk line had defined commercial domestic and international routes. Today we would simply call them a major airline. By 1978, only ten of the original trunk line carriers existed and there had been no new entrants to the market allowed since 1938. In addition, the energy crisis in 1973 – 1974 saddled the remaining airlines with very large fuel bills that could not be passed on rates leading them all to have large losses and face the potential of bankruptcy.

- <u>Bankruptcies</u> – While we have mentioned a few bankruptcies there were several significant bankruptcies that affected the decision to deregulate. With the rail industry, by 1960 one-third of the entire rail industry was bankrupt or nearly at it. Because the ICC controlled rates, they made rates low for bulk products like agriculture, metals and mining which was the sweet spot of rail and the majority of their volume while setting high rates for consumer goods effectively enabling truck competition to become the dominant shipper of this category. Besides the lower tariffs, railroads lost money and their infrastructure suffered badly. The 1970's was one of the worst decades for rail safety with one rail company alone experiencing about 650 derailments alone due to poor maintenance.

We've already discussed a similar issue in the airline industry. By the late 1970's most of the transportation industries were under significant cost pressure due to waste, the inability to innovate, and cost exposure that came from regulatory compliance. The tipping point came from the rail industry. Penn Central transportation (Penn Central Railroad and its holdings) was the sixth largest corporation in America and the largest of the Class I railroads. It had originally been formed in 1846 and was considered one of the largest and most stable companies in the world. Then through poor mergers and financial dealings along with stifling rail regulation, the company suddenly filed for bankruptcy on June 21, 1970. The result was devastating to the industry and to the stock market. The company had about 200,000 employees at its height and was in virtually every retirement plan in the country. It was the largest bankruptcy in US history.

The government ultimately stepped in and created a new freight rail company, Conrail (Consolidated rail) and the passenger services were taken over by the National Railroad Corporation, or Amtrak. Both were privatized but Conrail improved its operations, become profitable and ultimately filed a public offering for $1.9B in 1987, the largest IPO in US history. After deregulation, both CSX and Norfolk Southern (NS) would jointly bid to buy the company and use it as a service provider which exists to this day.

With this as a backstop, we can now understand the value and approach that started with 4R Act in 1976. The Act was passed as the first stop-gap measure toward deregulation. The 4R Act. It provided a bridge of funding and support while providing incremental freedom on rates and tariffs, made it easier to complete filing for rail abandonment (a situation where a railroad closes a section of its system due to poor economic performance or duplication) and provided more clarity and support for mergers. The 4R Act started a groundswell of support for the deregulation of transportation and resulted in several more deregulation acts that ultimately enabled broad competition and market freedom for all transportation modes. The content, purpose, and scope of these resulting act varied by mode and a brief review of these is instructive as we look at how freight transportation in the US works today.

As the Railroad industry benefited from the 4R Act, it's a good place to understand how the rail industry finally was deregulated. The definitive piece of legislature that lead to the deregulation of the rail industry was the Stagger's Act of 1980 signed into law by then President Jimmie Carter on October 14, 1980. The Stagger's Act[4] was groundbreaking legislation that limited the powers of the ICC and gave the railroads broad freedom that included:

- Railroads could establish any rate they desired provided there was rail competition in the same area.

- Railroads could contract with customers provided the contract would not interfere with the railroad providing common carrier (public freight movement for anyone) services. To date, there has never been a protest submitted and contract carriage is a critical market tool for railroads.

- Generally, the ICC could not interfere with rates it might find discriminatory on its own but had to default to antitrust laws.

- The entire process and approach to rate making through rate bureaus or other mechanisms was eliminated.

The airline industry was deregulated through the Airline Deregulation Act of 1978[5]. Recognizing the situation in the rail industry, President Ford and his administration were already looking into airline deregulation due to rising fares, that no airline had been formed as a new entrant in the market since 1938, which followed the CAB(Civil Aeronautics Board) dragging its feet in many areas of capacity and entry into the industry. In addition, the airline capacity had been constrained at the route level resulting in over served routes and underserved routes. Over served routes mean airlines had half-full planes usually and unprofitable, forced routes in others. Many changes came from the Act but the most relevant were:

- Required the CAB to gradually eliminate their control over fare setting.
- The CAB was given specific timelines for processing requests including new air routes and the entry of new airlines.
- The CAB would have to show definitive proof that a new or changed air route would not serve the public good.
- Any American owned international carrier could immediately provide domestic services.
- Airlines could actively take over service on routes that were under-utilized by the competition.
- The authority for airline regulation was moved from the CAB to the Department of Transportation (DOT) and the CAB was dissolved in 1984.

Essentially, the airline industry experienced a regulatory overhaul that led to increased efficiency, new entrants and completion and lower fares. It also drove a shakeout between those airlines that could no longer compete efficiently and those that could. It removed constrains on the industry enabling to innovation and market adaptation. We'll see this in greater detail when we discuss transportation modes later in the book.

Unlike the other modes, the maritime industry did not so much deregulate as modernize. The Federal Maritime Commission (FMC) had determined existing regulatory restrictions were not like other modes but some of the regulatory practices were out of date and ineffective. The Shipping act of 1984 [6] was the first move toward regulatory modernization. It replaced the original shipping act of 1916 which had become inadequate for, among other reasons, its lack of consideration for containerization and container shipping. The legislation opened up competitive rating and the ability for Maritime shippers to enter into carriage contracts by filing them with the FMC. It also clarified the authority by which Maritime shippers could engage in intermodal service contracts with service providers in other modes. It liberalized the ability for Maritime shippers to enter into cooperative agreements (sharing freight, cross-contracting, etc.) by automatically approving the agreements if the FMC had not commented within 45 days.

It also set in motion a required study by the FMC on the status and efficacy of reforms. Then, in 1998, through the Ocean Shipping Reform Act (OSRA) was enacted. The purpose was specifically to simplify and increase the flexibility for ocean based shipping vessels to manage service contracts without oversight, supported rate confidentiality, allowed the FMC more latitude to exempt transportation existing statutes in places when warranted.

By this time the Federal Government was considering transportation deregulation, the motor carrier industry, e.g. the trucking industry, was a mess. Like the rail industry, the ICC's oversight had caused significant issues in capacity, tariff rates, and competitive positioning. The beginning of the end of this occurred with the Motor Carrier Act of 1980. The main provisions of the Act that helped liberalize the trucking industry to create new entrants and competition included:

- Allowing any trucking company acting as a common carrier to publish its own rates without having to go through a rate bureau.
- Removing restrictions from trucking companies enabling them to move any category of freight and deregulated routes and regional restrictions allowing carriers to move declare service areas across the entire country for any freight.
- Removing entry controls allowing companies the freedom to enter the market with relative ease.
- Allowing trucking firms to contract with customers without gaining approval from the ICC.
- Creating a new category of trucking devoted to helping shippers find the carrier most suitable for them resulting initially of the trucking industry.

The reforms had an immediate and positive impact on the industry as new entrants quickly entered the market and existing companies expanded the territories and lowered rates to meet the competition. By 1990 there were over 40,000 carriers or double that of 1980. As the early 1990's came bringing with it the concepts of lean / just-in-time manufacturing, the trucking industry was prepared to respond. Manufacturers found they could leverage transportation to enable them to dramatically reduce inventory resulting in highly efficient operations.

Today, we see the results of deregulation as we now have over forty years of history to consider. During this period, we've seen dramatic rises in new regulations across all modes. These regulations are focused on social issues that include safety, security and the environment. Few would disagree that deregulation was necessary and has had a major positive impact on the transportation industry. Many may suggest that social regulation has gone too far and is itself stifling completion while raising costs. This is to be expected. Regulation is rarely seen as a positive thing in an industry because it creates controls and constraints.

There will always need to be a process of checks and balances between regulating agencies and the industries they regulate. As of 2017, the global transportation market stood at $4.8 trillion annually of which 1.2 trillion is attributed to the US transportation industry and representing 6% of the total GDP of the United States.

REGULATION IN PRACTICE

An understanding of the regulatory eras and how we evolved into the modern transportation market is an important context to have as we now look at regulation in practice. There are three main areas of regulation in the US: Economic, Social, and antitrust. In this section, we will review the approaches to and areas of regulation in the transportation industry for these three areas.

Economic Regulation

In transportation, the primary purpose of economic regulation is to control or influence the process and outcomes of new entrants coming into the market, the economic impact of those in the market and exiting a specific market. Economic regulation is the most affected in terms of a regulated versus deregulated market.

In a <u>regulated market</u>, the government will, at a minimum, have controls on market entrance and on rate setting. The government determines it must ensure an industry or market is executed in the public interest and it believes that it must control these factors to ensure a predictable outcome. As we've seen from reviewing the eras of regulation, control of entry can either be very strict or as liberal as a government decides. There are several ways governments can control the entry process to be as fast or slow as desired and either inexpensive or very expensive in terms of cost of entry.

There can be many situations where it makes sense to ensure a slow and methodical process in a regulated environment. Ensuring the company wishing entry is stable, has the requisite background and skills, can ensure safety and security in its operations and will operate in the public interest is core to any entry process. In a regulated environment this is slower and more methodical but not in every instance. As we saw with the US ICC, the intent of the ICC was to severely limit new entrants into the market for rail and trucking and, then there were no new entrants into the market from 1938 until deregulation.

This is an extreme example of artificial barriers to entry but is not that unusual. In regulated environment, the government is ultimately responsible for the success of industries and one way to ensure an industry succeeds is by control the rates to the public and limiting competition to the few that can be well managed. This is counter to most principles of market economics but in a regulated environment market economics are not the priority.

Similarly, rate setting is controlled most often in terms of the maximum allowable charges, but it can also include the minimum charges to ensure rates do not have too high of a range. In most interests, the government will consider the health of the company's in the industry as they generally want stable companies, but rate setting is most often characterized as an artificial method that is not market sensitive and often leads to companies having financial challenges. Again, the goal is not so much fair market economics as it is market control and the desire to have very predictable outcomes.

---

[4] https://www.govtrack.us/congress/bills/96/s1946

[5] https://www.congress.gov/bill/95th-congress/senate-bill/2493

[6] http://www.cargolaw.com/shippingact.html

Balancing the two, market control and market economics is very difficult in a regulated environment because of the artificial variables created. Most regulated markets will be one of focused market control of rates and "good enough" service levels than high efficiency, productivity, and customer satisfaction.

Rates and Usage Fees in a Deregulated Market

In a deregulated market, the government does not set rates or participate as a business in the transportation industry. Instead, governments allow market forces to set rates, which we often call market rates, and these rates are driven by the consumer's willingness to pay for the services. There will always be a healthy tension in rate setting in non-regulated, open markets which is a natural give and take between the shipper and carrier as both want a little something different from the relationship with cost. Shippers want to pay nothing, and carriers want the shippers to pay high rates to optimize their profits. So, the laws of supply and demand will apply extensively in a non-regulated market finding various equilibrium points based on capacity and constraints primarily due to the economic environment although regulation can also play a role in this.

There are several ways the government can influence the market economically in this environment. Usage fees are one of the most basic ways. Usage fees are fees associated with transportation we would consider variable costs. Fuel, for instance, is a great example. The government charges a little over 54 cents per gallon as tax on diesel fuel (the primary fuel of the trucking industry). So, the more miles a company logs the more fuel tax it will pay. This is a classic example of usage fees.

Another is special permits controlled by the states. Permits are required for any truck either overweight or oversize in its load. Permit costs vary but if a truck is in an overage state it must purchase a permit for every state in which it will pass.

Social Regulation

Social regulation makes up the largest share of all regulations typically in a regulated or deregulated system. Given that the recognized purpose of regulation is to ensure that the needs of the public are met, it makes sense that safety, security and environmental regulation would be core to any regulatory system. Let's examine each area to better understand social regulation.

Safety Regulations

Safe operations, and safety of individuals is one of the most important aspects of regulation and in transportation, there is a myriad of safety regulation. If you thought about it, you might realize that equipment inspections and having equipment and maintenance standards are safety regulations. To accomplish the mission of transportation safety, our single agency is an objective voice in safety and then each major regulating agency for each mode has the mission to evaluate, develop, publish and ensure compliance of all mode-based safety regulations. Let's look at these agencies in more detail in terms of domestic transportation safety.

The National Transportation Safety Board (NTSB) is the overall agency for transportation safety, safety practices and accident investigation. Its mission is to be an independent and objective authority in evaluating the transportation safety of all modes of transportation. It has investigative authority for all aviation accidents and any major accident of other modes. Its organizational structure creates offices for aviation, safety, highway safety, marine safety, and railroad, pipeline and hazardous material safety. Remember, the NTSB does not have a regulatory mission as the dot's offices cover all aspects of transportation regulation. It does have the mission to be objective and use accident investigation to evaluate the effectiveness of the regulations in place and to make recommendations where needed on changes. These regulations come from an independent voice in the government and carry weight to other agencies charged with creating regulation. For trucking, the FMCSA[7] is the main trucking agency for safety and oversees hours of service and the Electronic Logging Devices (ELDs) that are now in use to confirm and ensure safe operations of vehicles. It also drives the standardization, safety practices and regulatory practices of every other aspect of the trucking industry including inspection standards, licensure etc. at a federal level. States also have a transportation safety mission especially around state based licensure of all classes of driver's licensing, education, training and road safety. The state's Departments of Safety include the State's Highway Patrol usually and is charged with transportation safety within the state. The State Highway Patrol oversees the implementation and compliance of regulation and the safe operations of vehicles on its roads. They also operate the weight stations throughout a state to ensure load and equipment compliance in the state along with permit enforcement.

In rail, the Federal Railroad Administration (FRA) defines the regulations that govern safe operations and equipment safety of rail operations and defining the standards for all road crossings that involve rail to ensure public safety. States may participate in a federal program to have federal FRA inspectors in the state to support the safety and inspection processes for compliance. The FRA also issues a National Rail Plan periodically that outlines the challenges, issues, and goals of the rail industry and provides objectives to help expand the industry. The national plan has two major priorities:

- High Speed Passenger Rail: The plan calls for regionalization of high speed in high population clusters (mega-cities) and then to later join these as a national system.

- Growth in intermodal Rail: The plan lays out the need and approach for growth using the intermodal segment of rail. Projects have been completed over the last six to eight years that have supported this goal. This includes:

- The Heartland Corridor: A public-private partnership between NS Railroad and the federal Highway Administration and three states to create a faster corridor from the Port of Norfolk through Columbus out of Harrisburg (OH) to Chicago IL. This involved increasing the clearances of tunnels and bridges throughout the route to enable double stack shipping container transportation.

- National Gateway Project: CSX rail has sponsored an ambitious project to link mid-Atlantic ports with improved intermodal rail capabilities to enable faster intermodal rail from any east coast port to the Midwest of the US. The first phase of the project, a new corridor between the Chambersburg, PA intermodal rail yard and the Baltimore, Ohio intermodal rail yard has completed. Other projects are underway.

The Federal Aviation Administration (FAA) defines the standards for safe operations, maintenance intervals, and more to ensure equipment safety and also has strict requirements for safely operating individual aircraft including the mandatory safety briefings done before flights.

Maritime Administration (MARAD) defines the US standards for safety of vessels, equipment, and operations. This covers the river, Great Lakes, coastal and intercostal shipping segments. Intermodal regulations are important in Maritime due to the large container shipping done throughout the world. They also operate the US maritime academy and certify merchant marines (individuals involved in commercial shipping, fishing and other maritime activities.)

Finally, pipeline safety is governed by the pipeline Safety and Hazardous Materials Administration which also handles all hazmat standards for marking, working with, inspecting and delivering hazardous materials.

Security Regulations

Transportation security has grown rapidly in importance from the 1990's to today. The focus of transportation security is relatively straight forward. Most transportation security is focused on the identification and interdiction of four main types of cargo:

- Counterfeit Products

- Illegal Drugs and Substances

- Terrorism and smuggling

- Human Trafficking

Transportation security is a risk management activity. There is not enough inspection resources to look at every truck, package and container that enters the US. Applying risk management principles to identify cargo of the highest risk and need for inspection is a critical element of the system. Every country has a border protection scheme it uses. In the US, Border Security is done through a mixture of physical assets like the TSA, the INS, The US Coast Guard and the Department of Homeland Security. Customs enforcement also plays a major role in transportation security and will be covered in the next chapter.

Besides the physical assets, there are regulations that govern the requirements for documentation, notice and document transmissions before entering a country that create information flow about the cargo, the ports used by the vessel, the cargo manifest and other commercial documentation to determine the legitimacy of cargo and the potential risk the cargo and the ship have relative to others. For instance, a ship that has passed through areas known for terrorism, counterfeiting or smuggling, may be flagged to be inspected when compared to other ships that have travelled to ports considered trusted.

Transportation security leverages a layered approach that helps manage the security risk. There are three core layers: Intelligence, Screening and Inspection.

Intelligence provides a critical link in understanding the current global situation including known threats, indications of escalation, reporting on events, like drug movements, areas where recruiting is high for human trafficking, and potential terrorist threats. This intelligence can come in many forms including from national intelligence agencies like the Central Intelligence Agency (CIA) and the National Security Agency (NSA), and on a domestic front through the Federal Bureau of Investigation (FBI), and local law enforcement. Allied countries, including countries in the United Nations, also work together to share intelligence. The gathering, interpretation and dissemination of intelligence is typically on a classified level and supports threat warnings and declassified reports that help inform the Department of Homeland Security (DHS) and the Customs Bureau Protection agency (CPB).

Screening recognizes our inability to inspect every single piece of equipment shipped between countries. Different countries have different approaches to screening. In the US, that primary screening system is the National Targeting System (NTS) that is part of DHS. The NTS system, defines the security criteria that become the screening variables that define potential risk levels for cargo security. The variables are part of the Automated Targeting System (ATS) that evaluates inbound documents from cargo carriers in air and maritime to determine if a specific load or container needs to be inspected. While all cargo is scanned in ports for radioactivity, only those identified by the ATS system or identified as a random candidate for screening are typically inspected.

Inspect, or inspection, is the final area of focus for cargo security. Inspections may be chosen randomly and through the screening processes of the ATS. When a cargo load or container is identified for inspection, the Customs Bureau Protection agency (CBP) is accountable for the inspection process based on the normal procedures by the CPB for cargo. In 2016, over 11.9 million containers entered the US. Of that number the ATS system identified about 72,000 containers for inspection, or about 0.06% of all containers.

Critical International Regulatory Agencies (Safety, Security and Environment)

Two other international Agencies are worth discussion because of their impact on US transportation.

The International Maritime Organization (IMO) is a body within the United Nations focused on safety, security and the environment in global maritime shipping. The IMO works with counties with global shipping ports, the major shipping carriers and the major shippers to define standard for international maritime shipping. The IMO, since 1959, has as its core regulation the Safety of Life at Sea (SOLAS)[8] convention. SOLAS is actually a treaty signed by all member nations of the UN. It provides conventions, standards, and regulations for international safety, security and environmental regulations for ships at sea. It is generally considered the most important treaty in international transportation. It has fourteen areas that cover:

- Provisions for the control of ships when in ports of entry and exit throughout the world

- Construction standards of ships to create waterproof areas for crew and passengers to survive when water is taken onboard a ship

- Fire protection, fire detection and fire extinction include the require intervals for mandatory training and testing of the ship's procedures

- Life savings appliances and arrangements that define the standards for life saving equipment and the minimum required based on a ship's size and operations

- Radio communications including protected frequencies, the requirements for the Global Marine Distress Safety System (GMDSS), Emergency Indicating Radio Beacons (EPRIBs), and Search and Rescue Transponders (SARTS)

- Safety of navigation including the definition of the minimum acceptable level of navigation on board a vessel, the maintenance of meteorological equipment for ships; ice patrols, requirements for re-routing a ship and the requirements for maintenance of search and rescue services. It also sets forth requirements and protocols for ships to engage in area where there is a distress signal

- Carriage of cargos is included and requires secure and process cargo based on type, risk, and perishability

- Carriage of dangerous goods covers the specific areas of hazardous materials including the marking, labelling and stowage protocols for any hazardous materials or other dangerous goods

- The nuclear ships section covers standards, protocols, maintenance requirements and the requirements for handling radioactive materials on board ship and in disposal

- It defines the international Safety Management Code which governs the requirements of safety operations while onboard a ship

- Safety measures for high speed watercraft

- Special measures to handle maritime security for the ship, ports, and the interactions of cargo with both

- Safety measures for bulk cargo and bulk carriers

- The requirements for verification of compliance with SOLAS

- Safety measures for operating in polar water

Besides the above measure, the IMO is also active in environmental regulation through SOLAS and its amendments. Of note are agreements related to the treatment of sea water used for cooling ship engines (often called bilge water). As this water mixes with oil, grease and other substances, SOLAS requires this water to be purified before it returned to the sea. More recently, SOLAS has completed and is working on ballast water. Ballast water is sea water taken into the ballast tanks of ships to help them maintain their position and stability in the sea. Ballast water is taken on and released throughout the shipping process. The challenge is that the release of ballast water can introduce new species into ecological environments throughout the world creating unintended consequences related to marine life, national predators, etc. The IMO has developed a strategy to limit this and is getting global compliance.

The International Civil Aviation Organization (ICAO) [9], founded in 1940, is an agency of the United Nations that works with all member states to define the safety and security measures for international passenger and cargo flights. There are 192 members and the organization develops standards and practices that help drive safety, security, and environmental improvements in the airline industry for passengers and cargo.

---

[8] http://www.imo.org/en/About/Conventions/ListOfConventions/Pages/International-Convention-for-the-Safety-of-Life-at-Sea-(SOLAS),-1974.aspx

The current strategic objectives for the IACO are:

- <u>Safety</u> – This is driven by the IACO Global Safety Plan (GSP) which emphasizes state based monitoring and management of safety

- <u>Air Navigation capacity and Security</u> – This area is related to upgrading global infrastructure for air navigation and developing global standards and procedures for air navigation and safety along with optimization processes to add capacity

- <u>Security and Facilitation</u> – Defines IACO's role in air transportation security with an emphasis on their facilitation mission

- <u>Economic Development of air Transport</u> – Defines IACO's role in support economic policies and development within in global air industry

- <u>Environmental Protection</u> – Helps to define and support the implementation of environmental policies within the UN and within the IACO specific for air environmental improvements

Environmental Regulation in the US for Transportation

The primary regulatory agency in the US for environmental matters is the Environmental Protection Agency (EPA). The EPA defines environmental standards for all facets of the US Government, consumers, and industry. The EPA studies environmental issues and impacts and creates regulatory standards for environmental impact and ensures industry and others conform to those standards. Environmental regulation that covers transportation is part of the EPA and specific transportation regulatory agencies. The foundational areas of environmental regulation from the EPA are related to air, water, chemicals and toxins, public health, and land usage, waste and remediation. The EPA has also increased its research and regulation around sustainability in the areas of energy, food waste, recycling, and transportation.

Within transportation, the Department of Transportation (DOT) has a primary mission for environment regulation and oversight. They do so through their influence with the EPA on transportation environmental issues and the resulting National Environmental Policy Act (NEPA). NEPA covers issues related to the development, implementation, and use of transportation infrastructure, the fuel and emission standards including the Corporate Average Fuel Economy (CAFÉ) standards, and specific NEPA procedures for each transportation mode implemented by the transportation agencies. This process forms a core of environmental regulation and management that covers planning and execution at a strategic, industry, and transportation mode level. For hazardous materials, the Pipeline and Hazardous Materials Safety Administration (PHMSA) administers environmental regulation for both the pipeline industry and all hazardous materials regardless of mode of transportation.

Antitrust Regulations

In discussing the history of transportation regulation, we have covered most of the key regulatory laws set up to define the concept of antitrust and how it is administered. This includes the creation of the ICC, the Sherman Antitrust act of 1890, the Clayton Act of 1914 along with the creation of the Federal Trade Commission to oversee mergers and acquisitions, and the Robinson-Patman Act of 1936.

This legacy of regulation has given the case law to define two kinds of antitrust violations:

- The Per Se Violation - The Per Se violation under antitrust is a situation where a company's actions constitute a breech in the law making the action illegal. Because it is illegal, by law, there is no requirement to prove that any party was harmed; it is simply illegal. Acts like price-fixing (colluding to keep prices high), market-fixing (colluding to define markets between two competitors to ensure no overlap), or price discrimination (a process whereby a company charges two largely different prices for companies virtually similar) are all examples of the Per Se violation.

- Rule of Reason Violation – with a Rule of Reason violation, the affected party must show they were materially harmed to show an antitrust violation. The reason for this is that areas, like pricing and competitive practices may be legal when practiced. However, there can be a thin line between what is acceptable and an antitrust violation. Most Rule of Reason violations involve the "unreasonable" restraint of trade, or an attempt to cause a competitor to cannot effectively compete in an open market. This can include any corporate action to include mergers and acquisitions, price setting and pricing practices, specific customer relationships and conditions, and specific practices in competing with others. The challenge is showing that the restraint in trade in question constituted harm.

The US has a deregulated transportation industry that supports market growth through competition, efficiency and customer satisfaction. The transportation industry is the most regulated industry in the US. As we have seen, developing the body of regulatory law has happened over the last 100+ years. It started with the recognition of the need to protect cities and others from predatory business practices. It evolved to setting safety, security and environmental standards.

---

[9] https://www.icao.int/Pages/default.aspx

Often, the standards set for the transportation industry has helped it to develop and grow because all competitors and customers work with the same equipment and that equipment is portable between all modes. Containerization has also dramatically improved the flow of goods through transportation and the regulatory standards for handling containers has led to increased safety while the security regulations governing entry, movement and exit has led to strong increases in the security of cargo globally.

Regulations exist to serve the public needs and interests. When citizens or consumers gain the value driven from the safety and efficiency of the transportation system, they also experience the positive impact of regulations. Ultimately, it is that measure, more than other that must be evaluated when looking at the effectiveness of freight transportation in the supply chain.

CHAPTER 3: GLOBAL SHIPPING AND CUSTOMS

INTRODUCTION

As we will find, understanding the importance of the global regulatory environment helps to put the global shipping process and the role of customs in a greater perspective. The process of globalization has been an active part of society since the first wanderers banded together to form a tribe. Generally, we can think of globalization[10] as a sociological and economic process of integrating societies to create value in economic trade, development through the free flow of investment and capital, and the ability to leverage lower costs of labor with a result in losing the leverage but the gain of a new economic market. The steady process of globalization has created the need for freight transportation at the levels and volumes we see today.

Unlike domestic shipping, shipping freight globally is more complicated. The complications arise primarily because when we think about global trade, we must consider:

- The cycle time from order to deliver will often be in months, not days. This is due primarily to the elongated shipping cycle of using container or bulk carriers' ships, and the gateway process (like trade clearance through customs) that are needed to exit one country with freight and enter another.

- International and country-based regulations that govern the processes, standards, and behaviors of freight at rest and under movement. With international shipping, more regulations must be addressed for security, border entry, cargo designation and more. The shipping documentation also is more complex due to things like duties and import fees and their lack of global standardization.

The Financial Transactions Typically Require Banks that act as intermediaries in the buying and selling transaction. The broad term for this is "trade finance" and is a specific set of processes that banks use to ensure the integrity of a global purchase. These financial transactions are for more business-to-business type of purchases that involve large sums. For individuals using eCommerce, specific financial processes occur but these are generally obscured from the consumer. Trade Finance uses the bank to validate the buyer and their ability to pay for the goods with the seller's ability to product and deliver the goods. This will be discussed later but in most B2B transactions today, banks provide the trust needed for a trusted transaction.

---

[10] 1978 World Commission on Environment and Development (WECD)

Purchases and payments involve <u>currency conversion</u> that must be defined and consistent between both parties. Currency conversion is needed where the buy and the seller are not using the same currency. Since currency fluctuates, the trade contract must define when a specific currency rate will be referenced as part of an exchange. In addition, the revenue created from these transactions have potential taxation consequence depending on whether the buyer or seller have operations in these countries.

In the next section, we will review the global trade process to understand the roles and requirements to effectively manage global shipping along with the understanding of the role of customs in the shipping and receiving of freight.

THE GLOBAL TRADE PROCESS

Like most things in the supply chain, there are consistent and replicable processes that are most often used for global trade. These processes drive the trade process from the point of ordering through invoice and payment reconciliation. We will introduce a few new terms in this process and the different companies that are involved to ensure the transaction goes as expected. As we go deeper into the process, we will introduce specific documents, i.e. paperwork, that must be completed and the optional documents that might be needed based on the product, the locations of the buyers and sellers and the nature of the transaction itself. Finally, we will discuss how transportation is used and how it is contracted in an international setting using <u>Incoterms</u>; a set of standard terms specific to the transportation movements in a trading contract.

To begin, let's look at a global purchasing transaction. Figure 3 shows the basic outline of the transaction and how it moves from planning through execution at a general level. Like in all purchasing transactions, there is a buyer and a seller. Instead of a traditional purchase order, international shipments use the trading contract. This serves the same purpose as a purchase order but contains additional information required in these transactions.

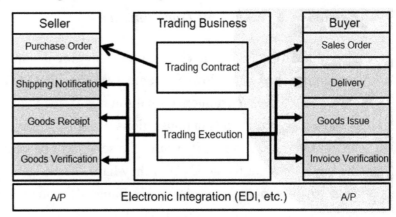

Figure 3. International Trading Transaction Flow

The trading contract forms the foundation of the terms of the sales of the goods to the buyer. At the most basic level, the trading contract will define:

- The identities of the buyer and seller

- A detailed description of the goods to be purchased and delivered

- The classification of the goods using the harmonized classification categories

- The price to be charged for the goods

- The payment terms by defining one of the eleven standard Incoterms

- Delivery details including the expected cost of transportation

- The currency that will be the foundation of the exchange, typically US Dollars or the exchangeable currency of the country of the buyer.

The data in the trading contract will be a basis for the other required shipping documents. From the trading document comes trading execution that involves:

- Setting up the trade finance aspects of the transaction which typically involves the creation and movement of letters of credit as the foundation for the ability of the shipper to pay and whose release pays the seller when the goods have been received.

- Determining the shipping terms that will define the execution of the shipping process by defining which of the eleven Incoterms will govern the shipping.

- The creation of specific international shipping documents that will govern the trading execution process.

Financing the Shipment: Trade Finance

One of the most important considerations in global shipping is ensuring the payment of goods is accomplished so it allows for some assurance that the goods are received and what they are expected to be. In most international shipments, the value and cost of the shipment is high compared to other kinds of transactions. Because of this, banks often act as intermediaries to broker the transaction, so it ensures the seller will be paid for the quality goods it delivers and the buyers pay for the goods after they have determined the seller's goods are in order. The basic process to do this is outlined in Figure 4. The process starts when the buyer and seller have completed a sales contract. The buyer (importer) will request a Letter of Credit to govern the international shipping transaction. Some companies have credit lines available and simply ask the bank to put the Letter of Credit together while others must request credit and then have it resolved with the Letter of Credit. Regardless of its origin, once the Letter of Credit (LOC) has been completed, the importer's bank (the issuing bank) provides the importer with a copy

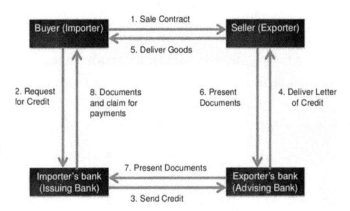

Figure 4. Trade flows using a Letter of Credit (LOC)

and forward the LOC to the exporters bank in their home company (the advising bank). The seller (exporter) will receive the LOC from their bank and then will complete the purchase by fulfilling the order and arranging for the shipment process based on the Incoterm agreed upon in the trading contract. The shipping documents flow from this process and are used to execute the shipment from the exporter's country to the importer's destination point. This includes the clearance of the goods through the exporter's customs process and the importers customs process.

Once the goods have been delivered, the shipper sends an approval to their bank (the importers bank) who then sends the money via electronic transfer to the exporter's bank. The exporter's bank then alerts the seller that the transaction is complete, and the money is available. This ends the financial reconciliation process for the international shipment.

One of the newer areas of both hype and promise in the supply chain is the use of Blockchain technologies. Blockchain is a set of technologies that create secure, trusted transactions between two or more parties. It does so by carrying every element of the transaction in digital form in "blocks" that are chained together from first to last. It is a interesting technology because these transactions create high data security with each block being cryptologically secured based on the information in the previous block (or from a key derived for the first block). This makes the transactions virtually tamper proof and counterfeit proof. It also means all the data created in the transaction is in the transaction throughout its life.

For many, the payment process that uses letters of credits and banks as intermediaries could go away for Blockchain transactions. This would work for payments because the transaction could carry the authorization to initiate the electronic transfer of the money upon completion of receiving the goods.

In theory, the electronic receipt used to validate the goods via bar code scanning and counting at the destination point could be the trigger to execute the pre-authorized money transaction to complete the payment. While in the early stages, Blockchain is much more than just hype and several pilots by major corporations are underway to test the efficacy.

The Use of Incoterms in International Shipping

Optimization of the supply chain often involves standardizing processes, practices and data to create a core common set of transactions, languages, and outcomes that are replicable and predictable. Through this lens we explore the concept of Incoterms in global shipping.

Incoterms have their principal foundation in 1936 when the International Chamber of Commerce (ICC) created the International Rules for the Interpretation of Trade Terms (Incoterms).. The initial Incoterms were modified in 1953, 1967, and 1976 to create the foundation we now draw upon from today. Subsequent changes were made in 1990 to accommodate intermodal transportation, in 2000 to better spread the allocation of loading and unloading costs and adding two additional terms to equal thirteen Incoterms. The most recent change, done in 2010, decreased the number back to eleven Incoterms resulting the terms we have today. The initial Incoterms were modified in 1953, 1967, and 1976 to create the foundation we draw

We will likely see a new release of Incoterms in 2020. The impact of security issues, among others appear to be a strong part of the discussion for the changes. What does Incoterms do in the shipping process that makes it worthwhile? Incoterms helps to simplify the terms associated with a shipping transaction to one of eleven set of standard terms to make it easier for buyers and sellers to set and understand who is responsible for the cost of the shipment, the cost of insurance and the scheduling of transportation to include when and how the transfer of liability will occur between the seller and the buyer in an international shipment. Figure 5[11] provides the current set of Incoterms based on the 2010 standard. One way to look at Incoterms is the progressive nature of the responsibilities the buyer or seller have to the transportation process. In reading Figure 5, we start at the top left with "Packaging". Based on the

Distribution of costs according to the Incoterm negotiated in the contract

SPECIFICATIONS	Departure from ware-house	Main transportation not paid by the seller			Main transportation paid by the seller				Shipping charges paid by the seller until reaching destination point		
Incoterm / Cost	EXW	FCA	FAS	FOB	CFR	CIF	CPT	CIP	DAT	DAP	DDP
Packaging	S	S	S	S	S	S	S	S	S	S	S
Loading from warehouse	B	S	S	S	S	S	S	S	S	S	S
Pre-carriage	B	S	S	S	S	S	S	S	S	S	S
Export customs clearance	B	S	S	S	S	S	S	S	S	S	S
Handling at departure	B	B	B	S	S	S	S	S	S	S	S
Main transportation	B	B	B	B	S	S	S	S	S	S	S
Transportation insurance	B	B	B	B	B	S	B	S	S*	S	S
Handling at arrival	B	B	B	B	B	B	B	B	S	S	S
Import customs clearance	B	B	B	B	B	B	B	B	B	B	S
Post-carriage	B	B	B	B	B	B	B	B	B	B	S
Unloading into warehouse	B	B	B	B	B	B	B	B	B	B	S

S: Cost paid by the buyer
B: Cost paid by the seller

Figure 5. INCOTERMS - 2010 version

Incoterm chosen, we then read under that Incoterm to determine which party pays what part of the shipment costs. At the extremes are EXW (Ex-Works) and DDP (Delivered Duty Paid). All transportation under EXW is paid by the buyer. Under DDP, all transportation costs are paid by the seller. Anything in between has costs split either favoring the buyer or seller at some level. We need to create context for the figure and then discuss its meaning. Looking down the left side of the chart, we see the eleven terms available to any shipping transaction. The chart stars with the seven general terms usable by all modes and begins with EXW and ends with DDP. The last four are available only to maritime based transactions and are specific to international maritime shipping.

Using Incoterms has dramatically helped the process of global shipping through the clarity it provides. Based on the terms, carriers, insurance companies and even customs have a more immediate understanding of the terms and from who to expect interaction and payment.

Shipping Document Requirements

Now that we understand how the transaction will be funded and what terms are available for the international shipment, we turn to understand the requirements for documentation in the international shipping lifecycle. The following are typically the required documents needed to execute a global shipment:

- The Commercial Invoice – The Commercial Invoice is a critical and required document for every international shipment and includes:

  o The time and place in which the merchandise was sold

  o The seller's and buyer's full names, addresses, corporate tax ID numbers and the contract information for both for the transaction

  o A detailed description of the goods that will include:

    - Product number, general product name and line detail for each item in the order

    - Any grading or quality associated with a specific line item good

    - Marks, numbers of symbols that identify the good

    - Currency of exchange for the invoice

    - Country of origin of each good

---

[11] https://iccwbo.org/resources-for-business/incoterms-rules/incoterms-rules-2010

- Quantity and price per unit

  - The country of shipment

  - Any certifications required by the buyer's country

  - Any US Government issued certifications for the products

  - US Export Control information which will typically be a number within the Commerce Control List managed by the Bureau of Industry and Security and provides a numbering system for every commodity, technology or software to be imported or exported. This number will determine, based on the origination and destination country whether there is additional export or import licenses and fees that may apply to the transaction and that must be included in the Commercial Invoice.

  - The point in the transportation process where the title of the goods will transfer from the seller to the buyer. This is also defined and must match the Incoterm chosen for the transaction.

  - The method of payment, to include the Letter of Credit

  - Relevant law or other aspects that will govern the transaction

- <u>Certificates of Origin</u> – Products may have to provide certificates of origin showing where the product was made and what % was made by country, etc.

- <u>The Packing List</u> – this list provides a detailed accounting for the entire shipment for each product. It identifies the product number, description, and total quantity for each item in the shipment. The packing list will often be used by any freight forwarders that use it to create the bill of lading or the bank for the Letter of Credit.

- <u>Bills of Lading</u> –, a bill of lading authorizes the holder to the title of these goods. Every carrier must have a valid bill of lading for their shipment to show they may manage those goods (versus being stolen). In international shipping, there are several ways we use bills of lading:

  - <u>Domestic bill of lading</u> – For any local, in country transportation movement, the carrier must have a bill of lading authorizing them to manage the goods and it must be transferred from that carrier to whomever (freight forwarder, the company or an international carrier) will continue to manage the shipment to an international destination.

  - <u>Ocean bill of lading</u> – The Ocean bill of lading, as the name suggests, is required for any international shipment using the maritime mode. There are typically two kinds of these:

- **Straight bill of lading:** Applies to a specific consignee only. The consignee takes control of the goods by presenting the bill of lading by presenting it as an original, signed version.

- **Negotiable bill of lading:** This bill of lading is based on the order of shipping and is signed by the shipper and presented to the seller's bank in their home country.

- <u>Airway Bill</u> – The airway bill is a bill of lading for air, or the airway bill. This is a non-negotiable bill provided to the carrier for authorizing to move goods through the air mode.

- <u>Entry in the AES Systems</u> – The Automated Export System (AES) is run by the US Chamber of Commerce requires a shipment to be entered into system if the value of the purchase order is over $2,500. Often the company in the US does this but it can also be done by a freight forwarder or other transportation service provider if allowed

- <u>Consular Invoice</u> – Although rare today, a consular invoice provides a version of the commercial invoice in the language of the country providing detailed information on the merchandise being shipped. It is reviewed and approved by a consul at an embassy which certifies the document. The document is usually used to aid in determining import taxes. There are still about fifteen small countries that require this

Besides the above, international shipping may require additional documents if the shipments involve dangerous goods, if the countries involved require an import or export license.

CUSTOMS AND GLOBAL TRADE

The above covers most of all shipping transactions. As one can see, funding the transaction, defining terms, and then ensuring all the paperwork is in order are all important to the successful delivery of goods. The one critical area left to explore in international shipping is the process used to move goods in and out of a country's sovereign borders. To do this, we look at the role of customs in the global shipping lifecycle

---

[12] https://www.cbp.gov/travel/clearing-cbp

The concept of customs has evolved from an agency of the government that collects taxes and customs fees as part of revenue generation for the government to a screening and enforcement services with ensuring that freight coming into and out of the country meets all legal requirements for shipment. The <u>US Bureau of Customs and Border Protection</u> (CPB) leverages the intelligence, screening and inspection processes (Figure 6[12]) as core to its mission of safety and security.

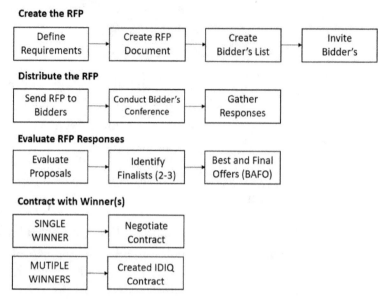

Figure 6. Customs Clearance Process - US

The customs process is built to evaluate, screen and review freight coming in and out of the country with a specific goal of ensuring goods entering or leaving the US have identified the appropriate freight category that ensures a clear understanding of taxes or import/export duties that may be due in a shipment. In addition to screening freight to ensure it is legitimate, the CPB also screens freight looking for specific threats or situations including:

- Evaluating freight for the potential of counterfeiting higher value goods and ensuring counterfeits are discovered and not allowed past the border

- Screening and evaluating freight for radioactivity and other threats of terrorism that may threaten the borders or US citizens

- Evaluating and ensuring incoming freight has not engaged in human offenses

The CPB does this through activities and regulations that help create predictability of outbound and inbound freight. The core of the CPB role in managing entry and exit of freight into the country is through the customs process itself. Figure 6 provides a view to this process. This process is the import view of customs clearance. The export view is similar just in reverse where all statutory licenses and permits are gathered, the documentation is prepared, and the goods are presented for evaluation and are inspected or allowed to pass with the goods then moving from the US to the carrier to be shipped internationally. From an import perspective, the goods are presented at the port and then transferred to a bonded area.

Bonded areas are secured storage areas in the control of the CBP and must be evaluated and cleared from the bonded area to be released. This is done by reviewing the import declaration, confirming the category and value of goods and then applying any statues related to import fees or taxes. Once it has been determined the duties and taxes, the goods are evaluated for inspection. Goods subject to inspection are reviewed, the freight category is validated, and the goods are inspected to ensure the only goods there are the once claimed. If no inspection is required, the goods may pass after they have passed the screen monitoring. Once completed, all documents are audited as a check and balance to the process. The goods declaration is then accepted, the goods are released, and the duty is arranged for payment either in advance or after final clearance. After the transaction is complete, it is subject to a post-duty audit and if any discrepancies occur that change the duties, the receiver is contacted to reconcile.

In our global business and consumer environment today, moving goods in and out of countries is more complicated than the process we use domestically but are there to ensure the effective flow of desired goods while prohibiting the entry of undesirable and illegal goods. The customs process is a necessary and intended choke-point in the supply chain that support the custom's mission.

Most governments also ensure the customs offices provide a mechanism for regular and trusted shippers to bypass several customs steps. For instance, the US has a commercial Fast-Track program that allow commercial entities like trucking companies and others to register and be authorized for an expedited entry process. Similarly, the US C-TPAT (Customs Trade Partnership against Terrorism) Program allows US and foreign entities to register, have an extensive review of their security operations and be certified to enter the US using an expedited process. The AEO (Authorized Economic Operator) program is like C-TPAT and is used in the EU to expedite customers operations of regular and trusted shippers.

Regardless of the approach to international shipping, the role of customs in ensuring border security and ensuring trusted and verified freight moves in and out of the border is a critical part of the global shipping supply chain. Understanding the processes, documentation, and clearance approaches is critical for any organization that needs to ship and receive goods globally.

CHAPTER 4: TRANSPORTATION PRICING

INTRODUCTION

Like virtually everything else, the services provided by transportation providers costs money. Transportation pricing comes from the process of rate making that considers many aspects and factors in moving goods both domestically and internationally. Most often, the cost of transportation is based on either a flat rate which covers the cost of all aspects of transportation unless there is a specified additional charge or a metered rate usually as a rate per mile plus any authorized additional charges, or surcharges.

In this chapter, we will discuss how transportation pricing is developed, how rates are calculated, and how the transportation company needs to understand its cost structures to set pricing that can make the company profit.

PRICING BASICS:

Understanding Market Price

In a regulated market, the government will set the maximum, and sometimes minimum, price that can be charged for transportation. This was traditionally done either as a rate per mile or rate per pound. When a government deregulates the market, it allows market forces to determine the price. This is done primarily through the normal economic models that set prices in any market. We consider a market price to be the price that a customer will accept for a transportation transaction. We consider the price to be "what the market can bear" and will generally be in a consistent range under normal circumstances. If either the demand for shipping or the available capacity of carriers changes significantly, the market will go through a time of chaos while rates change and find an equilibrium. While supply and demand plays a large role in market pricing, it is only one factor. Other factors play an equally important part in how market prices change. Market forces are those variables that impact the consumer's interest in paying a specific rate for transportation. There are several market forces that drive the market price for transportation. Below are five specific forces that affect market price day to day:

- Build Your Own – Even before understanding the market for transportation pricing, a company makes a more fundamental decision. For some this is a serious consideration for others, more of a passing thought. The first thing a company must decide is whether to build its own transportation infrastructure or to outsource it to a third Party. Companies that use trucking exclusively might evaluate whether it makes sense to own their own trucks and drivers. While this is not a trivial decision, it is easily analyzed and is done by understanding the magnitude of its own transportation needs.

Companies with simple and straightforward transportation needs, like the need to pick up suppliers from a few local suppliers and deliveries within a few hours of its facility may buy its own trucks and hire drivers, especially if it does not require CDL licensing which usually happens if a company can use box trucks rather than cab and trailer configurations. Understanding its own capacity and frequency of transportation allows a company to evaluate the purchase a few assets, consider the cost of maintaining and insuring them, the fuel cost, and the cost of the drivers. If it economically makes sense, a company might try to manager it won transportation fleet instead of using third parties.

- Supply and Demand / Economic Conditions – When thinking about supply and demand for transportation we typically look at the total amount of freight (demand) against the available capacity to ship (supply). There are several factors that may affect this. The economy plays a major role in the supply and demand of transportation. When the economy is expanding the demand for many goods, industrial and consumer, rises increasing the demand for freight. To meet supply, carriers will work to increase their capacity over the short to mid-term to meet the demand. Should the demand fall off suddenly, the carriers will find themselves with significant excess capacity without demand. For some modes, like motor carriers and rail, it is possible to reduce capacity relatively quickly. The typically approach for these carriers to is have about 80% of their transportation assets owned and active and about 20% through leasing arrangements that can be terminated on notice within 30 to 60 days.

Other modes, maritime and air along with pipeline do not have the same ability to rapidly reduce capacity. The purchases of aircraft and ships, even in a leasing situation, typically have a much longer lease cancellation notice period making it more difficult to manage short and mid-term capacity. One might have noticed that in large economic downturns, like the Great Recession of 2008-2009, airlines may end up in chapter 11 reorganization with bankruptcy protections. This is one mechanism used by these companies to renegotiate contracts, payment terms, etc. to remain healthy.

- The ability to create a full shipment - Different modes have different standards for weight and volume (density) that defines the rate category used to calculate a rate for transportation. If the shipper can fill up a standard piece of transportation equipment (truck trailer, shipping container, rail car, etc.) it is considered a "full load". If the shipper cannot fill the entire piece of equipment, we refer to that as a "partial load". Partial loads will be more expensive on a rate per mile or per pound than a full load. The reason for this deal with partial loads use consolidation techniques to combine partial loads into full loads for segments of the transportation of shipment. These methods, which will be discussed in the modes section, keep the load from costing twice as much as a full load through this consolidation approach.

- <u>The likelihood of a load at the destination of a shipment (Back Haul)</u> – Another aspect that affects market rates is whether the carrier shipping the load can find another load at or near the destination of the shipment. We call this a backhaul although the load doesn't have to take the driver back to their origination point. Part of the cost mechanics of transportation involves the need for chains of shipments where a carrier leaves an originating point and then arrives at a destination with the ability to get the next load near the destination. The more remote a destination is, in terms of potential shipping volume, the more likely the rate will be higher. This is done because carrier must cover the cost to return with an empty load or to travel beyond the immediate vicinity to get another load. In both of these instances, the carrier must "deadhead" to another origination point. Deadheading is something carriers work hard to avoid because the company makes no money but must cover the variable costs of the fuel, driver labor etc., without revenue. In addition, drivers will typically get paid around 20 – 30% less for deadheading if they are employed by the carrier whereas independent carriers usually get nothing. Finally, and more related to motor carriers than others, deadheading that involves carrying an empty trailer is much more dangerous than having a full load. Trailers that are empty are half as heavy as they normally will be and things like high winds or other rapid changes can more easily cause the driver to have an accident.

- <u>Lane Characteristics</u> – Another factor that drive rates is the lane that a shipper needs to use to get their goods shipped. Lanes are a defined set of at least two points, often cities but they can also be a general region, zip code, or a location like a port, that define the origination and destination of a shipment. Lanes are serviced by transportation carriers who create routes (driving directions) to operate in the lane. To service a lane, a transportation carrier must allocate equipment (trucks, airplanes, rail engines and rail cars, etc.) and operators (drivers' pilots, engineers, etc.) as dedicated assets of the lane. Lanes are populated by transportation providers based on the demand for shipping between those points. The more customer demand there is for a lane, the more likely many carriers with a large of amount of capacity will be available to ship goods. High traffic lanes will are cheaper per mile than lanes that are less trafficked. This results directly from supply and demand. Shippers must expect to pay more for shipping to less dense or trafficked areas than others. The one exception to this may be found in the international maritime shipping space. With international maritime, many people use the same ports of exit and entry causing increased port congestion. When a port is over-subscribed, i.e. has more ships want to enter the port than port capacity, the port will increase the port fees due to supply and demand. There, shippers may use other nearby ports or other transit styles, like going through the Panama Canal to avoid the west coast prices.

SHIPMENT CHARACTERISTICS THAT AFFECT RATE PRICES

The items above are general considerations for market prices. These factors impact the market in terms of raising or lowering rates for either a mode or all modes of carriers based on these conditions. Besides this, there are several factors that drive individual rate making that include:

- Shipment Characteristics – The characteristics of the shipment has more impact on the cost to ship goods than most other factors. Shipping Characteristics include:

- Volume and Weight (Density) - Understanding the density characteristics of an average load for the company, whether full or partial, helps the company gain insight into the transportation strategies in terms of frequency of transportation and mode. The overall density of a product will point us to specific modes depending on the total weight of an average shipment. The shipping needs to move 100,000 or more tons will be handled by large bulk carriers like rail or ship simply because of the need equipment that can handle high weight. Generally, however, the more flexible and quicker shipping carriers, air and truck, can carry around 20 – 25 tons although air can carry perhaps up to 100 tons with larger, dedicated freighters. Regardless, the difference is striking. Typically, the denser and heavier something is, the cheaper it will be to ship primarily because they require little extra work to create the shipment. Highly dense items, like iron ore, grain, and coal, need minimum handling and do not have significant protection needs, i.e. they may not need covering, although grain will, and they require no special handling

- Value - The total value of a shipment also plays a role in the cost of shipping. Virtually all goods are shipped with insurance but the more valuable the goods the more the insurance will cost. More important, the value of the goods reflects on the other aspects of the shipment in terms of increased packaging, more careful handling, and an increased need for security that all reflect in the cost to transport. Typically, the higher the value of a good, the more it will cost to ship. Further there is a direct correlation between density and value. Items that are very valuable typically have a small density and require extra measures to ensure they are stable and secured when shipping them.

- Distance - Distance plays an important role in understanding the potential cost for transportation. Typically, the further the shipment must travel the more the shipment will cost. On a cost per mile or pound basis, however, the further a shipment goes the lower the cost per mile or pound although the greater the absolute cost.

- Time - All things being equal, if the shipment does not have a significant time constraint, it will be much less, even dramatically less to ship than if there is a high time constraint.

The primary reason for this is that time constrained items are moved exclusively by the air or truck mode which, from a ton-mile perspective, will cost around 15 – 17 cents per ton-mile for truck and 85 cents to $2.50 per ton-mile for air. Compare that to about a penny per ton-mile for international maritime shipping and 2 to 3 cents per ton-mile for rail.

- <u>Access to Goods</u> – The ease at which the carrier can get to the goods is also a factor in the rate. For instance, the standard for truck is a loading dock. If a customer does not have a loading dock there will likely be an upcharge due to the inconvenience.

- <u>Mode Choices</u> – The choice of a specific mode will drive rates differently. The shipment characteristics may specifically suggest a mode. For instance, a shipment of a two-hundred tons of goods equals 400,000 pounds in the US or 181,437 kilograms. This weight is most economical when sent using a "low and slow" mode like ship or rail. Similarly, time plays a critical role in mode choice. Even if a shipment is 400,000 pounds, if it is 2,000 miles away, if there isn't enough time to use rail or ship, then the shipper must resolve to either truck or air. Clearly, this creates a significant cost impact as 400,000 pounds could be put into just two or three rail cars but if using truck, and assuming 40,000 pounds of freight per truck, we must have ten trucks to do the same job.

- <u>Freight Surcharges</u> – Freight surcharges are added charges to a standard transportation rate based on industry practices and specific shipping decisions and needs. Surcharges are additional costs specified in the rate quote. Some surcharges are fee based and some are based on the base freight. Surcharges are required based on the shipment itself and its characteristics rather than a specific customer need. Below are common surcharges used in shipping:

  - <u>Fuel Surcharge</u> –, Every mode will charge a fee for fuel. These rates are based on different variables. Some can include regular indexes for fuel etc. while others are a percentage of additional cost based on the current fuel rate. Regardless of the charge, it most often a small percentage of the base freight cost. Different modes may have different words for fuel surcharges. For instance, in maritime shipping the fuel surcharge is called a bunker adjustment fee.

  - <u>Security Charges</u> – Many international shipments using air and maritime will charge a security surcharge to cover the additional security processes, customs process etc. that must be cleared to have an authorized international shipment.

  - <u>Terminal Handling Fees</u> – These surcharges are common only in air and maritime and involve the costs of working within and through an international port.

o Currency Exchange Fees – International shipments are also subject to currency exchange fees as they pay carriers in local currencies

o Equipment charges – Some modes will add a surcharge for equipment when a shipper wants specialized equipment. This is true in the motor carrier and rail industries. For instance, using a "Reefer", or refrigerated units will always have a surcharge.

o Location Characteristics and Needs: Several assessorial charges come from the characteristics of the origination location and the destination location. These surcharges include:

- Liftgate – If a location does not have a loading dock it will require a truck with a liftgate to allow for pallet loading on the ground.

- Limited Access – If a location is not easily accessible by the carrier equipment (this is most common in motor carriers) then a surcharge will apply to cover the additional time and effort needed to secure the load. Limited access facilities may include schools, prisons, military installations and others.

- Residential Pick up or Delivery – Surcharges apply to any delivery or pickup in a residential zone. Interestingly, the driver of this surcharge is location verification software that uses zoning rules and other factors to determine location categories. It is not unusual to have a professional building (medical, law, etc.) to be in a zone that results in a residential surcharge.

- Convention or Trade-Show – A common surcharge for location is the convention or trade-show surcharge. Like residential surcharges, additional charges are added if the driver, again, dominantly motor carrier, must pick up or deliver to a convention center or major trade-show location. Typically, a driver must find the person who can tell them where to drop the load, they must find another person who can accept their manifest, it may involve long wait times, etc. Charges offset the additional work and hassle of delivery.

- Freight Assessorial Charges – Similar to surcharges, assessorial charges are additional charges beyond the freight rate. Some companies mix the surcharges and accessorial charges together as one category and others use both categories. We will separate these in categories with the notion that assessorial charges are usually base on customer specific needs or desires. Below are typical assessorial charges that can apply:

- Insurance – Although insurance is technically options, it is always used to ensure damaged, delayed, or stolen goods are covered.

- Notification of Shipment Status – a common accessorial is shipment status. Usually an extra charge, notification provides visibility to the shipment and automated notifications when shipments are delayed and delivered, etc.

- Blind Shipment – Blind shipments enable a third Party to manage the transportation movement with neither party knowing the identity of the other.

- Wait Time – Wait time occurs most often because the shipper or the receiver are congested during pickup or delivery causing the driver to wait. Usually, some amount of wait time is free, typically 30 minutes or an hour and after that wait time is charged on an hourly basis usually at 15 minutes, or any part thereof basis.

- Hazardous Materials (Hazmat) – Hazmat may be charged as a surcharge but normally falls under an assessorial charge. Usually, hazmat charges are based on a cost per pound of hazmat material with a minimum charge that makes taking the risk worth the cost.

- Demurrage / Detention – Maritime carriers must ensure their ships are loaded in a reasonable amount of item. Carriers need their equipment back after the shipment is done. Carriers provide a time window for using and notice of the available of the equipment to be returned. If that time window is exceeded the carrier charges for 'leasing' their equipment on a daily, sometimes hourly, basis. This is also true in maritime. If a ship takes too long to load, the port will charge demurrage for tying up the loading area.

As one can tell, the concept of a transportation rate and the resulting market price, based on customer acceptance, is based on many factors. Ultimately, the rate charged by the transportation company must be both competitive and profitable for a company to stay in business. The market competitive dynamic is always changing the carriers must know and adapt to these changes quickly. Still, if a rate to a customer is not profitable, the company loses money. Understanding the costs associating a shipment and with the allocation of company overhead into the rate is critical in understanding the total cost impact and, therefore, the potential profit in a market rate. Now that we have discussed a market price and things that go into it, let's look at the other side of the equation: understanding the cost basis of the company.

CARRIER COSTS: CREATING PROFIT FROM RATES

Understanding Costs: Variable and Overhead Costs

Like any other business, a transportation carrier will always seek to optimize their profits by charging as much as the market will bear and ensuring their costs are well below what they charge. Since they don't know specifically what the market will bear until a customer says "yes", carriers must have a very strong understanding of their cost basis. There are different ways to go about this. For our purposes, we will use a costing approach that considers the variable costs associated with an "average" shipment and the overhead cost that must be added to achieve the cost basis of the company. This final cost, or the market cost, helps the company know how much potential profit is in a rate. This often will help to set discounting policies and analyze the revenue and profit the company is making through transportation services.

Determining an Average Cost per Load

The first thing we need to understand is "What will it cost for me to run a typical shipment". While there is no hard and fast "typical shipment", a company can derive a profile of a shipment by looking at their historical contracts and their spot market deals (more on this later). We will use a hypothetical trucking company (we will typically use trucking companies for our examples as trucks are typically involved in over 85% of all shipments in the US) that operates seven lanes and had about $20 million in revenue in the last fiscal year. Table 4 shows the lanes, costs, and revenues based on the past fiscal year. Each lane in Table 4 has a breakout of the variable costs that make up a normal shipment by lane. These costs include the cost of the driver, meals and incidentals during the trip, the fuel cost (fuel surcharges help offset some of this and are included in the revenue number), an allocation for vehicle insurance, registration, and maintenance, and a basic order processing cost. This creates a cost per shipment for each lane, which varies widely based on the lane distance.

Lane	Miles	Driver Cost Per Load	Fuel Cost	Insurance / Other	Cost	Orders	Rev Per Order	Total Miles	Total Revenue	Total Cost	Gross Margin
				Current Lanes, Cost and Revenue Experience from Pervious Year							
Lane 1	811	649	$ 239.61	$ 8.50	$ 896.91	1,150	$ 1,711	932,650	$ 1,967,891.50	$ 1,031,446.50	47.59%
Lane 2	922	784	$ 272.41	$ 8.50	$1,064.61	922	$ 1,945	850,084	$ 1,793,677.24	$ 981,570.42	45.28%
Lane 3	345	293	$ 101.93	$ 8.50	$ 403.68	898	$ 728	309,810	$ 653,699.10	$ 362,504.64	44.55%
Lane 4	687	550	$ 202.98	$ 8.50	$ 761.08	1,354	$ 1,450	930,198	$ 1,962,717.78	$ 1,030,502.32	47.50%
Lane 5	5,321	3,831	$ 1,572.11	$ 17.22	$5,420.45	354	$ 11,227	1,883,634	$ 3,974,467.74	$ 1,918,839.30	51.72%
Lane 6	80	68	$ 23.64	$ 8.50	$ 100.14	587	$ 169	46,960	$ 99,085.60	$ 58,782.18	40.68%
Lane 7	792	673	$ 234.00	$ 8.50	$ 915.70	645	$ 1,671	510,840	$ 1,077,872.40	$ 590,626.50	45.20%
Totals:						5,910		5,464,176	$ 11,529,411.36	$ 5,974,271.86	48.18%

Table 4. Transportation Lane Cost Mechanics

After this, we see the orders associated with the lane. The spot market orders are orders that come in randomly from shippers who do not necessarily ship regularly. Contract orders are the carrier's customers who have signed contracts with an average rate based on the contracts in the lane. Spot Market and Contract rates have different averages so it's important to have the order flow for each represented to get a meaningful answer. To get the revenue per order, we take the spot orders and the contract orders and multiply them by the lane distance and the average rate for each type of quote and then combine them and take an average. We multiple the total orders for each lane by the distance to get total miles and the revenue per order times the total of orders to get an approximate revenue number. Total cost comes from multiplying the shipment cost times the total of orders.

With this information, we can derive the average revenue per load ($1,950.83), the revenue per mile (Total Revenue / Total Miles) at $2.11 per mile and the total cost per load ($1,010.85) and per mile cost (Total Cost / Total Miles) at $.1.09 cents per mile. With this, we now have half the answer to understand our expected total cost, or market cost per mile.

Determining an Average Cost per load for Corporate Overhead Costs

To be profitable on each lane, we need to add in our expected operating and overhead costs associated with running the company. We are interested in an apple to apples comparison, so we want to take the total overhead costs of the company annually and divide it by the expected number of miles driven. This gives us a cost per mile we can add to the variable cost to determine the total market cost for the company. One important note. The miles driven is considered a forecast for the company. It's fine to base a baseline on the most recent fiscal year but the company must ultimately factor in expectations of growth in costs, shipping rates and miles driven unless they are forecasting the exact same as the previous year (which company's rarely do). For our purposes, we will leave this out of

Corporate Costs	
Cost of Sales	$ 922,352.91
Cost of Operations	$ 1,152,941.14
Facility Costs	$ 345,882.34
G&A Expense	$ 537,684.47
Interest Expense	$ 59,742.72
Total Costs	**$ 3,018,603.57**
Total Miles	**5,464,176**
Cost Per Mile	**$ 0.55**

Average Cost Per Mile	
Corporate Cost / Mile	$ 0.55
Load Cost / Mile	$ 1.09
Average Cost / Mile	$ 1.65

Table 5. Overhead Allocation Cost

discussion other than to say that armed with the expected average market cost per mile, the company can effectively project their next fiscal year by creating a sales revenue forecast that resolves into an expected number of miles driven which is then applied to our average market cost per mile. Table 5 shows an example of these corporate costs and how the come together to give us the overhead rate per mile. As we can see, the overhead costs are divided into the baseline of 5.4 million miles taken from the previous year which results in a $0.70 centers per mile allocation. This number, when combined with the $1.09 cents per mile we get a cost of $1.79 per mile for the average market cost per mile. If all remains the same, i.e. the revenue per mile and the average market cost per mile, the company can expect to gross profit of $0.48 cents per mile or a 23% gross margin.

Analyzing Market Pricing and Cost per Mile calculations

We now have a picture of our business much clearer in terms of what we can and what we must charge to be profitable. With our small transportation company, we expect to be at an average market cost of $1.63 for the next fiscal year. Based on an analysis of our current contracts the contract rate will probably be around $2.11 per mile. The current spot market rate will be around $1.94.

The above is simple example. To do this the company has several more important considerations in looking at the cost and the potential market price:

- New Contracts and Contract Renewals – One of the major issues that a company must understand and work aggressively is their contract rates for both new and existing contract renewals. In today's market, contracts are often two years and may have an option for a third. Many shippers are reluctant to sign longer term contracts because the transportation carrier market is considered a commoditized market with rates going down, rather than up, in a normal year. The amount of a drop varies but changes of 2 to 3 cents per mile to 10 cents a mile. If capacity is constrained, the spot market rates will go up, but the contract rates will be the same if the contract is in force. Transportation Contracts will also have volume commitment from the shipper in terms of number of full shipments and the expected total miles used to fulfill those shipments. If the customer does not use all the shipments, they will be charged up to the minimum so companies are very careful to ensure they will use all committed elements of the transportation contract. Contract renewals are often a source of in-year rate reduction because of become of this commoditization. For example:

    A customer signed a contract two years ago and the total contract rate was $2.15 cents per mile for a committed 3,000 total shipments (1,400 the first year and 1,600 the second) with a total aggregated mileage of 782,000 for the contract. This resulted in a total two year contract value of $1,681,300. However, the company doesn't receive revenue until they ship. So, from a fiscal year perspective, if the shipments didn't start until July of that year, the company will likely only realize $420,000 revenue in that fiscal year. For the next fiscal year, they will have twelve months of shipping resulting in about $850,000 in revenue and then in the third fiscal year, which is the second half of the second year of the contract, they will experience revenue through June of that year of about 411,000 and then the contract ends if not renewed. So, the company has that and other contracts starting at the beginning of the fiscal year but to realize an entire twelve months of revenue, they will need to renew the contract before June 30 of that fiscal year. When they do, there is a high likelihood the rate will go down unless additional volume or other services are added. In our case, let's assume there is not, and the $2.15 contract rate is dropped to $2.05 per mile because of favorable market rates. The result of this is that the company will have 10 cents *less per mile charged than it thought for the second half of that year. This results in a revenue shortfall of around $40,000 that must be made up somewhere else.*

It's easy to assume that a $40,000 drop from one customer isn't such a big deal for a $20M company. The challenge carriers face is that this change will be true for many as 20 – 30% of its customers in each fiscal year if not more. To overcome this, the company needs to sign new business in the current fiscal year. The strong preference is to get customers early to take advantage of having months in the current year to get revenue, but this will not typically be the case. Renewal dates vary and so the company must manage new contracts and contract renewals aggressively to succeed

- Spot Price Fluctuations – Another important aspect is to monitor spot price fluctuations. In our example we expect the spot market to average around $1.94 over the fiscal year. Variations on this, up or down, create a sensitivity to the revenue and cost of the company. How sensitive depends on the percentage of orders that are spot versus contract orders. For our company, about 31% of our orders are spot market orders. It makes up about 25% of revenue. A 5% drop in the spot rate would have a corresponding negative impact on that revenue by 5%. A similar increase over the average would have a positive impact of 5% on revenue. Most companies watch their spot and contract rate averages at least monthly throughout the year so they can adjust forecasts or costs to meet their profit objective.

- Cost Inflation – In our example we took the information from the past fiscal year and applied to a forecast for the current. We considered no cost inflation related to employee wages (drivers and others), increased operations or facility costs etc. Because of this, our numbers, while directionally correct, must be adjusted to meet the next fiscal year's budget increases which will likely increase our average market cost per mile.

- New Regulations / Compliance Costs – As we saw in 2018 when Electronic Logging Devices (ELDs) went into mandatory compliance, new regulations may have a significant impact on capacity, driver cost, or other costs for compliance. These may blind side a company if they are not aware of the regulatory changes expected in a new year. Most companies stay ahead of this but even then, like the ELDs, it is very difficult to project the ultimate impact until it is actually happening. This may sometimes create a reactionary environment as the company seeks to respond to the change and maintain its costs and market pricing.

There are more factors, but these affect the cost and market prices in a typical carrier environment. As one can see, ensuring the company has strong fiscal cost accounting and allocation methods is critical to understand the total cost to the business of moving freight. Similarly, staying close to regulatory events and planning can help ease the issues of new regulations in the market.

We have look at market pricing and how customer acceptance of rate creates a market standard until the next customer accepts a rate and so on. We've also discussed factors affecting the rates that may be charged in the market. On the other side, we've looked at how we can create a cost basis for the company to understand its costs per mile so it can better ensure profitable deals.

In the final section we will look at rate making in practice to understand how modes ultimately create a rate presented to a customer. Like what we have done already, we will focus primarily on the trucking industry given its transparency and importance in the transportation sector. We will also touch on other mode's rate making approaches to provide a better overall understanding of how rates are done across all modes.

TRANSPORTATION ORDERS AND RATE QUOTES

Each mode of transportation has different approaches to determining the rate they will offer their customers. Rate making is similar across all modes, but each mode has differences in how they approach it. One of the best ways to examine this is to look at how trucking industry rates are created.

Trucking Rates: TL, LTL, and Quote Types

We have discussed in some detail the different considerations needed to form an effective rate for the customer and the carrier. The trucking industry handles rate making by classifying shipments in very specific ways.

The first way we classify a shipment in trucking is by determining if the load is a truckload (TL) or a Less Than Truckload (LTL). There are two principle ways we evaluate a load to determine this:

- Weighing Out – The most common way we determine a load is a truckload (TL) is based on weight. We'll go over specifics when we cover trucking but generally if a load weighs out at 35,000 pounds or more, we consider it a truckload. There are factors that can change this number including supply and demand, contract considerations and others but for now, we'll use this as our standard. Based on this any load that is less than 35,000 pounds will be considered Less Than Truckload (LTL). Weight is the primary determination of load but there is an exception

- Cubing Out – What if a shipper can fill an entire trailer rated for 35,000 pounds full of pallets with no space left but weighs only 15,000 pounds. Since the trailer can hold no more volume, wouldn't it be right to call that a TL instead of LTL. Yes! That is what we look at when considering a "cubed out" load. Sometimes, what we ship has more volume than weight and so if we fill the trailer with volume, we will consider that TL

- <u>Point to Point</u> – Transportation has been a rapidly changing market for some time. Distance used to play an important role in TL versus LTL but generally does not anymore. It is very possible carriers may consider weigh outs at 20,000 pounds as TL if they want to fill capacity. So, one might wonder, if there is a better hard and fast rule for determining TL or LTL. An additional way to think about this is based on what we expect to happen when a carrier receives a load. The point of determining LTL shipments is to understand how that shipment will be fulfilled. Since LTL has extra space in the equipment, we do not want to ship partial loads between the shipper and the receiver. In LTL, we use freight terminals (explained in the next section) to allow us to consolidate smaller loads into larger loads so the carrier can leverage their volume to keep their costs lower. LTL shipments do not go from the shipper to the receiver directly but instead go through freight terminals before getting to the final destination. Therefore, any load this is picked up at the shipper's point of origin and delivered directly to the received point of destination is, by nature of the shipment, a LT shipment. Anything that doesn't do this is LTL

We rate TL and LTL shipments differently, so this is an important factor before starting the rating process. The other area of immediate consideration is the quote being requested. Two ways companies can get a rate, or cost, for a shipment:

- <u>Spot Market Rates</u> – spot market rates are rates determined at the time of the shipment request based on overall market conditions. Some think of this as a "retail rate" which is a good analogy. Traditionally, spot market quotes were for non-contract shippers who only shipped occasionally or seasonally (<u>casual shippers</u>). Another category of customers for spot market rates are those who need to expedite goods and must use a specific carrier or service for this. To be clear, expedited rates are higher than typical spot market rates because of the immediacy of the shipment but many companies use services that provide spot market rates for this. Today, we are also seeing an increase in frequent shippers evaluating spot market rates to see if they can beat their contract rates. Distinguish this from the others. A shipper with a transportation contract will always ensure that they meet their minimum volumes. As we mentioned earlier, rates go down year to year. In a year where the spot market rates are high, they will likely ship more than their minimum through their contract carrier because it is more economical. In years where the spot market rate is lower than the contract rate, the shipper will use the contract carrier for the minimum and seek to source full TL to get a better rate. This is an important development in transportation because traditionally spot market rates were for casual shippers and was dominantly LTL. That now we are seeing TL shipments through spot market quotes to be contract rates speaks to the commodity nature of the industry but more important, to the significant increase in the effective value of automation in enabling these capabilities to be more seamless to the shipping company.

- <u>Contract Rates</u> – The other way that quotes are done is through contract rates. Contract rates are rates per mile, surcharge levels and accessorial costs put into a transportation contract at the outset of the relationship to govern the costs associated with that contract between the shipper and the carrier. We will cover transportation contracts in the next chapter but it's important to understand that the contract not has only rates but other compliance aspects that affect the total cost of transportation. Some of these are specific rules, like "no tolls" or "avoid congestion in specific areas". Others are specific terms that must be met before the carrier can charge the shipper. The most common of these is wait time. The most effective way to get the value out of contract rates is through a Transportation Management System (TMS). A TMS is part of a software category called Supply Chain Execution. The TMS is an anchor system of the shipper that allows them to codify their contract in the system, including business and compliance rules, along with rate structures that will be used. Further, a TMS can be integrated with a carrier directly or through carrier networks that automate the entire process of planning, getting a cost for the shipment (<u>shipment tendering</u>), scheduling, in-transit visibility, and Freight Audit and Pay capabilities. The TMS must be integrated electronically most often using <u>Electronic Data Interchange (EDI)</u> for orders, invoices and other things that are not time dominant and with <u>Web Services</u> for real-time integration. This creates a seamless capability for turning customer orders into shipments and getting the shipments to the destination at the lowest cost with visibility throughout the process.

Now that we've covered the characteristics of load and quote process, we can discuss each quote process in more depth to see how rates and shipments are done.

Spot Market Quoting

Companies that use spot market quotes will either call a carrier directly or may also call a <u>Freight Broker</u>. A freight broker represents multiple carriers and works like a matchmaker to match shippers and carriers to meet shipment needs.

We will discuss freight brokers more in the next section. Regardless of the source, the first thing that must be known in a spot market quote is whether the load is TL or LTL. If it is TL it is most often rated on distance between the shipper and receiver and then a rate is derived using a formula that considers the shipping characteristics and the distance. This is most often presented as a cost per mile but there are instances where a carrier may offer a flat rate for shipping that simplifies the cost because a flat rate is an "All-in" cost. For LTL, the process is considerably different and is one of the main reasons shippers us Spot Markets. To discuss LTL quotes, we need to step back and understand the concept of a freight commodity category.

Freight Categories

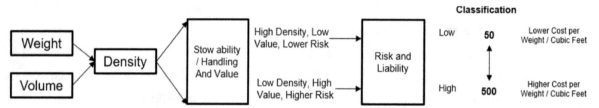

Figure 7. NMFTA Process to Determine Freight Classification

LTL freight will typically be combined with other shipments and then will use freight terminals to move the goods through the freight system to their ultimate destination. Freight companies consolidate these smaller orders into TL orders for the bulk of these movements. To plan for this consolidation process, an LTL freight quote must understand the nature of the freight itself. Specifically, the LTL carrier needs to understand the density of a typical pallet being shipped along with its value and liability and its ease of handling called stow-ability and handling.

As one can imagine, there are potentially thousands to millions of various combinations of these four characteristics of a shipment. This creates a complex system and around 1960, the National Motor Freight Transportation Association (NMFTA) create a consolidated table that took these many combinations and resolved them into eighteen commodity classes considering the characteristics of the freight in question. Figure 7[13] shows the generally approach that lead to the various classes of freight and Table 6[14] shows the NMFTA Table. The first step is to understand the density of the freight based on one pallet, or item if there is no pallet. Density is computed by taking the volume in three dimensions (length, width, and height) of the pallet or freight and the weight is divided into the result to get pounds per cubic foot. Density ranges from 50 pounds or greater down to less a 1 pound per cubic foot. The density is analyzed based on the stow-ability, handling and value creating factors that characterize high density, low value, and lower risk to a low density, high value, higher risk rating.

Density (Weight per Cubic Feet)		
Greater than or equal to	And Less than	Estimated Class
50	N/A	50
35	50	55
30	35	60
22.5	30	65
15	22.5	70
13.5	15	77.5
12	13.5	85
10.5	12	92.5
9	10.5	100
8	9	110
7	8	125
6	7	150
5	6	175
4	5	200
3	4	250
2	3	300
1	2	400
N/A	1	500

Table 6. NMFT Freight Categories

Based on these ratings and associated risks, the pounds per cubic feet are then aligned to the freight classes (Table 6) where we see the lower classification (50) is for freight very dense, like coal, iron ore, or similar, which will have a lower overall value and has basic handling to the highest classification (500) which represents light and lower density (volume higher than weight) items that are higher risk and higher value. The value comes from that fact there are eighteen classifications which allow us to characterize our freight pretty effectively. To get the specific freight class, we take the pounds per cubic foot and apply the number to the NMFTA Table following the number across to the freight class. We then use that freight class as part of the LTL quote. Remember, a rating engine has a set of base freight rates based on density, handling, risk value etc. and the freight classes point to a specific table by which the rate will be derived.

This means the table associated with class 50 will yield rates lower than class 65, 70, or even 400. If there is ever a circumstance where the density factor is available on two tables, e.g. a calculation of 12 pounds per cubic foot, one would choose the lower class, class 85 over class 92.5 simply because the rate table for eighty-five will be cheaper than 92.5. Once the freight classification is known and provided to the carrier for a spot market quote, the carrier can determine a base freight relatively quickly. The quote will reflect this base rate, a fuel surcharge based on the base rate, and other costs including other surcharges and assessorial costs. Once completed the total cost of the transportation along with a breakout of base freight, fuel surcharges and other costs will be provided to the shipper to either accept or reject. Remember that freight categories only apply to LTL quotes. Understanding the freight category helps the LTL carrier to consolidate like or near classes to ensure shipments have the right handling, security, etc.

Computing a Freight Category – Example

To compute a freight category, let's use an example shipment to understand how to this is done:

- Yolo Olive Oil Company has been shipped four pallets of olive oil to a client. Yolo Olive Oil is a Dayton, Ohio based business and the client is BNN Restaurant Group in Buffalo New York. They need to get a spot quote to determine the cost of the shipment so they can get the client's approval and finish their shipping order. The olive oil is shipped in five-gallon buckets and a standard 40"x48" pallet can hold 48 buckets if packed at 48" tall. The client order calls for 192 five-gallon buckets. In the distribution center, pallets are built with forty-eight buckets each and the pick ticket will call for four pallets to be picked and staged to the shipment area. Each pallet weighs 500 pounds. To compute a freight category, we do:

- [13] http://www.nmfta.org/pages/nmfc?AspxAutoDetectCookieSupport=1

- [14] ibid

1. **Convert Pallet dimensions to feet:**

   40/12 = 3.33 ft wide, 48/12 = 4 ft long., 48/12 – 4 ft high

2. **Multiple the three results to get the total cubit foot volume**

   3.33 x 4 x 4 = 53.28 cubic feet

3. **Divide the weight of ONE pallet into the cubic feet dimensions to get pounds per cubic foot**

   500/53.28 = 9.38

4. **Now that we know the pounds per cubic feet we use this factor to compare in the NMFTC Table. From the table above (and inset below), we find the 9.38 factor in the 9 – 10.5 category, or class 100. We will use class 100 as our category for the LTL freight quote.**

Class 77.5	Tires, bathroom fixtures	13.5 to 15 pounds
Class 85	Crated machinery, cast iron stoves	12-13.5 pounds
Class 92.5	Computers, monitors, refridgerators	10.5-12 pounds
Class 100	boat covers, car covers, canvase, wine cases, caskets	9-10.5 pounds
Class 110	cabinets, framed artwork, tablesaw	8-9 pounds
Class 125	Small Household appliances	7-8 pounds

Obtaining a Spot Quote

Once the freight category is known getting a spot market quote is relatively straightforward. To get a spot quote, one must call either a carrier directly or go through a freight broker. Freight broker's help companies find carries when they need one so this can be a very effective way to go. Usually, spot market quotes can be done on the phone or online. Figure 8 is a mocked-up example of an online form used for spot quotes. While this form may differ from company to company, the basic information is always the same in terms of origination, destination, and type of business, and

Figure 8. Example Quote Screen

items to be shipped. After the quote has been completed, the system will return quotes to the potential shipper. Figure 9 shows an example of the resulting quotes. Sometimes, quotes can be chosen, and a freight breakout will be shown between base freight, fuel surcharges, and assessorial charges.

Regardless, the shipper can review the quotes and pick the most appropriate for the situation. The quotes in Figure 9 are similar and you'll notice there are no guaranteed rates. Guaranteed rates are usually more expensive and would be further down the list.

These were not shown to conserve space. If a guaranteed quote is needed, one can choose the quote that best fits for that. Guaranteed quotes are just that, the shipment is guaranteed to be delivered by a certain day and time and the shipper pays a premium for this, typically 25% to 100%.

Once a quote is chosen, the shipper will put in the specific company information for the origination and destination locations along with any other freight characteristics or services needed and then will arrange for payment.

	Transit Time*	Discounted Price
Carrier 1	1 Business Day(s)	$142.32
Carrier 2	1 Business Day(s)	$159.47
Carrier 3	3 Business Day(s)	$186.26
Carrier 4	1 Business Day(s)	$207.02
Carrier 5	1 Business Day(s)	$216.61
Carrier 6	2 Business Day(s)	$222.59
Carrier 7	1 Business Day(s)	$224.06

Figure 9. Quote Results

Contract LTL Shippers

Although different than TL contracts, companies that regularly ship LTL also enter into shipping contracts. Carrier costs as computed using the LTL approach of freight categories etc. but there are deeper discounts for regular shippers so it's advantageous to have a contract if a company is shipping LTL regularly.

Another benefit of regular LTL shipping is an arrangement for Freight of All Kinds (FAK) based rates. Many LTL shippers have multiple products they need to ship with several freight categories. When multiple products are shipped in a single shipment, the company can ask the LTL carrier to apply an FAK approach that looks at all the freight categories and allows a single category for rating. Let's say a shipper is regularly moving ten pallets with freight categories ranging from 50 to 100. The shipper can ask the LTL carrier to rate the load using freight category 65 or 70. By doing this, they will receive a slightly higher rate than the fifty but a lower rate for those about 65 or 70 which can reduce the cost as much as 25% sometimes.

As we have seen, quoting LTL business is different than TL. This is not done without reason. The LTL business model involves the use of freight terminals, multi- points of pickup and delivery and a very different approach for consolidating and moving freight. We'll see this in more detail in the Chapter 6: Motor Carriers where we will discuss these different business models in more depth.

Contract Quotes

The most important thing a contract quote recognizes is that the shipper has at least one if few contracts with carriers. We will discuss contracts in the next session but generally there are two contracts that shippers sign with carriers:

- Open Contracts – An open contract is one where the shipper and the carrier have developed a standard set of terms but have not agreed to any pricing but have the standard prices, base freight, surcharges, assessorial items set up in the contract. In these contracts, the shipper would contract the carrier directly, either thought he phone, email, or through an integrated system between the two and offer a freight load. At that point the shipper needs service, they would either send a tender (an order for transportation services) to the carrier with a price they will accept, or they would leave that blank and ask the carrier to given them a price. Regardless of the method, both the shipper and carrier can accept or reject the bid based on cost, delivery timing or other reasons.

- Committed Contracts – A committed contract is one where the shipper and the carrier have created a contractual relationship that includes some minimum amount of volume committed for the shipper and carrier to exchange freight. The minimum committed volume creates a bigger discount for the shipper but if the shipper does not use the capacity, typically in truckloads, they must pay for whatever is not used. Usually, the shipper commits to a volume it knows it will move safety and will get a deeper discount than an open contract.

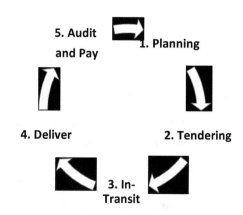

Figure 10: Transportation Lifecycle

With a committed contract, the terms are completed, and contract pricing is added to the contract creating the maximum the carrier will bid for a shipment. Most contract quotes will use a Transportation Management System (TMS) as a core part of their transportation planning and execution process. Planning and executing transportation orders is well defined (Figure 10). Every shipment starts with planning. Here, the transportation planning is based on receiving an order that needs to be shipped. Usually companies are taking and receiving orders throughout a business day and as the orders are received and processed, they initiate order picking in a warehouse or distribution center. Once the orders are assembled, they are then staged to be shipped. Simultaneously the orders are being sent to the warehouse or distribution center, they are also sent to the TMS system for load planning. Load planning allows a transportation manager to identify orders that need shipping and understanding the characteristics of that order including what it is, where it is going, when it must be there, etc. A planner will be confronted with a list of orders like Figure 11 In this example. Customer orders are grouped by Load ID the load itself. In the

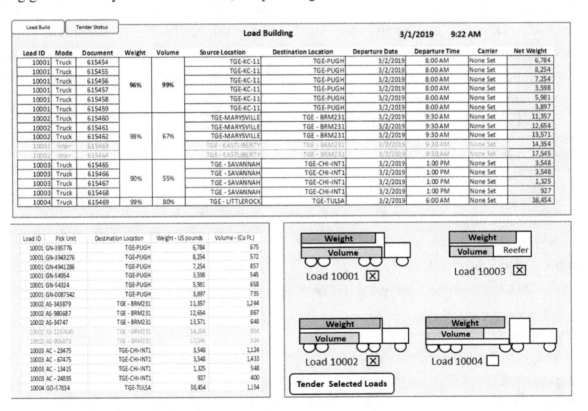

Load ID	Pick Date	Pick	Drop Date	Drop	Trailer	Carrier	Distance	Reference	TruckStatus	Load Status
10001	3/2/2019	GenCo	3/4/2019	DR Distro	Van - 48'	Not Set	897	T-271	TBD	Planned
10001	3/2/2019	GenCo	3/4/2019	DR Distro	Van - 48'	Not Set	897	T-271	TBD	Planned
10001	3/2/2019	GenCo	3/4/2019	DR Distro	Van - 48'	Not Set	897	T-271	TBD	Planned
10001	3/2/2019	GenCo	3/4/2019	DR Distro	Van - 48'	Not Set	897	T-271	TBD	Planned
10001	3/2/2019	GenCo	3/4/2019	DR Distro	Van - 48'	Not Set	897	T-271	TBD	Planned
10001	3/2/2019	GenCo	3/4/2019	DR Distro	Van - 48'	Not Set	897	T-271	TBD	Planned
10002	3/2/2019	Asan Mtrs	3/5/2019	MEL Inc	Van - 53'	Not Set	1,211	none	TBD	Planned
10002	3/2/2019	Asan Mtrs	3/5/2019	MEL Inc	Van - 53'	Not Set	1,211	none	TBD	Planned
10002	3/2/2019	Asan Mtrs	3/5/2019	MEL Inc	Van - 53'	Not Set	1,211	none	TBD	Planned
10002	3/2/2019	Asan Mtrs	3/5/2019	TVN Co	Container - 53'	Not Set	1,327	TV-11	TBD	Planned
10002	3/2/2019	Asan Mtrs	3/5/2019	TVN Co	Container - 53'	Not Set	1,327	TV-11	TBD	Planned
10003	3/2/2019	Acme Inc	3/6/2019	Sun Whse	Reefer - 48'	Not Set	1,857	Ac-999	TBD	Planned
10003	3/2/2019	Acme Inc	3/6/2019	Sun Whse	Reefer - 48'	Not Set	1,857	Ac-999	TBD	Planned
10003	3/2/2019	Acme Inc	3/6/2019	Sun Whse	Reefer - 48'	Not Set	1,857	Ac-999	TBD	Planned
10003	3/2/2019	Acme Inc	3/6/2019	Sun Whse	Reefer - 48'	Not Set	1,857	Ac-999	TBD	Planned
10004	3/2/2019	Gordeon	3/2/2019	Gordeon	Lowboy	Smith Inc	385	G-00349	Ready	In Pick

Figure 11. Transportation Load Planning Screen

planning screen, we would not expect to see carriers already identified but sometimes, where a single lane is managed by one carrier, for example, the carrier may already be known. The goal is to ship the individual orders together into a single customer shipment wherever possible.

In this example, all loads can be combined except for load 100002 from Asan Motors. Here we have the same Load ID's but we have two delivery locations so the load will need to be split as the planning gets underway. From this screen, the planning team would choose the orders for the

Load ID	Mode	Document	Weight	Volume	Source Location	Destination Location	Departure Date	Departure Time	Carrier	Net Weight
10001	Truck	615454			TGE-KC-11	TGE-PUGH	3/2/2019	8:00 AM	None Set	6,784
10001	Truck	615455			TGE-KC-11	TGE-PUGH	3/2/2019	8:00 AM	None Set	8,254
10001	Truck	615456	96%	99%	TGE-KC-11	TGE-PUGH	3/2/2019	8:00 AM	None Set	7,254
10001	Truck	615457			TGE-KC-11	TGE-PUGH	3/2/2019	8:00 AM	None Set	3,598
10001	Truck	615458			TGE-KC-11	TGE-PUGH	3/2/2019	8:00 AM	None Set	5,981
10001	Truck	615459			TGE-KC-11	TGE-PUGH	3/2/2019	8:00 AM	None Set	3,897
10002	Truck	615460			TGE-MARYSVILLE	TGE - BRM231	3/2/2019	9:30 AM	None Set	11,357
10002	Truck	615461			TGE-MARYSVILLE	TGE - BRM231	3/2/2019	9:30 AM	None Set	12,654
10002	Truck	615462	98%	67%	TGE-MARYSVILLE	TGE - BRM231	3/2/2019	9:30 AM	None Set	13,571
10002	Inter	615463			TGE - EASTLIBERTY	TGE - BRM231	3/2/2019	9:30 AM	None Set	14,354
10002	Inter	615464			TGE - EASTLIBERTY	TGE - BRM231	3/2/2019	9:30 AM	None Set	17,545
10003	Truck	615465			TGE - SAVANNAH	TGE-CHI-INT1	3/2/2019	1:00 PM	None Set	3,548
10003	Truck	615466			TGE - SAVANNAH	TGE-CHI-INT1	3/2/2019	1:00 PM	None Set	3,548
10003	Truck	615467	90%	55%	TGE - SAVANNAH	TGE-CHI-INT1	3/2/2019	1:00 PM	None Set	1,325
10003	Truck	615468			TGE - SAVANNAH	TGE-CHI-INT1	3/2/2019	1:00 PM	None Set	927
10004	Truck	615469	99%	80%	TGE - LITTLEROCK	TGE-TULSA	3/2/2019	6:00 AM	None Set	38,454

Load ID	Pick Unit	Destination Location	Weight - US pounds	Volume - (Cu Ft.)
10001	GN-395776	TGE-PUGH	6,784	675
10001	GN-3943276	TGE-PUGH	8,254	572
10001	GN-4941286	TGE-PUGH	7,254	857
10001	GN-54954	TGE-PUGH	3,598	545
10001	GN-54324	TGE-PUGH	5,981	658
10001	GN-0087542	TGE-PUGH	3,897	735
10002	AS-343879	TGE - BRM231	11,357	1,244
10002	AS-980687	TGE - BRM231	12,654	867
10002	AS-34747	TGE - BRM231	13,571	648
10002	AS-2237645	TGE - BRM231	14,354	854
10002	AS-906873	TGE - BRM231	17,545	924
10003	AC - 23475	TGE-CHI-INT1	3,548	1,124
10003	AC - 67475	TGE-CHI-INT1	3,548	1,433
10003	AC - 13415	TGE-CHI-INT1	1,325	548
10003	AC - 24895	TGE-CHI-INT1	927	400
10004	GD-57834	TGE-TULSA	38,454	1,154

Load 10001 [X]   Load 10003 [X]

Load 10002 [X]   Load 10004 [ ]

Tender Selected Loads

Figure 12. Transportation Load Building Screen

shipments they will build and then load building. Once the orders have been selected, they will flow to the load building screen. Some TMS systems can allow the customer to configure the system to do automated load building or to manually load build. In Figure 12, we have an example of several loads being built.

You'll see in the load building screen we have the same Load ID numbers and now the loads are being allocated into the equipment identified in the load planning screen. This is an interactive screen where the load planner, or the system, will allocate the specific order line items into the equipment either by choosing the load or by dragging and dropping the load into the specific equipment. You'll notice that in this example, we are building four loads. As we add orders, we see the depiction of the equipment fill up with the load build screen keeping a running total of the total percentage of weight and volume capacity used. The screen will not accept orders that exceed the weight or volume capacity of the equipment. You'll see in load 10002 from Assan Motors, the line items from Easter Liberty cannot fit into the truck and are shaded to show they were not included. The builder will return these orders to the load planning screen so they can be built later. With the other Load IDs they have all be built and will generally weight out. Once the load builds are done, we select the loads that need carriers and then choose "tender Selected loads" (inset right) to begin getting a rate quote from a carrier for the load.

If the carrier doesn't respond within a few seconds, it will then send a request to the second carrier and so on until it gets a satisfactory quote. Once a load has been sent out for tendering, the status of the process can be found by looking at the tender Status Screen (Figure 13). This screen shows the progress of each tender and, when accepted, will automatically approve the load and send

Pickup Time	Delivery Date	Delivery Time	Tender Approach	Carrier Name	Total Cost	Status	Carrier	Dispatch #	Trailer #	Driver	Comment
8:00 AM	6,784	675	Performance	Longmount	$827.98	In-Process	Longmount	T-1275	E-343	Smith	
9:30 AM	11,357	1,244	Cost	J.J. Yeley	$1,098.12	Accepted	J.J. Yeley	D=5697	Z-111	Jones	
1:00 PM	3,548	1,124	Preferred Carrier	CSX	$382.34	Rejected					Cost too low

Figure 13. Tender Status Screen

to the carrier for dispatch, or, if the comp any prefers, it can have an associate specifically release the tenders to the carriers. In our case, we are showing it being done automatically. Of the three quotes sent, one has been accepted and dispatched, one has been accepted

Pickup Time	Delivery Date	Delivery	Tender Approach	Carrier Name
TGE-PUGH	6,784	675	Performance	Longmount
TGE - BRM231	11,357	1,244	Cost	J.J. Yeley
TGE-CHI-INT1	3,548	1,124	Preferred Carrier	

CSX
Edwards Int'l
JJ Yeley
Longmount
NS

Tender Screen / Menu

and one has been rejected due to cost. The tender, which was sent to a carrier with an open contract (a contract without specific rates set), will go back to the tender Screen to either go to multiple carriers or to have the cost adjusted to where the carrier will accept the load. With open contracts where there is not a specific rate, this can occur.

Once the loads have been accepted and sent to the carrier for execution, the carrier will schedule load for pickup and then manage the load from pickup through delivery. If a company has a TMS and it's integrated with its carriers, the TMS can often provide visibility into the status of the shipment until it is received. Transportation Visibility is one way this is done by using the carrier telemetry in the transportation equipment to identify where it is geographically throughout its journey. The system can pick up location and can compute, based on standard speeds and other data, whether the shipment is still on-time for delivery or if it may be at risk to be late. In addition, the carriers themselves can report issues during the shipment, to include delays able to be used by the company to respond, rather than to react to changes during the shipment process. The TMS may also have a Control Tower, which is a module of the TMS system specifically built to provide this visibility along with metrics, revenue reporting, and cost management. Control Towers are often more sophisticated than the diagram, but it is a good example of supply chain visibility. In the example, we can see that one shipment has been delayed and has their shipment status updated along with the new delivery window. Many control towers will allow the user to click through to see more detail as to why it was late, whether a claim has been filed etc. These can be very helpful to ensure that the follow-on processes that need to happen for a late shipment are easily done. The Control Tower will also note changes or updates to the dock scheduling and will identify when a shipment is complete which then triggers the last part of the lifecycle, the audit and pay portion.

Audit and Pay also leverage the TMS to close the transaction lifecycle through invoice and payment. Using a TMS allows the company to include the rate structures, the surcharge rates and assessorial rates along with business rules for compliance to govern the use of tolls, wait time, and other factors that may increase the cost of the shipment. Most audit and pay systems begin with an invoice from the carrier. The invoice is then matched with the bill of lading and may also include a delivery receipt. Each charge of the invoice is checked against the contract profiled in the TMS to ensure the rates and charges are valid and consistent with the contract. Any charges that are not compliant will be rejected and the invoice will only apply to those valid charges for payment. Payment is most often done via electronic ACH (Automated Cash Handling) directly between the company and carrier's banks.

Transportation pricing is a complex process in today's global transportation market. Carriers must understand their cost basis for operating both on a variable and fixed basis and be able to understand the rates they can afford to give to clients. If those rates are not competitive, they will either have to reduce their costs, profit, or may not survive as a carrier. Carriers also must deal with wage increases, changes in fuel costs and more while keeping their rates competitive. For most carriers, contracts are the lifeblood of their business allowing a more predictable workload allowing for better capacity planning and allocation. Carriers also respond to the spot market where they have excess capacity to enable them to create more revenue and more capacity efficiency.

Shippers need to manage their transportation costs aggressively to ensure their product prices and ability to serve customers enable the company to create a profit. Based on the company's size and supply chain efficiency transportation costs can be from 3% to 10% of revenue. A $2B manufacturer, for instance, will experience transportation costs on the order of $60M to $100M annually. Managing these costs effectively is critical for the company. Effectively developing carrier relationships, entering into transportation contracts that enable more predicable pricing, and managing the carrier's performance to ensure the company gets the most out of the relationship are key practices for the modern shipper.

Tender – The Transportation Order

In transportation, we often use the word Tender to denote a transportation order to the carrier. Often the question arises "Why do you call it a Tender rather than a transportation order"?

We use the word "Tender" to separate the process of acquiring transportation services, which is also a kind of an order, from the customer order that we are fulfilling to try and avoid confusion. After all, if someone said they are having a problem with the "order" and they mean getting a transportation carrier for a load, it could easily be confused with the actual customer order resulting in misunderstandings. So, the word Tender has taken on the meaning of a transportation order.

The logical next question is the origin of the word tender. In our case, the word "tender" is a noun that goes back to the ancient Greek civilization. The ancient Greeks had vast navy that included many kinds of ships from military to trade. Compared to the ports that were available, many of the Greek ships were so large they could not easily port. Other times, they wanted the navy at sea to protect the local land areas. To service these ships smaller ships, or "tenders" would be dispatched to provide people, supplies, and even cargo. The word caught on through the ages and is a convenient term to use for a transportation order.

CHAPTER 5: CONTRACTING FOR TRANSPORTATION

INTRODUCTION

Contracting for transportation is an important part of the overall shipper-carrier relationship for companies that regularly ship goods. A transportation contract is a legally binding document that defines the legal terms of the shipper-carrier relationship between one shipper and one carrier. Contracts are confidential and will contain sensitive and proprietary information that can include performance metrics and service levels, pricing information, and more. Besides legal terms which are standard in the industry, the transportation contract defines the parameter of the relationship between the shipper and the carrier in terms of the services offered to the shipper, the performance required by the carrier, and the costs the carrier will charge for these services. These items taken together form the contract that will define and govern the relationship from the date it is signed until the termination of the contract.

In this chapter we will explore the approaches to creating and entering into transportation contracts. We will discuss the major items included in the contract along with trade-offs that are often considered during the contracting process. We will also discuss the Request for Proposal (RFP) process which is a formalized process used to create a competitive bidding environment as a precursor to entering into transportation contracts. Finally, we will look at how we manage changes and the performance of contracts using amendments and balanced scorecards.

Company may have very specific ways they approach carrier selection and contract development. There are often many approaches to reach the same outcome and contracting for transportation services are no different. The approach we present here provides a general understanding of transportation contracts and an understanding of how the RFP can create better practices to ensure carrier competition, flexibility for the shipper, and an opportunity for carriers to be more than just a vendor to a shipper.

While we will generally focus on transportation carriers in this chapter, it's important to note that companies will contract for transportation and logistics services from more than just carriers. As we will see in Chapter 10, there are several ways that companies outsource transportation and logistics services. Contracting for carriage, or creating a transportation contract is arguably the most common form of transportation contract and is discussed here. The process to enter into these contracts and the terms are very similar. What differs are the specific services, the performance service levels, and the prices.

By understanding the contracting approach, the services and performance levels of transportation contracts, one will gain insight into the overall process of developing and managing relationships with transportation providers and how to leverage them as partners.

VALUE IN THE CARRIER – SHIPPER RELATIONSHIP

What's the value of a relationship? To open up and endless debate, try and get someone to articulate the value of a business or customer relationship. There are as many ways to evaluate the value of a particular relationship as there are ways to define it. For most businesses, customer relationships have some identified value. We categorize our customers into segments based on the revenue generated from them in many companies. More savvy companies can actually measure their customers in terms of profitability; a much better metric however one-sided. How do customers measure the value of their relationship with a company? Customer satisfaction is one way and there are many ways to measure this. Companies find that customers who value the relationship they have with them tell other people about their satisfaction. The same is true about dissatisfaction. In a world of social media and online reviews, we can quickly get a perspective on a company just by looking at what its existing customers think of it.

One way we think about relationships when we are the buyer of services is to differentiate a supplier between a "vendor" and a "partner". This is common language in most companies and the two represent very different relationships. Here the term 'vendor' may have a slightly negative connotation or may have a connotation for those suppliers that are not strategic to the company. Vendors are transactional in nature and, to a buyer, a good vendor gives them what they need and little else. If a vendor has a problem with supplier to a company, they likely won't be a supplier long because there is little loyalty or connection between the companies.

Compare that with a supplier as a partner. Partners are more strategic and more valuable to the company. They are most often characterized by the way they exceed the needs of their customers, or provide very critical services with great reliability and capability. They developed a relationship that has allowed them to go from vendor to partner by earing that right. Partners have problems like vendors do but with a partner, the history of value provided allows them some understanding when things don't go well, provided they solve the problem and not repeating it. Just as vendors is partners, partners can also lose their status and be vendors.

In today's complex supply chain, companies need TSPs that can become partners to them. Not only do these companies need exceptional services in areas where they choose to outsource to a third party, but they also desire the value that partner can bring in terms of their understanding of the market, ideas for improvements and more.

At the most basic level, most shippers want the same things out of their carriers:

- Reliable, consistent on-time delivery of their shipments

- The right equipment available for their various kinds of shipment

- Solid customer service that is responsible when things are going right

- The lowest possible price

- Ease of doing business with the carrier. This could be through automation or through simple processes straight forward

These are considered the basic requirements for a successful carrier relationship. How the carrier conducts their business, how they provide flexibility and support as the company adjusts its needs based on market factors and growth, and how they respond when things don't go well drive the value the shipper sees in the relationship.

What about the carrier? If a carrier could define a relationship with a shipper, carrier will often look for

- A customer that needs transportation capacity where the carrier has the most capacity available

- A price high enough to optimize its profit in the lanes where the customer ships

- Schedule flexibility and enough notice for new shipments to ensure the carrier can effectively manage its capacity

- A customer interested in developing a deeper relationship

As we can see, there will always be some difference, especially with price shippers and carriers both recognize the value of a relationship for shipping goods.

TYPES OF TRANSPORTATON CONTRACTS

Virtually every shipment done between a shipper and transportation carrier will involve a contract. This is true from the smallest spot market deal to the largest multi-year transportation relationship. Contracts, if nothing else, define the process of liability transfer between the shipper and the carrier and defines the price and basic terms of a shipment. These basic terms are needed to meet the needs of Generally Acceptable Account Practices (GAAP) and regulations like Sarbanes-Oxley that defines effective risk management accounting in business.

Table 7 provides a basic list of the contracts that shippers use with carriers based on their shipping frequency. One of the most common ways shippers' contract with carriers is through a standard carrier contract template. These contracts are basic terms between the carrier and the shippers and define the specific requirements of one shipment. They are used each time a shipment is done and covers only that shipment. This is true of the casual shipper, whether using an online freight board or going to a carrier directly and a volume based shipper that uses the carrier's standard contract. This contract sets for a standard set of terms of conditions, including basic performance metrics, but defines the rates and charges for that shipment only. The advantage of this is simplicity. Standard carrier contracts need not be negotiated they are not negotiated and can be completed quickly. The major disadvantage is that they do not take into any shipping volume beyond that single shipment and the prices and surcharges are likely to change shipment to shipment. In addition, if a shipper uses any online service, like a freight board where they can post their freight request, etc. there will likely also be a user agreement or similar that the shipper must accept to use the online system, even if free.

Type of Shipper	Definition	Quote Approach	Contract Type
Casual Shipper	An infrequent shipper that typically shippers no more than a few times a month to a few times a year	Spot Quote on Freight Board	Terms and Conditions of Freight Board
			Standard Carrier Template Contract
		Carrier Direct	Standard Carrier Template Contract
Volume Shipper	A shipper that has a regular set of shipments it does as part of its business to include weekly shipments to multiple shipments per day	Carrier Direct	Standard Carrier Template Contract
		Contracted Carrier	Individualized Shipper-Carrier Contract

Table 7. Contract Types

The other major kind of contract is an individually negotiated contract for transportation services often negotiated and written for multiple years. These contracts allow the shipper to take advantage of its shipping volume, setup specific terms for areas like performance and sets up an ongoing rate structure. These agreements seeks to create a more detailed and longer relationship between the shipper and the carrier. This often results in greater discounts based on the volume a shipper will commit over time and discounts based on the length of the contract. In addition, the contract may define more specific service and performance requirements that may also include penalties for non-performance. The advantage of these contracts is that the shipper can define what they want out of the relationship and, subject to negotiation, get it from the carrier. The advantage to the carrier is also that the carrier can work to define reasonable performance and services up front that will be consistent through the life of the contracts and have a certain amount of committed volume they will move throughout the life of the contract. This gives the carrier a regular stream of revenue which is more predictable than the other ways they contract for services.

CONTRACT CONTENTS

Most transportation contracts are constructed in similar ways and each company will have some variation based on the legal authorities that put together the initial contracts, lessons learned from previous contracts, and specific negotiation experience. In this section, we will discuss the basis approaches to structure of the contracts and standard terms that will be found in most contracts. Then, we will discuss how the transportation services are added to the contract along with specifically negotiated areas like performance and service levels. When considering multi-year contracts between shippers and carriers it's important to remember that the resulting contract will have areas that will not change and some areas that could change based market changes, the relationship needs, or other factors. The structure use to create the contract should be considered to allow for changes without having to renegotiate the major elements of the contract.

Contract Structure and Flexibility

Contract structure can be very simple sometimes and will need to be considered more deeply in more individualized contracts.

Standard carrier contracts will most often have a single structure that defines the terms, the services, and the pricing all within one integrated document. This can be done because there will be virtually no variation between shippers and so one template works for all.

Negotiated contracts may be structured to enable a consistent set of terms while allowing some flexibility in how the services, pricing and performance are presented. Often, these contracts are structured to have legal elements, like terms, definitions of services, and other covenants that will not change in the first part of the agreement and then use appendices or addendums to capture cost and performance elements. The contract itself allows for modifications of the appendices or addendums without having to renegotiate the other aspects of the agreement. This allows for flexibility in adding to or changing services, pricing, and other operational factors with simple agreement.

Basic Terms and Conditions

Transportation contracts have a structure generally consistent with similar contracts and we won't get into the specifics of a basic contract structure. For a transportation contract, there are a set of terms that are both consistent and important in the contract. Below are the most common terms used in a transportation contract:

- Domestic Terms – The set of terms will typically be included in domestic based transportation contracts.

- <u>Definitions</u> – Most contracts will have a definitions section that provides the legal or contract based definitions of key terms used in the contract. These definitions may include a definition of the shipper, the carrier, what constitutes freight or shipments, hazardous goods, lanes, routes, and more. Anything that the drafters of the contract believe could be unclear, in terms of definition, will be defined in this section.

- <u>Term</u> – The contract will define the specific dates in which the contract will be valid. The start date is usually the day the contract is signed, and the end date will typically be measured in years from that date.

- <u>Transportation Services</u> – The contract may use this section define the entire scope of transportation services used in the contract or may generally define transportation services and reference an appendix that more deeply defines the specific services, and performance requirements, of the contract. This section can be moved to an appendix so it can be modified occasionally without fully re-negotiating the contract.

- <u>Costs</u> – The contract may have detailed costs or may reference an appendix that covers the costs, surcharges and fees associated with the services provided. Like transportation services, this section is good to use in an appendix so modification and changes can be made occasionally.

- <u>Payments and Payment terms</u> – The contract will define how payments will be made, how disputes of payments will be reconciled, and the specific terms of payments required between the shipper and carrier.

- <u>Liability</u> – The contract will define the liabilities between the shipper and the carrier and when the liability of goods move from the shipper to the carrier and to the receiver (the destination of the shipment).

- <u>Documents</u> – The contract will define what documentation is required for shipping. This will usually include directions for bills of lading, packing lists, invoices, receipts, and other documents used in the contract.

- <u>Damage and Claims</u> – The contract will define damage and loss and the process for claims due to losses or issues with the shipment process.

- <u>Limitations of Liability</u> – Claims, which are part of the insurance process, may be used if there is damage or loss in the shipment and the shipper is typically paid for the value of the actual loss and are not addressed in this section. This section normally defines the limitations of liability for the carrier based on loss, damage or poor performance. Typically, liability is limited to the freight charges related to the shipment with liability associated with it. Similarly, costs or penalties for poor performance will be covered here if they are not covered in a performance appendix.

- Other contractual terms – Other terms which are more consistent with any contract include things like governing law, confidentiality, definitions of contract breech and their consequences, termination of the contract, notices (the addresses to which official correspondence is sent) and more.

- International Terms – besides any domestic terms, if the contract covers international shipment there will be a few additional terms that include:

    o International air – If using international air, the terms will include the definition and use of the airway bill, a replacement for the bill of lading in domestic transportation, and any specific terms related to the receiving, delivery, and notifications done specifically for air. The terms may also include any additional customs requirements, any specific security notifications or requirements, and the specific airport to airport designations of the shipment.

    o International Shipping – If using international shipping, there will be several additional terms that include a definition and use of Incoterms, the carrier's responsibility, inspection of goods, any liens used on the goods to secure payment for shipments, and others terms specific to the use of documentation, the process of customer clearance and receipt of goods, etc.

Contracted Transportation Services

Transportation services definitions are another major part of the transportation contract and are used to clearly define all the services that will apply to the contract. Some contracts may include all services provided by the transportation carrier and designate the specific services. This section will often include:

- Transportation – Defines the specific approach and use of transportation for the client (shipper)

- Equipment – Defines the kinds and nature of equipment available to the shipper throughout the term of the contract

- Surcharges – Defines all specific surcharges, like fuel, that apply to the contract

- <u>Assessorial Items</u> – This defines any accessories that may apply to the contract like the definition of wait time, additional services, like storage, notifications, etc.

Service Levels and Performance

A final and very important part of the transportation contract is the area of the contract that defined acceptable service and performance benchmarks and their consequences if not met. In looking at what performance metrics to choose, it's important to remember the adage "You get what you inspect". You need to choose the metrics to measure specific to the outcomes you want to achieve. For instance, if one were to measure the carrier's ability to arrive exactly at prescribed in the tender the carrier, over time, will ensure they are always there exactly at the time defined. Is this valuable? I'm sure to some it will be valuable. Is it more valuable than on-time delivery? Most likely it is not. Too many performance metrics makes it very difficult for the carrier to perform. Too few and the shipper doesn't achieve their outcomes. So, what are the right measurements for performance of a carrier? Since we are talking about logistics, the answer is "it depends". When developing a performance scorecard for a transportation carrier, some of the most common metrics are:

- Percentage of On-Time Delivery $= \dfrac{\text{\# of On Time Delivery Shipments}}{\text{Total Shipments}}$

- Percentage of Damaged Shipments $= \dfrac{\text{Total \# of Damaged Shipments}}{\text{Total Shipments}}$

- Equipment Availability $= \dfrac{\text{Shipments With Requested Equipment}}{\text{Total Shipments}}$

- Shipment Claims Percentage $= \dfrac{\text{Total \# of Damaged (Claimed) Shipments}}{\text{Total Shipments}}$

- Claims as a % of Freight Cost $= \dfrac{\text{Total Loss from All Claims}}{\text{Total Freight Costs}}$

- Claims Cycle Time $= \dfrac{\text{Total Days to Resolve Claims}}{\text{Total Claims in the Period}}$

- Freight Bill Accuracy $= \dfrac{\text{\# of Error Free Freight Bills}}{\text{Total Freight Bills Received}}$

Other metrics can be used to measure the effectiveness of carriers. The key to metric choice is to ensure that you choose metrics for things that, when measured, drive the outcomes the company is trying to achieve.

REQUEST FOR PROPOSAL PROCESS

How Transportation Services Are Procured

A company wishing to buy transportation services has several approaches they can use. The choice of method will often be based on the cost or value of the service to be acquired, potential market competition for that or service, how much the company already has suppliers in which it is satisfied, and the time the company wants to have those services. Often, companies will use a decision process like Figure 14 to determine the best method for the purchase.

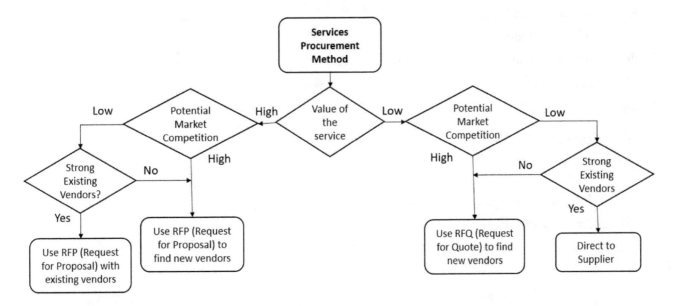

Figure 14. Decision Matrix for Vendor Sourcing

What is a Request for Proposal?

A Request for Proposal (RFP) is a formal process that seeks to create competition among potential suppliers when purchasing a product or service. The RFP could cover a single purchase or for contracted services over a period. The value of an RFP for the buyer is relatively obvious: Ensure competition to get the best combination of price / functionality / and customer service for a procurement situation. The value to the suppliers is not always as clear. Suppliers typically prefer to sell their solutions directly to the customer and not through a process that involves competition. Because of this, there needs to be enough incentive for the suppliers to be willing to do the work required to support the process and create a competitive proposal without knowing the odds they will win. Similarly, effort to use an RFP for purchasing is significant and RFP's are not always the best way to buy products or services. Further, if existing suppliers are already well known, and the overall value of the services is smaller, using a Request for Quote (RFQ) with existing suppliers may be the better choice. Direct purchasing from a source is warranted when there is little competition and you have a strong relationship with at least one supplier. If the value is high, even with existing suppliers, it's good to use an RFP to ensure one gets the most out of competition.

One very important thing to remember if contemplating using an RFP for securing transportation services is the quality and completeness of the RFP. There's an saying "Garbage In / Garbage Out" which suggests that effort should create a strong up front RFP to ensure the company receives quality

responses. Creating an RFP takes considerable work and effort, but it is rewarded when the bidders understand the business and its need and can respond so it creates success when the company moves to use these services.

Executing an RFP Process [15]

RFP's with high odds of success are typically done using the stages in Figure 15. While beyond the scope of this book, let's review the key and what happens in each.

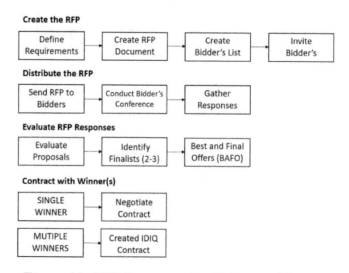

Figure 15. RFP Process using Stages and Decisions

Step 1: **Create the RFP.** Creating an RFP takes time and involves evaluating the company's needs, understanding its history related to transportation, and developing the specific requirements that are needed to enable the company to use outside transportation carriers. This requires collaboration with all impacted parties and some companies will use third party consultants to help with the process to manage the complexity of the process and ensure the resulting RFP product will meet the company's needs to acquire high quality carriers at the best price.

Step 2: **Identifying Bidders.** This is done by using existing suppliers or new suppliers that pass the defined viability and performance standards that are preset as part of the RPF.

Step 3: **Distribute the RFP** – We only send the RFP to those bidders that have committed to review and bid on the opportunity. A key part of this phase is sending the RFP and the following up with a Bidder's conference. The Bidder's Conference is a one-time only event used to go into further detail about the RFP and answering questions from the vendors. After this is over, there is generally no more contact until submissions are in.

Step 3: **Evaluate Responses:** Once the RFPs are received the RFP team will evaluate the responses. This is usually done using a Red-Yellow-Green-Blue method where red is a disqualification, yellow gives the vendor once review and fix any requirements they are missing, green meets all requirements and blue exceeds requirements with additional services the RFP team finds valuable. This is an important distinction because if a vendor exceeds the requirements in an area the RFP team feels is value added, they can award a small amount of extra points to that area of evaluation. We generally accept these proposals as higher value so they can also cost up to 15% more, on average, and still win.

Step 4: **Identify the Winner(s):** In the final step, we identify the winner(s) and move to create a contract with them. This can be done by choosing one winner, or the company can choose two or more winners and then create a contractual vehicle that allows for only these winners to continue to compete on price, delivery time, or other factors and award the business to the best supplier for that specific load, or tender. When the US Federal Government does this, they refer to this a contract among multiple winners as an IDIQ, or Indefinite Delivery, Indefinite Quantity contract. Basically, you award a contract without a specific commitment, or with a minimum commitment that covers less than 50% of your expected traffic and then uses bids for each load with the winners bidding competitively against each other.

MANAGING CONTRACTOR PERFORMANCE

Once we have the appropriate transportation providers and contracts and they are configured in our TMS, we can effectively execute on the movement of goods through the supply chain. Likely any supplier situation, monitor and evaluate the supplier's performance periodically and we've covered a number metrics that can be used for this purpose. The shipper will experience the normal issues with transportation like a need for a piece of equipment that isn't available, a late or damaged shipment, and perhaps even some price inflation throughout the term of the contract. Managing the issues as they come up is important to ensure the flow of the supply chain meets the shipper's needs, especially as it relates to customer delivery. This is typically done on a monthly or quarterly basis.

---

[15] Heartland Professional Services. 2016

It's also important to periodically score and evaluate carriers against the performance metrics and between each other. TMS systems will often allow for specific rating rules that can be linked to performance including, among others, choosing the best performing carrier for a specific lane or situation. To do this, we will create a consistent balanced scorecard for our transportation carriers and will typically create a "report card" (a balanced scorecard that looks at the last quarter's performance for all areas managed) to evaluate carriers.

The report card can be sent to the carrier for their review and comment, and, for the most important carries, it's typical to have a carrier performance meeting at least annually but often quarterly. Let's look at constructing a balanced scorecard and its use in a quarterly performance meeting to understand the value and approach of this method.

The Balanced Scorecard[16]

The balanced scorecard is an evaluation instrument that uses a point system to evaluate the most important part of the relationship and performance of supplier. Points are allocated to different performance criteria based on their importance, so the most critical items have higher point totals creating a balance between scoring and performance priorities. Figure 16 shows an example of a balanced scorecard used or a transportation carrier

Performance Criteria	Maximum Score	Carrier Score	Comments
On-Time Delivery	25	15	Missed multiple Delivery Windows
Quality	20	17	Two loads with Damage
Billing Accuracy / Claims Settlement	15	13	Need new contract for Claims
Carrier Responsiveness	15	12	Did not have Reefers in two situations
Customer Support	10	10	No consistent contact person
Safety and Driver Courtesy	8	8	Excellent
Account Management	7	7	No issues
TOTAL	100	82	Carrier Probation Indicated Carrier Imposed $15,000 Performance Fine

Figure 16. Carrier Balanced Scorecard

relationship. There are seven criteria with the first three being 60% of the total scorecard.

A good performance is usually 90% or better and preferred performance is often above 95%. Because of this, the company cannot ignore the other four criteria but will put more emphasis on the first three or four than the others. We expect this because of the way we create the scoring. This is the balance we want to strike in the balanced scorecard. Companies will maintain their scoring standards for performance levels. Typically, the vendors will fall into one of several categories. Below is the structure used by the company to review the carrier:

- 95 – 100: Exceptional – Will likely direct loads to this category of carrier because of the strong performance. We might even consider this the "Tier I" carriers.

- 90 – 95: Very Good – These carriers have overall strong performance and will also draw a good amount of workload to bid on. Sometimes also considered Tier I, they may also be considered Tier II carriers.

- 85 – 90: Marginal – These carriers have had a mix of good performance and issues and are considered solid carriers but with marginal performance. Often the company will work with these carriers to understand the issues and work with them to incrementally improve. These carriers will still be used but will typically only get the loads the pervious tiers do not take.

- 80 – 85: Probationary – Carriers that fall to this level have a level of performance that has been problematic for the company over the most recent quarter. Sometimes a poor quarter results in a very strong carrier falling into this category and other times the performance loss is more systemic. Regardless of the reason, carriers in this category must formally recognize their short coming, provide a root cause reason for the poor performance and must development an improvement plan for improvement over the next quarter. These carriers may have their loads restricted or they may continue to bid on loads as a marginal carrier. Carriers consistently in the probationary category will likely be moved to poor if they cannot improve.

- Below 80: Poor – Carriers that fall into this category will often be replaced or removed from the carrier program unless they have suddenly had a change of performance after having a very strong track record. In those cases, they are treated more like probationary carriers. The shipper may provide them a month to month analysis by severely restricting their loads and evaluating each one. More often, they are simply informed they will no longer be a carrier to the company.

It's important that the scoring process be quantitative, but we also must recognize that part of the evaluation is also subjective. Keeping the subjective scoring to the smaller items is the best approach when there is a subjective item. The balanced scorecard forms the primary content used in a supplier performance management discussion with the carrier. Conducting these reviews is an anchor to the supplier performance management of the carriers and it's important to understand the purpose and approach for these meetings.

Supplier Performance Management

The discipline of supplier performance management is just about as important as effective customer management. In today's supply chains, the relationships with suppliers of all kinds can be differentiating in the market. Where company may have traditionally looked at these relationships as "vendor management", most businesses today understand there are two roles our suppliers can take: Vendor or Partner. Suppliers can be evaluated using the same Pareto analysis we do with customers or even inventory. Most often 20% of the suppliers will drive 80% of the cost of the inventory. Transportation isn't that much different. Typically, 20% of the carriers will drive 80% of the execution. We know statistically that motor carriers will be most of our transportation moves but companies that ship globally must look beyond the motor carriers to develop strategies relationships with other modes. While much has been discussed in business journals about the value of partnership in business, understand the difference between and vendor and partner relationship with suppliers. Pareto is one effective way to segregate those companies where we need partnership versus just vendor execution. The criticality of the supplier is another way to think about the need for partnership. Regardless of how we define those suppliers we categorize as vendors or partners, it's important to understand the expectations that go with these categories:

- <u>Vendors</u>: Sometimes companies use the term vendor to denote a supplier that may have issues with the company or be perceived as negative, but this is not the way we should look at the term. Better, a supplier considered a vendor is one where the relationship with them is generally transactional in nature, has limited overall business with the company or the business done is a commodity to the company without a large impact on the business. Since it's not practical to treat all suppliers as partners, we need strong and effective vendors that do what we need when we need it without a lot of fuss. We put a premium on vendors that have very strong technologically driven processes with very responsive and effective customer service at a price considered advantageous in the market.

- <u>Partners</u>: Suppliers that become partners are typically strategic or mission critical along with higher spend that makes them part of that top 20% of supplier spend for their category. More important, supplier who become partners provide more than just the service we contract them to do. Often, supplier collaboration with these suppliers yields improvements in the business for both companies. They may provide insight into the market or they may share the expertise they have to help the company. The ultimately value in a supplier partner is the intersection of importance, usually based on the amount we spend with the supplier, and the value add they can provide us as a company.

As one can imagine, we treat partners differently than vendors in the company and transportation is no different. The highest performing carriers will often have opportunities to demonstrate partnership with the company. These carriers may recommend changes in how the company does things to streamline or improve their overall transportation capabilities. Sometimes the company may want to pilot a new technology or system and these suppliers are often the partners that help them test the solution before its implemented. Sometimes, the carrier can provide additional flexibility, or recommend a different approach, when the company is struggling to solve a problem on its own. Regardless of the approach, the partnership between the company and the supplier is value to both. Most often it's the carriers we see as partners part of our quarterly supplier program and we use that time not only to evaluate the performance of the carrier but also to discuss the overall relationship between the two and ways they can benefit each other.

We've discussed the concept, but we need to illustrate how this works in practice. Let's draw from an example where a partner supplier was evaluated as having lower performance and, through the supplier performance meeting and the spirit of partnership exhibited, the outcome proved very different.

An Example

In the following example, we will not use the real names of any companies to discuss an experience that happened a few years ago between a manufacturer and one of their best carriers.

- Background: Johnson and Benson (J&B) Carriers had been a carrier to Westmoreland Manufacturing for the last fifteen years. Throughout that time, they had consistently outperformed most of their competition and had become a value partner to the business. During the most recent economic downturn, both Westmoreland and J&B went out of their ways to help each other. Because they had few loads to move, the company ensured J&B got its share of the loads to ensure it stayed viable. J&B reduced its rates 20% even though they had contract rates in force. Both knew that if they helped each other it would ultimately be good for both. After the economic downturn business boomed. J&B added to its fleet to meet a larger share of the Westmoreland business and, due to its ultimate expansion, Westmoreland added more carriers but ensured J&B had a few dedicated lanes besides competitive lanes. Both thrived and all seemed well.

- Situation: About 12 months ago, Westmoreland began to more aggressively implement transportation-based technology to help them manage their increased volume of shipments. They upgraded to a more enterprise centric TMS with deep integration. This allowed them to improve their compliance analysis, move completely to electronic tendering, enabled shipment tracking, and allowed the company to implement freight auditing as part of its carrier payment process. About six months ago, the company implemented a new yard management system to help manage the increased volume of trucks coming to the factory to pick up loads. From the company's perspective, the changes had been effective and while there were issues along the way, the operations of the company seemed to benefit from these changes. J&B strategically decided to invest in technology that would ensure they could integrate with Westmoreland to meet their needs for electronic tendering, invoicing and payment through electronic means. They had completed the integration right after the company went live with their TMS. The companies signed a new three-year contract two months ago that changed their balanced scorecard in minor ways so they could use standardize reporting from the TMS as part of the calculations for on-time delivery, quality, etc. The contract had been configured into the TMS at the beginning of the month.

- <u>The Issue:</u> Jayne Hayes, the supplier management representative in charge of the J&B relationship had scheduled their quarterly performance review for the following week and was pulling together TMS reports and gathering feedback on the performance for J&B. She did this as a matter of routine and had been doing so for two years. She had planned on using their standing agenda as she was anticipating another quarter where J&B would mimic their scores of the previous eight-quarters; somewhere between 96 and 98. It was about 10:00 am a week before the meeting and she had just printed the performance reports from the TMS. As she got her third cup of coffee, she turned her attention to the reports thumbing through them to look at the claims experience, contract compliance and on-time delivery scores. She saw they had two claims for the quarter and had had a shortage of refrigerated trailers (reefers) and then she looked a the on-time delivery and almost spilt her coffee. Over the last three months, the company had progressively got worse at on-time delivery. The most recent month suggested that the company had an on-time delivery rate of just 80%. The company standard was 95% or higher for Tier I and Tier II carriers. In J&B's history they had never had a month this low. She thought for a moment and remembered they had just updated the configuration of the contract into the TMS. It occurred to her that perhaps the configuration had been done wrong and this was skewing the results. So, she went back through their carrier profile only to find that the configuration was perfect. She looked at the report again and her only conclusion was that J&B had missed those deliveries.

Figure 16 (from a previous example) was the final scorecard she created. She knew that when she sent it to J&B it would likely spark controversy because she had not heard from them about missing delivery windows and, normally, if they missed something they always emailed or called her. She composed an email to her client representative at J&B and confirmed the time of the supplier meeting the following week. She then forwarded that email to the head of procurement, Julia Warner. Julia replied to her email almost immediately asking if the report was correct. Jayne told her that, based on her analysis, it was. Julie suggested that she attend the meeting because she figured J&B would likely send someone more senior given the significance of the report. Jayne told Julie she would welcome her attendance and then sent the meeting invitation. Sure enough, just as she finished this, Chris, the account representative from J&B replied to her email thanking her for her report, indicating he was confused by it but would research it before the meeting, and then let her know that Ted Janson, the Chief Operating Officer (COO) would likely attend the meeting. Jayne was glad that Julia had suggested she attend. She assured Chris that Ted would be most welcome, recognized his concern about the score card and assured him they too were confused by it and were looking forward to "digging in" to find the answers. This air of professional was not lost on Chris. He had always like Jayne and knew Westmoreland was known for their professionalism even when things were tough.

<u>The Meeting:</u> On the following Tuesday, the companies got together to conduct the J&B carrier's quarterly supplier meeting. Because the scorecard would move J&B from an Exceptional Rating to a Probationary Rating, Jayne wanted to make sure they had the right people in the room who could discuss and respond to the issues that the scorecard would raise. For Westmoreland, there was Julie, the head of procurement, Jayne, the supplier management representative, Jose Martinez, the head of the Materials Planning and Logistics (MP&L) Sara Sanders, the team lead for receiving, and Harrison Jackson, the lead for carrier invoicing and accounts payable. Fred Thomas, the legal representative that completed the contract, was scheduled to be in the meeting and indicated he might be late. He openly questioned his need for the meeting due to his schedule of meetings that day, but Jayne indicated he was needed if questions came up he could answer. He agreed but said he'd probably be about an hour late. When J&B arrived, they had Chris Aleppo, J&B's account manager for Westmoreland, Ted Janson, the COO, Ito Satori, the head of dispatching for J&B, and Wanda Samuels, the head of customer service. The room was initially tense as the groups introduced themselves and went through the normal pleasantries to break the ice.

Jayne asked the group to please take their seats and then looked to Julia to being. Julie looked at the group and said, "By the time we're done, this may be one of the strangest meetings I've ever attended". Then, looking to Ted, she said, Ted, you and I go back 20 years and in all that time, I don't think we've ever come together over a situation like this. I'm not sure what's happened but I want to say at the outset, that we know the quality and partnership that J&B has had with us for that 20 years and there's no intent here to throw J&B 'under the bus'. Following Julia's lead, Ted said, Julia, I appreciate you saying all that. Like you, we're confused as to how we got here so I'm hoping we can have a robust and open discussion. Helped by this team, I think we'll discover what's happened and what we need to do". And with that the team looked to Jayne.

As you all know I completed the most recent balanced scorecard for J&B and our findings suggest that J&B has fallen from last quarter's ninety-seven rating to a rating of eighty-two. At first I thought there might be a mistake in our system or how we configure things, but I couldn't find one. I contacted Jose and asked if his team could identify the specific dates and loads that were not on-time. It took until this morning so I apologize that we couldn't send it to you earlier but perhaps that's our best place to start. The group agreed and Jose passed out his analysis and report. "As you'll see", he began, "of the sixty-eight deliveries made by J&B in the last quarter, 13, or 19.11% of these deliveries were late by 30 minutes or later to the dock". "As you know", he continued, "we have a 15-minute window and deliveries that are over 30 minutes late are tagged as late for scorecard purposes. I have the truck number, dates, and delivery times in the report for your reference. I realize you many need to take some time to review it", he began, when Ito Satori, politely said "I apologize for cutting you off Jose, but I brought my dispatch report of every delivery over the last 90 days and have the truck numbers, dates and times."

He passed a copy out to all members and said, "The confusing part on our end is that we have a record of only two late deliveries during this time and both were related to an equipment malfunction. In both of those instances we called the receiving clerk and they were able to give us a new gate time", he said. This drew confused looks from all the members at the table as they received both reports and digested the information. Jose offered, "Ito, I am aware of those two issues, but they were not tagged as late". This only further drew puzzled glances from the group.

Over the next hour, the teams poured through the numbers, hypothesized on what might have happened but generally could not come up with a satisfactory explanation of why J&B had no record of missed deliveries and Westmoreland had a report full of them. While no one wanted to suggest that anyone was openly lying, the mood in the room became tense because no satisfactory answer was emerging. The group agreed to take a 15- minute break and adjourned.

When they got back together, it was getting close to lunch time and there was a slight impatience in the room. Just then Fred Thomas walked in apologizing for being late and asked innocently "What did I miss?" Julia gave a slight laugh and told him, "Well Fred, you didn't miss a thing, but we have a bit of a mystery we're trying to unravel." She asked Jayne to quickly summarize the group as a way of catching up Fred. Fred listened intently as Jayne explained the discrepancies in the reports and the confusion it was causing. After she was done, Fred asked simply "Can I see the reports please." They were quickly produced, and he peered at them first with an air to understanding what was in front of him but then his expression intensified as he focused in on the two reports comparing them together. After a moment he said, "Well, this is quite a dilemma. One report says you guys are failing, while the other…." his voice trailed off as he noticed something on a report for the first time.

Without further explanation, Fred rapidly flipped back and forth between there reports flipping pages quickly as he was comparing something between them. Finally, he sat back with an amused expression on his face. He looked at Julia and at Ted, acknowledging him for the first time with a "Oh, hey, Ted", and then continued with "I know the problem. It came so quickly because Ted and I had long conversations about this very issue". As if to dismiss the entire issue, he brightened and said "It was a logical and natural mistake. In fact, it makes perfect sense to me now". Julia, not so much losing her patience as wanting to look some productive conversation going back at Fred and said "Uh, Fred, ya gotta help me out here, what makes perfect sense". Fred, coming to himself said "Oh, shoot Julia, sorry about that, I was playing the conversation back in my mind". Looking to Ted, he said, "Ted, remember when we were talking about how we would be configuring the contract into our TMS and that we would be able to track performance of all of carriers"? Ted acknowledged the conversation with a nod but did not reply.

"We have a blanket template in our TMS that allows us to preconfigure our standards terms and agreements in it", Fred went on. "After we got the yard management software, they asked the IT folks to change one of the configuration items for delivery. Frankly, I'm not sure why they did it and I only heard about it in passing…" he said his voice pondering. "Oh my, you're right Fred", said Sara Sanders suddenly, "we did have IT go in and change the delivery parameter from the gate to the dock so we could monitor how well the software worked" she said with an air of triumph in her voice.

Now Jayne was catching on, "So you're saying that since we implemented the yard software package, we have been measuring delivery to the dock?" she asked wonderingly. "Exactly", Fred nodded, "the thing is, that's not what the contract said, is it Ted". Ted, now smiling said, "No Fred it's not. I remember we had quite a debate over that point and you finally agreed that holding me accountable to a delivery to a location I can't control isn't terribly fair and may lead to unintended consequences. You finally agreed with me and the contract's delivery point is the gate". "That's the problem with people who make good logical arguments, he said slightly laughing, and "I have a hard time disagreeing even if I am a lawyer!". The group laughed harder than they should have finally releasing some tension from the room. Wanda, who had been quiet up to this point, chimed in with "But wait, even with the gate as the delivery point, why were still late thirteen times. What's the distance of the gate to the dock? It shouldn't take that long, should it", she observed.

The room was suddenly quiet as this revelation took hold. Jose whistled slowly under his breath "hmm, I wonder if we might not have a different problem. Have we been able to measure how well the yard management system is working"? Everyone looked at each other. After a moment, Julia offered "well, apparently either none of us knows or we haven't", and then she went on, "I'll get in contact with Estaban our Yard Manager and see what I can learn". Then, thinking for a moment she went on. "Ted, I wonder if you might help if we need it", she said. Ted looked at her saying "What do you have in mind". Thinking as she spoke, she said, "Now that we have a handle on what's going on, it might be helpful if we had a carrier that could help us track the cycle times from the time you get to the facility, through the gate, and to the dock. If we could somehow have a time stamp for each of those events we could compare those against our systems and see if we're getting the same results. If we are not, then we have a bigger problem than we think". Ted pickup up where she left off, "and we could help you figure that out". "Exactly", she said. Looking at Ito Satori, Ted said "Ito, we've just completed the Electronic Logging Device implementation, right"? Ito nodded in the affirmative. "Well then", Ted said smiling, "Looks like we can do this and check our own ELD quality at the same time. I can have our IT people build a report that takes the telemetry from the ELDs at those points and then have a report sent to you daily". Julia seemed pleased by the response and said "Ted that would be terrific. I'll let our folks know and between us I believe we can figure this out". Then, turning to Jayne, she said, "Well Jayne, we still have the matter of the scorecard.

Do you want to do the honors or shall I"? "Not a problem boss", she said smiling as she took the paper scorecard from the middle and rip it vertically". Then, looking at Chris, she said laughing, "I'll get you the REAL ONE tomorrow". With that, she adjourned the meeting. The next day, Chris forwarded the email to Ted he had got from Jayne. It included the new scorecard along with a message of thanks. Ted opened the scorecard to find the modified score. "97", he said with satisfaction. As he got up to relay the news to Cliff, the company's CEO, he thought about the meeting of the previous day. "We'd be nothing without partnership", he said out loud to no one.

Many different approaches companies use to contract for these services but in the end most companies want the same thing: An efficient transportation network that delivers goods on-time at the lowest possible pricing with suppliers they can trust. Contracting for transportation services is a core part of developing carrier relationships. It provides the company with a core set of third party services it can leverage to drive efficiencies in logistics and transportation along with the potential for these relationships to go well beyond just the value of moving goods.

Effectively managing these carrier relationships is a critical part of achieving the company's end goals for transportation. Building relationships, using the balanced scorecard as a way of driving improvements and efficiencies with carriers and within the company creates a 1+1=3 kind of value. Ultimately, transportation can be a differentiating capability within the company when it has achieved a set of suppliers it trusts, and customers are satisfied due to the consistency and flexibility it provides in delivery.

CHAPTER 6: MOTOR CARRIERS

INTRODUCTION

You say motor carriers, and others say trucking. In this chapter, we'll generally say trucking when talking about motor carriers. The trucking industry is the largest domestic transportation industry accounting for over 70% of all transportation carrier spend in the US. We discussed the role of regulation in trucking previously along with the strong impact the US interstate Highway has played in the role of trucking.

In this section we will discuss the role of trucking in global transportation with an emphasis on practices in the US. We'll discuss the different trucking companies, the equipment available to match loads, the standards for the equipment and the requirements for being a truck driver. We'll also talk about the life of an Over the Road (OTR) or line-haul truck drivers. Most of this transportation involves truckload (TL) hauls over relatively long distances.

Long distance trucking is not the only way we move goods with motor carriers. In this chapter, we'll also discuss the role of Less Than Truckload (LTL) and how, using freight terminals, they drive efficiency for customers whose load doesn't fill a truck fully.

While we have many topics to discuss, it's important to remember the role of trucking in the supply chain and why companies choose the trucking mode of transportation versus other modes. There are primarily three reasons companies use trucking for their transportation mode:

- Speed: Trucking, when compared to other modes, is fast. For transportation under 500 miles there is likely no other answer that is as fast and affordable as trucking.

- Location Flexibility: Generally, if a truck cannot reach a destination then it's probably not reachable. Trucking gives us the flexibility across the supply chain whether it's last mile delivery, working with intermodal transportation to pick up goods inland and deliver them to their planned destination or simply enabling small loads to move between many locations with efficiency.

- Load Flexibility: Trucking also can carry loads that other domestic modes will struggle to move. Have you ever seen a truck carrying a house between locations? How about two trucks each carrying half of a double-wide trailer. Or maybe you've seen trucks carrying long wind-mill blades. Thanks to the road infrastructure and the evolution of equipment for trucks to use to carry loads, trucks can carry irregularly sized items near impossible to move otherwise.

DEFINING THE MOTOR CARRIER SEGMENT

One would think the motor carrier would be relatively simple to define but part of the flexibility that the trucking segment brings is in its diversity. There are several ways we can define segments within motor carriers and in this section, we'll cover the major ways we look at the segment. Figure 17 [17] summarizes the overall trucking industry in terms of its makeup and size for 2017. The $700B industry comprises private and for-hire (common) carriers and less than load (LTL) carriers and

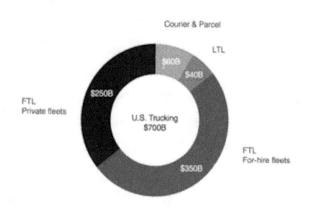

Figure 17. Makeup of the Motor Carrier Industry

courier and parcel. While courier and parcel are different, the fleets we are looking at in this segmentation all fall into the general category of a truck we often call a "tractor-trailer". What exactly is this vehicle?

What is a Truck?

There are different trucks in commercial trucking. The Federal Motor Carriers Safety Administration (FMCSA) is the principle regulating agency for motor carrier definitions, equipment, operations and safety. The most basic definition given for a motor carrier is "A motor carrier transports passengers or property for compensation" [18]. There are also licensure requirement for operating trucks in certain categories. When looking at freight hauling, we find multiple definitions of a commercial vehicle [19] and their associated licensing requirements:

- Gross Vehicle Weight Rating (GVWR) of 26,000 pounds or more - These are most often "big rigs" most people think of when they think of trucking. These vehicles most typically operate with a tractor and a detachable trailer and require a Commercial Driver's License, class A, (CDL-A) to operate. Vehicles in this category include any trailer connected to a tractor. We'll cover the equipment involved in this segment later in the chapter.

- GVWR under 26,000 without a detachable trailer – This category covers many kinds of commercial vehicles including busses and commercial transportation vehicles and some construction vehicles and tow trucks. It also covers commercial delivery vehicles often called "straight trucks" or "box trucks" because the tractor and trailer are integrated. These vehicles typically require a class B driver's license.

---

[17] Bls.org. Motor Carrier Segment. 2017
[18] FMCSA 49 CFR
[19] ibid

- Hazardous Material (HAZMAT) Carriers not covered above – Any vehicle of any kind that transports hazardous materials is considered a commercial motor vehicle and is bound by commercial trucking regulations. Drivers of these vehicles must be certified for carrying hazmat. Further, if the vehicle meets the definitions below, they also require additional licensure. Drivers of these vehicles typically require a class C driver's license.

- Vehicles that do not meet other criteria – Any commercial vehicle, typically passenger transportation related, also are covered under the regulation. They require a class C driver's license.

Truckload or Less than Truckload

Another important way we segment motor carriers is whether they will provide services for full trucks only (truckload, or TL) or if they will also accept partial loads typically called Less Than Truckload (LTL). This used to be a designation that also defined a specific company as LTL companies employ freight terminals as part of their operations and TL companies do not as they pick up at one origination point and deliver directly to a specific destination. In addition, there used to be a general rule that any load under 500 miles was typically an LTL load and only long distance, over 500 miles and often over 1,000 miles were considered TL. This is not a good way to look at the market any more. For one, LTL companies are forming partnerships to move freight within their regions and then hand it off to partners to provide TL across the country. For another. TL companies have learned there is sometimes value in carrying a partial load between their delivery point and their next pickup point. Using freight terminals is now the best way to think of this distinction. A company with a freight terminal network that allows them to pick up freight from multiple companies locally and transport it to many destinations is the true LTL model.

Even with these definitions and approaches, we also need a standard by which we can create a full truckload both to determine a reasonable cost for the load and to understand how much we can haul in one load. In trucking, our weight is limited by the federal standard for total GVWR. An entire load cannot exceed 80,000 pounds when considering the truck tractor, the trailer, and the freight itself. The size of the truck and the weight of the trailer both affect the weight available for the load. Figure 18 shows an example of how this weight breaks out.

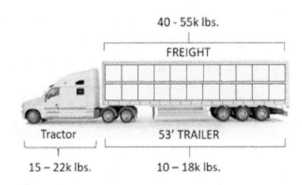

Figure 18. Total Gross Vehicle Weight by Vehicle Sections and Load

Different sizes of tractors and trailers will carry different weight so the weight of these two will vary by the size of the tractor, the size of the trailer and the materials used in making the trailer. Generally, the tractor is typically between 15,000 and 22,000 pounds. Similarly, the trailer, in our case the largest trailer available at 53 feet will weigh between 10,000 and about 18,000 pounds (Figure 18). The federal standard for the entire rig, truck, tractor, and freight, is 80,000 pounds. So, a typical full freight load with weight will run around 40,000 to 55,000 pounds. This is slightly above what most companies will consider a standard load at 35,000 pounds. Sometimes we meet our maximum weight at about the time we fill up the trailer with palleted goods. Other times, the pallets are so heavy, we are constrained by the weight and don't use up the volume. When this occurs, we call the load a "weigh out".

While weight is the primary way we define a truckload a TL or LTL, we can also look at volume. Trucks may carry more bulky and light items especially when considering moving consumer goods. When the truck fills up with pallets before achieving the 35,000-pound minimum weight, we call this "cubing out". We've filled the dimensions of the trailer with no ability to add more. We also consider this to be a TL load.

Other Size Standards

Besides weight, there are also other standards governing the length, width, and height of trucks and trailers:

- Length – The Federal Government defines the maximum length standard for trailers in the US at no longer than 56 feet. For most box trailers, or dry vans, the industry standard for the longest vehicle is 53 feet.

- Width – The Federal Government also defines the maximum width of a trailer at 102 inches which can also be 2.6 meters (102.36 inches) if they are metric based. Interstates average a 12-foot lane, so this provides just under two feet of clearance on both sides. In urban environments where the road width can be as small as 10-feet it leaves only about 9 inches on each side for clearance. Height – Each state defines its required maximum height for truck clearance. These vary but are generally between 13' 6 inches and 14-feet. In urban areas with interstates they must be at least 14-feet and on rural interstates the clearance is 16 feet.

Parcel and Courier

Until recently, companies involved in transportation did not look at the parcel and courier segment the way they did the other segments in the motor carrier industry. For one, courier services are typically smaller companies that deliver small packages throughout the day in large urban centers or are based on small envelopes that require overnight or faster delivery (express). In addition, Parcel is a specialized class of freight that involves individual packages traditionally under seventy pounds and with dimensions that are less than 165 inches in length and width. Parcel is generally received in individual packages requiring a different business model to handle it as freight. Companies like UPS, Fedex, DHL and various country's postal services typically have handled parcel delivery. Parcel delivery has become a core part of eCommerce both in the US and globally. This has had a disruptive effect on transportation costs to the consumer and especially within retail business. The traditional freight model in retail involves moving goods from manufacturers in large quantities of pallets to distribution centers and then later shipped to retail locations. Those goods are then stocked at the retail store until consumers come and buy them. With eCommerce, many of those traditionally pallets are now becoming parcels shipped from a central distribution center, or eCommerce fulfillment center directly to the consumer's home. Most recently, retailers, both local and online, are engaging in even faster delivery with providing same day delivery. This is having a disruptive effect on retail and is also affecting the transportation industry company's work to take advantage of these new needs. LTL companies are developing home delivery and parcel services in the regions in which they operate. We will discuss this in more detail in the chapter: Omni-Channel Commerce transportation later in this book.

EQUIPMENT IN THE MOTOR CARRIER MODE

As we will see as we explore all the modes in this section, using specific equipment is a major part of the efficiencies and standards needed to create predictable loads. This is important as understanding the capacity of the various equipment helps transportation planners to determine their typical load plans, identify the most effective equipment for the load and communicate so it is common for all involved. In this section, we'll cover some of the major equipment available in trucking along with some of the standard sizes for that equipment. We'll do this using some these categories: Boxes, flats, tanks, specialized.

Boxes

The first category of trailers are boxes. These are built to primarily carry palleted freight but in one instance it is built to carry freight that cannot be crated or palleted. Figure 19 pictures these trailers.

- The Dry Van – The Dry Van, sometimes called the Box Trailer, is one of the most common trailers on the road. It is a enclosed trailer typically made from steel and/or aluminum. The most common sizes are 28-foot, 40-Foot, 42-Foot 45-foot, 48-foot and 53-foot but other sizes can be found. Dry vans are used extensively to move palleted goods that must not be exposed to the elements.

- <u>Refrigerated Van (Reefer)</u> – The Reefer is a version of a dry van that includes a refrigeration / freezer unit to keeps palleted goods refrigerator or frozen throughout the transportation movement. In looking at the Figure 19 it should be apparent that a Reefer trailer is a dry van with a cooling unit and that is what it is. Common sizes for Reefer trailers are 28-foot, 32-foot, 36-foot, 40-foot, 48-foot, and 53-foot.

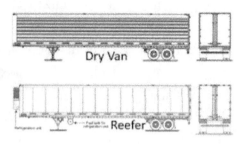

Figure 19. "Box" Based Trailers

Flats

Our next category are trailers that have a wide and flat surface for moving freight. These trailers provide little protection from the elements and rarely are configured to carry palleted items. Figure 20 provides pictures of these trailers.

- <u>The Flat Bed</u> – The Flat Bed trailer is the general hauler in the trucking segment. It has a long base and can carry bulk goods that require no significant protection from the elements. Load are usually covered in canvas besides being tied to the trailer as part of their movement. The most common sizes are 42-Foot 45-foot, and 48-foot. These trailers are about five feet off the ground and can generally carry up to 48,000 pounds. Flatbed trailers can only carry goods up to 8 ½ feet in height so if a load is higher than this, a different flat based trailer is needed.

- <u>Drop Deck / Double Drop Deck</u> – These trailers will typically have at least two levels enabling taller cargo to be moved besides other cargo on the higher level.

Pictured is a standard drop deck. Double drop decks have a back deck slightly higher than the center deck that is the lowest. Most drop deck trailers are 48-feet in length.

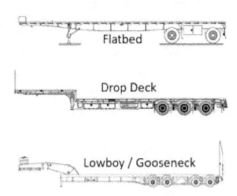

- Lowboy / Gooseneck Trailer – The lowboy and the gooseneck trailers sit lo w to the ground compared to other kinds of trailers. These trailers can carry freight up to 12-feet tall with a maximum weight around 48,000 pounds.

Figure 20. "Flat" Based Trailers

They are effective with items very dense, heavy and compact. Typical loads for these trailers include very large vehicles (dump trucks, military tanks, etc.), industrial machinery like large generators and other items that are tall, bulky and heavy.

Tanks

Tanks based trailers are enclosed tank based configurations used primarily to move bulk goods in them. This can include virtually any liquid or gas, but some trailers can carry bulk agricultural items like grain and corn. There are also tank trailers open at the top to carry bulk items like coal, iron ore, and scrap metal. Figure 21 shows these trailers.

- Tanker Trailer – The tanker trailer is the probably the most recognizable tank based trailer. Tankers carry liquids of all kinds from food grade chemicals to oils to dangerous hazardous materials. They also carry gases under pressure which is typically a hazardous material. Typical trailer sizes are 42-feet, 45-feet, 48-feet and 53-feet.

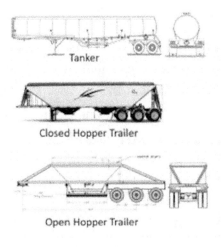

- Closed Hopper Trailer – This tank carries dry bulk goods like rice, corn, flour, sugar and more. The trailer has a broad long top "door" that opens to accept bulk goods and then has doors at the bottom of the trailer that open to allow the goods to flow via gravity into a container for storage.

Figure 21. "Tank" Based Trailers

- <u>Open Hopper Trailer</u> – This tank is more of a bucket than a tank. It carries bulk items but provides little protection for goods. It has an open top which can be covered with canvass to stop spillage if the load is too high. Like the closed hopper, it also is delivered through doors at the bottom of the trailer that uses gravity to empty the load.

Specialized

The final category of trailers are specialized trailers. These serve a very specific purpose and not available to be used for much else. This doesn't reduce the value of the trailers as much as their demand must be carefully monitored because if the equipment isn't available it will be very difficult to execute on the loads these specialized trailers are used to move. Figure 22 shows these trailers.

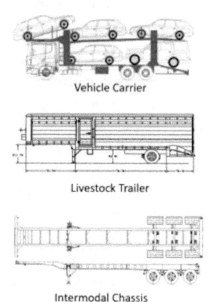

Vehicle Carrier

Livestock Trailer

Intermodal Chassis

- <u>Vehicle Carriers</u> – Vehicle carriers move cars and other smaller vehicles between destinations. The vehicle carriers can be configured to carry between 5 and 9 cars or light trucks depending on the size of the vehicle which never exceeds 53 feet.

- <u>Livestock Carriers</u> – Think of a dry van with a lot of slots for air and you have a livestock carrier. Livestock carriers must contend when moving livestock. Livestock moves under 500 miles are generally straightforward. For over 500 miles drivers must stop overnight on their journey for a ten-hour rest break. In some networks, the driver has interim locations in which to offload cargo overnight and in others the animals stay in the trailer. Heat and cold issues, water and even feeding become significant issues for this live cargo.

- <u>Intermodal Chassis</u> – intermodal is a rapidly growing segment of transportation and requires specialized equipment when working with shipping containers. A shipping container looks and acts and works much in the same way as a dry van but the container isn't in a trailer configuration so it can easily be stacked on rail equipment in a double stack configuration or on container ships. Because of this, shipping containers moved by tractor- trailers require a specialized chassis for the shipping container. Containers are placed on top of the chassis and locked into the chassis creating an integrated trailer container.

Longer Combination Vehicles (LCV) [20]

Longer Combination Vehicles (LCVs) are truck vehicle configurations that either exceed the mandatory weight limit of 80,000 pounds and/or exceed the federal length standard of 56 feet. Between 1956 and 1991 the government allowed states to determine whether they wanted the operations of LCVs in their states. In 1991 they removed the option and banned LCVs from those states that did not allow them. Because of this, the standards for LCVs haven't changed since June 1, 1991. In 2004, the Federal Motor Carrier Safety Administration (FMCSA) implemented training requirements for all LCV operators. This can be found under part 380 of the electronic Code of Federal Regulations (CFR) 49. The requirements call for in-class training and a driver's test on an LCV configuration. Successful completion allows the driver to drive LCV combinations. LCVs are more prevalent in Canada than they are in the US. In the US twenty-three states allow LCVs and most LCVs operate in the western part of the US. States that use LCVs ensure licensure and certification along with the LCVs allowed and the LCV length and weight combination standard. Figure 23 shows three typical configurations of LCVs and Figure 24 shows the areas in the US where these are allowed (primarily the northwest section of the US). LCVs are controversial overall due primarily to safety concerns.

Studies have shown that LCVs are more susceptible to roll-over and accidents primarily due to their size. But they are very efficient when compared to normal truck operations. There is renewed interest in LCVs as "road trains" to help increase the total freight moved through trucking in the US. We likely will not see any significant changes in the foreseeable future. The

trucking industry is already dealing with driver shortages, congestion around populated areas and are more expensive at carrying bulk freight than other modes like rail.

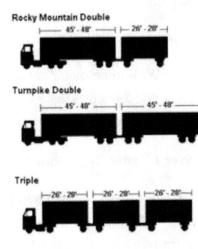

Figure 23. Popular LCV Combinations

---

[20] https://www.fmcsa.dot.gov/regulations/rulemaking/03-20368

MOTOR CARRIER OPERATIONS

We see trucks on the road all the time as we go through our life. Motor Carrier operations are the processes and practices used to ensure that carriers have qualified drivers, meet regulatory requirements related to driver safety and ours of service along with the specific operations involved in line-haul, or TL loads and LTL loads. In this section we'll cover the specific licensing requirements for drivers along with special endorsements some driver's need to do their job along with exploring the processes and life of a line-haul, or TL driver. In

Figure 24. Areas of Permitted LCV Operations

addition, we'll cover LTL carrier operations, explore the use of freight terminals and discuss how this affects LTL drivers. Motor Carrier operations have seen significant changes in the last decade and the approach used in trucking today differs greatly from the past. Understanding the key issues and the approaches to mitigation gives us greater insight into how trucking works from a practical viewpoint.

Largest Variable Costs

Within the motor carrier industry, there is a moderate amount of capital investment and several variable costs that go into every shipment. Labor, and fuel are the largest of the variable costs and drives about 65% of the cost of the shipment.

Driver License Requirements

Truck drivers are required by federal law to obtain a Commercial Driver's License class A (CDL-A) before operation a tractor-trailer. As this is a federal standard it applies to all states uniformly. Drivers can obtain the license only through bureau of motor vehicles in one state. To apply for a CDL-A, the driver:

- Have a regular, valid driver's license with no active suspensions or revocations

- Be at least 21 years of age (for interstate driving)

- Must show proof of citizenship

- Must pass a general background check and have no disqualifying factors per CFR 49-part 383.51 disqualifying factors

- Demonstrate fluency in speaking and writing in the English language

In addition, the driving candidate must pass a medical examination that includes hearing, vision, blood pressure and blood sugar. Drivers cannot obtain a license if they are insulin dependent through a needle, have narcolepsy, have blood pressure that could interfere with driving or a sugar level above 200. Drivers who have sleep apnea used to be disqualified but now may be allowed if they can certify the use of a sleep apnea machine, C-PAP, that mitigates the condition.

Drivers that qualify must pass a written test and a driving test. The road test includes a pre-vehicle inspection, demonstrating basic vehicle controls and a road test. Once a driver has completed their testing, they receive a learner permit which allows them to drive in the presence of an experience driver or training driver. The time they must drive like this varies by state but once they have met that requirement they can complete the driver's skills test and get their CDL license.

Obtaining Endorsements

Drivers that do not anticipate operating with any special equipment or requirements require no additional endorsements to operate. A few endorsements must be obtained depending if the driver is interested in operating advanced equipment. These are:

- "H" Endorsement – The H endorsement certifies the driver to operate with hazardous materials. To do so a driver must pass a 30-question test on hazardous materials operations, complete an expanded background investigation and agree to be fingerprinted.

- "N" Endorsement – The N endorsement certifies drivers to operate tanker truck. Tankers carry liquids and gases that may also be considered hazardous materials. To complete the tanker endorsement, drivers must pass a written test on tanker operations for both liquids and gases.

- "T" Endorsement – The T endorsement is used for drivers that will operate multiple trailers as either a double trailer or triple trailer. This is required due to additional axles that must be managed when moving these trailer configurations. To obtain the endorsement, the driver must complete a test on these configurations.

- "X" Endorsement – Because so many tanker drivers will likely carry various hazardous materials, drivers can opt to get both the N and H endorsements simultaneously by applying for the combined X endorsement. This saves time and allows the drivers a more comprehensive view of their role in moving these goods. More information will be provided on hazardous materials in the Pipeline and Hazardous Materials section.

Motor Carrier Operating Authority

For a motor carrier company to operate, they must obtain <u>Operating Authority</u> from the FMCSA to move freight. There are several kinds of operating authorities, but our focus will be freight commodity based. We covered much of this in the regulation chapter but it's also important to understand Operating Authority as it relates to motor carrier drivers. Besides trucking companies, the driver's themselves can work with carriers in several ways:

- <u>As an employee</u> – This is the most common way drivers begin their careers. Employees are provided with a truck; the company covers all their major expenses and pays the employee a rate per driven mile. The employee works exclusively for the company who assigns them loads and coordinates their time off. The employee works under the motor carrier authority of the trucking company that employs them.

- <u>As a Lease Operator</u> – Some drivers may want more independence than being an employee but do not want to operate their own business as an independent operator. For these drivers. Leasing on to a company is the approach. This involves a driver leasing a truck with a specific company for typically one to three years. The drivers are paid more per mile or paid on a percentage of load basis and act as an independent contractor. The company will find shipments for the driver and the driver will have some freedom in how long they are out on the road. In terms of pay, the company which covers the fuel, maintenance, repairs and insurance deduct these from the cost of the load and then either pays the driver on a cent per mile (CPM) basis or as a percentage of the load. The driver covers their own costs and benefits like any other independent contractor. At the end of the lease period, the driver can purchase the vehicle (if they haven't already through the lease program) or resign a new lease. The driver works under the motor carrier authority of the company that contracts with them and often make from 60 CPM to $1.00 per mile or more.

- <u>Owner-operator</u> – the owner-operator is a trucking company of one. Owner- operators must secure their own Operating Authority from the FMCSA and must operate their own business including the ownership of the truck, all the costs associated with operating the truck, they must find their own loads, and manage the invoicing and payment processes for the loads they run. Often, drivers will have a good amount of experience before considering this approach and will have carrier and broker relationships it can work with to find loads.

Line-haul / Full Truck Load (FTL or TL) Trucking

The most common truckload today involves long distance transportation from one point of origin to one point of destination. These line-haul loads are transported by Over the Road (OTR) drivers that stay out on the road for multiple weeks at a time. The Bureau of Labor and Statistics estimates there are about 1.8M tractor-trailer drivers in the US [21]. The OOIDA foundation did a survey[22] of owner-operators and professional employee drivers and found:

- The average professional driver has about 25 years of experience

- They drive about 110,000 miles or more per year

- 54% were away from home for 200+ nights per year in the last year

- If an owner-operator, they probably started their business at around 37 years of age

- 95% of drivers run solo

- Owner-operators average age is fifty-five and they typically make over $50,000 per year

- Professional Drivers average age is fifty-five and average $38,000 - $40,000 per year

Drivers are given loads by trucking company dispatchers if they are employees or by contacting the company through a job board or via phone or email to see if one is available. There are typically two kinds of loads: The "Drop and Hook", or the "Live-load / Unload". A drop and hook load involves a driver arriving at the pickup location and finding the shipping office and checking in. With a drop and hook, the trailer is already loaded so the driver must simply "drop" an empty trailer, if they have one, and "hook" the new trailer and leave.

These are straight forward and take little time once the driver has been given their load. The live-load, or live unload is the opposite. In these situations, the driver, who will typically have an empty piece of equipment (trailer, flatbed, etc.) checks in with the office and is told to back up to a specific dock point. They then wait while the trailer is loaded, or if it is a delivery, unloaded. This can take from 15 to 30 minutes to more than an hour. While the driver is waiting, they are burning their hours of service time available for that day so the time they must wait is important to be kept to possible.

---

[21] Bureau of Labor and Statistics Jobs Outlook 2018.

[22] OODIA Foundation, Owner-Operator and Professional Driver Facts. 2018.

A Day (or Week) in the Life

John Rafferty is a Line Haul (Long Distance) driver who has been on the road for over 20 years. His home base is near Winchester, Virginia. He's been off the last five days after having spent five weeks on the road. Last night he checked in with his dispatcher and told them he was ready to get back in service. They gave him a load for pickup in Valley Forge, PA. Today is Sunday and he needs to be there by Monday afternoon at 3:00 PM to make his dock time. Winchester is about 4 hours from Valley Forge so around 9:30 am on Monday, he heads out for Valley Forge.

Traffic was normal for this time of year and he arrives at the factory at about 1:30 pm. He relaxes for an hour in his sleeper cab catching up on email and completing his initial paperwork in his ELD. Through the ELD he lets the dispatcher know he's arrived but, he didn't need to do so as the ELD and GPS already told them. Still, he's "old school" and likes to talk to dispatchers occasionally. At about 2:30, he checks in with the gate and they clear him to dock ten on the backside of the factory. Once there, he pulls the truck up to the door that says "shipping" and checks in. He gives the clerk the load number and they hand him his bill of lading and packing list. He does a quick check of the load already loaded and ready to then backs his truck up to it, secures the load, and leaves. "Right on-time", he says, looking at his watch which reminds him it's 3:15 and time to move. His destination is a distribution center in Stockton California. He punches the address into his GPS and sees that it's about 2,934 miles to his destination and will likely take five full days of driving. The Pennsylvania Turnpike would be quicker, but the shipping contract says, "no tolls", so he heads out on Lincoln Highway out of Valley Forge to avoid it.

He makes good progress through the Pennsylvania foothills and down to Morgantown, WV before finding a truck stop outside of Wheeling West Virginia to stop for the night. He checks at home around 9:30 pm. He watches some TV for about an hour and goes to sleep.

He wakes at 5:30 am on Tuesday morning and checks in with the truck stop to get a token for a shower. The shower helps wake him up as does the coffee he buys as he gets back into his truck for a full day of driving. His wife had packed him two sandwiches before he left, and he have one as he gets his day going. At 7:30, or 10 hours since he stopped, he gets back on the road. He enters Ohio and get an in-cab signal to stop at a weigh station about two miles after crossing the border. It's a straightforward process. He shows his paperwork and his ELD, they check it and do a walk around inspection of his truck and he's back on the road about 90 minutes after he stopped. With his pre-pass he should be able to get through the rest of Ohio without stopping. He's back on his way at around 9:00 am and drives steadily through the day stopping briefly outside of Indianapolis for a quick break.

He makes it through Indiana and Illinois without incident. As he got near the Iowa border there was a construction zone that cost him two hours. He used the time to call home and even helped his daughter with some of her homework. At 9:00 PM he stopped in a truck parking lot near Iowa City, IA. He still had food from home, so he put on a movie, ate the food and went to sleep. At 6:00 am, he woke up and made his coffee and at around 7:00 fired the truck up for another day.

It was lightly raining in Iowa City when he left but the storm blew over and the sun came out about the time he made it to Lincoln Nebraska, so he found a truck stop and took a two hour break to get fueled up, a shower, and something to eat. Another six hours of driving and he could see the signs to Cheyenne Nebraska. He looked at his watch and it was just turning 8:00 pm. He stopped on the entrance ramp to the interstate off state highway 122 because there were no truck stops and he had hit his maximum for the day. Dinner consisted of microwave chili, a peanut butter and jelly sandwich, and two antacid tablets to make sure the chili didn't keep him awake all night. A quick text to the wife and by midnight he was asleep.

He was sure it was Thursday when he woke up around 5:30 am and looked out his cab window at the generally light traffic of the interstate. He remembered a western store in Cheyenne where he had bought a pair of boots two years back but since he was already past, it was a fleeting thought. This morning he put some cream in his coffee. He normally drank it black, but the chili had given him enough acid from the night before. He was back on the road at 6:00 which was the earliest he could take off and stay compliant with his ELD.

It was about two hours to Rawlins Wyoming. He remembered this place right off the interstate near a truck stop called Millie's. He decided he'd get there for breakfast. He made good time and pulled into the lot around 7:45 noticing the sign however, "Trucker's Welcome". Milly knew how to do breakfast, but she also had installed showers for trucker's that visited her instead of the truck stop next door. He ordered the "Paul Bunyan" breakfast and headed to the shower to clean up. Feeling refreshed, he tucked into the breakfast was on the road in less than an hour.

From Rawlins, he didn't stop until he got to the other side of Salt Lake City, Utah where he stopped for fuel. While there, he noticed one of his tires had gone flat, so he took an hour to change that. His watch said 3:30 pm and his ELD had him clocked at 7 hours of drive time today.

He made good time but Reno, Nevada was seven hours away and the best he could do was get to some nowhere town called Golconda in Nevada. He called his wife and told her. His wife just laughed and said, "Golconda is important to somebody so don't call it a nowhere town"! It reminded him how much he missed her and their two kids when he was on the road. He found a Walmart parking lot in Golconda and went in and replenished his dwindling suppliers for his mini-fridge and the cabinet that held his foodstuffs. It was now 7:30 pm and found himself again at the mercy of his

ELD and the 10 hours break he had to take. He noticed there was a theatre nearby and went to see what was playing. After looking at the ticket prices, he went back to his cab and put on a game on his satellite TV and settled in. He didn't finally get to sleep until well after 11:00 pm.

He woke up around 6:00 am and noticed that he had slept in a little longer than he had intended. His delivery in Stockton wasn't until 4:00 pm that day but he was always leery of the bay area traffic. "It shouldn't be too bad", he thought to himself, "I should be able to stay east of Oakland and that should keep things light". Another quick cup of coffee, back to black this time, and he was off.

He pulled into Reno, Nevada around 8:30 and decided he better clean up before his delivery. He found one of his favorite truck stops and got in line for a shower token. He noticed some one-armed bandits in the game room and remembered he was still in Nevada. He absentmindedly put in a dollar and hit the buttons only to realize the machine reported that it had rewarded him with $10. Not being one to look a gift horse in the mouth, he cashed out and went to the McDonalds in the plaza and treated himself to breakfast while he waited for his shower.

He got back on the road about 10:00 am for what he hoped would be a short three-hour drive to Stockton. Traffic was light and he made good time so he called ahead to the Stockton Distribution Center at 2:00 pm and told them he was and wondered if he could get an earlier dock time. They told him they had nothing open now but to come by at 3:00 and they would see what they could do. He arrived at the gate at 2:45 and saw there were about a dozen trucks ahead of him. "So much for early this time", he thought to himself and sure enough when he checked into the gate he was told it would be about two hours before he could deliver. With time on his hands, he checked in with the company's dispatch team and asked them to see what was available.

He had reached Fred who had been a dispatcher with the company for over a decade. "How was Golconda", Fred asked him with amusement in his voice. Fred had looked at the ELD data and saw that John had done his last rest break in Nevada. "So good they should actually put in on the map" came John's reply. Fred was looking at the job board and said, "You've got about what, 20 hours left this week?" "Yeah, that's about right" replied John. Fred, continuing to search the board said, "Let's see if we can end your week in a place a little bigger than last night, shall we", and with that noticed a load he thought might work. "Hey, this might be good for you. I've got a load that needs a pickup in San Jose and a delivery in Denver. That'll pretty much finish you for the week and you can do your 34 hours in Denver. How about that?" he asked. "That sounds about right", John said, "It's been awhile since I've been to Denver. Might make for a nice day or two." With that, Fred told him he'd send the details via the ELD shortly.

About an hour later he was headed to San Jose to pick up his next load. With week one almost over, he knew he still had about four weeks to go. He calculated that he'd make about $1,700 this week by the time he reached Denver. "Not a bad start" he thought to himself as he headed down I-680 in the heart of Silicon Valley on his way to his next load.

John, like most of the Over the Road (OTR) drivers create the extensive trucking networks that existing in the US. In any recent year, the drivers in the trucking industry travel about 279 billion miles as part delivering about every consumer and industrial good one can imagine. Collectively, they moved 10.42 billion tons of freight, or enough material to make 1,571 new Hoover Dams every year which could produce enough electricity to power 2 billion people, or about 1/3 of the global population!

Less than Load Trucking (LTL)

Although not as big or pervasive as TL trucking, Less than Load (LTL) trucking provides a flexibility and management of freight equally as critical. LTL represents a different approach to trucking and moving loads. Instead of point to point, LTL operations can move small loads of freight from many origination points and deliver them to just as many destinations, so it makes shipping smaller loads economical and practical. It creates different options for shippers to meet their business needs and provides a speed and flexibility difficult to match. It also creates a very different lifestyle for the drivers.

The key to the business model is how the LTL networks are created using freight terminals. Because of the point to point nature of TL loads, there is no need for anything between them. In LTL, we use freight terminals of various kinds to create a network and service area that allows a company to plan and execute freight needs quickly and efficiently. To understand LTL networks, we need to break down the facilities and networks built in LTL. To begin, let's look at the terminals used in LTL shipping:

- The LTL Network – As we look at how loads are managed in an LTL environment, we need to understand the network and facilities involved in LTL delivery. Figure 25 provides a simple LTL network that involves a Midwest LTL company with pickup and delivery service areas in most major cities along with break-bulk facilities in centralized areas that enable the sortation and movement of goods outside of the Pickup and

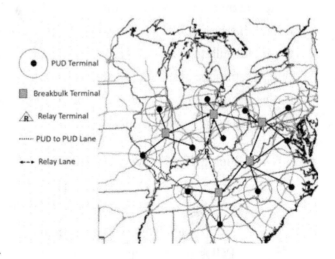

Figure 25. LTL Carrier Freight Network Example

Delivery (PUD) service area to move goods between PUD terminals. Notice how the PUD terminals are centrally located around the most likely areas of volume. These are denoted by dark black dots with a circle around them that shows the general service area. Locations outside of the service area will typically have a premium for delivery added to the cost of the shipment. Similarly, the Break-bulk Terminals (grey squares) are located along major interstate routes and generally spread out between clusters of PUD terminals. One of the key factors involved in an LTL network is that LTL drivers generally work through their day and are home at night. Because of this, some LTL networks will also use Relay terminals (triangle with an "R" in it) to help them keep moving freight in one direction but allow the drivers to can return home. In our case, we have one relay terminal near Cincinnati Ohio that helps us bridge the break-bulk facility in Toledo Ohio with another break-bulk facility near Knoxville, TN. With a basic understanding of the network and service areas in Figure 25, we can now look deeper at all three kinds of these facilities; PUD, break-bulk, and Relay terminals and their functions. Most PUD terminals will deliver freight during the earlier part of the day and then pickup and return freight to the PUD terminal at the end of their shift. Freight bound for another PUD terminal is then loaded onto trucks and driven through the evening to their respective Break- bulk Terminals or, if there is a direct PUD to PUD connection to the PUD terminals. In our network the only PUD to PUD connections are between Atlanta (bottom of the diagram), Nashville, and St. Louis, Missouri. These connections are only done when a high volume of dedicated freight moves between these terminals.

Most will travel to Break-bulk Terminals. Drivers will arrive at the break-bulk facility and back their load into a docking point where the freight will be unloaded and sorted and staged for the next destination of the freight in the system. There will usually already be previous loads sorted and loaded so when the drivers get to their locations, they will typically go to the other side of the facility where they will be dispatched back to their home base with a load that has freight for that destination. This is true of drivers moving from PUD terminal to Break-bulk terminal and back, and for those drivers that move freight between two Break-bulk Terminals. We'll now discuss each kind of terminal in the network and how it works both independently and within the network to enable freight to move between shipper origination points and destination points.

- Pickup and Delivery Terminals (PUD) – The first terminal is the Pickup and Delivery Terminal which enables the LTL Company to service a specific area with the terminal for picking up or delivering LTL loads. The terminal size varies based on the demand in the service area. The service area concept is very important. For PUDs to work the drivers from the terminal need to run routes that deliver and pickup freight. The number of stops on the route will be directly related to the size of each load. LTL companies typically use 53-foot dry van trailers (the largest legally available) which can hold 30 pallets in a single stack or up to sixty pallets if double stacked but also may use smaller box trucks (trucks without a separate cab) that can carry 10 to 12 pallets for smaller loads. Some LTL companies also use refrigerated vans or box trucks as part of a "cold- chain" (a supply chain focused on refrigerated or frozen based products) operation. Most PUD terminals have a service area in a 100 to 150-mile radius from their terminal depending on the state and connected to a break-bulk facility to enable movement between other PUD terminals. This is done to optimize intrastate hours of service. Some PUD terminals may be directly connected to other PUD terminals if there is enough freight volume to dedicate a lane between them. These connections can only move freight between the two service areas and provide no break-bulk capabilities.

Drivers can typically work up to 12 hours, or even 14 hours with some exemptions, and will be home every night. There are a few ways LTL terminals develop their routes. The approach is based on the customers and the characteristics of the freight and typically include:

- Deliver to Pick up Routes – The most common kind of route involves a driver leaving the PUD terminal with a full truck made up of multiple deliveries to customers. The driver delivers the freight to the customers on the route and then, when empty, picks up freight from customers as they return to the terminal. Figure 26 shows an example of this. Notice that the terminal loads the truck in reverse, i.e. the farthest delivery from the terminal is loaded first etc.. Trucks are loaded in reverse order with the farthest delivery point in the front of the truck and the delivery point closest to the terminal in the back, or closest to the

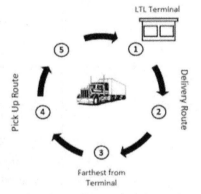

Figure 26. Delivery with Return Pick up Route

trailer door. As drivers arrive at their delivery locations (1, 2, and three in the diagram), they use a live unload approach until the last delivery leaves the truck empty. The driver will proceed to the pickup point farthest from the terminal (number 4 in the diagram) and then go to each pickup point using a live-load approach until the truck has completed the pickup route. The driver returns to the terminal where the truck will be emptied, and the freight will be sorted for delivery.

- PUP Delivery and Pickup – Another approach to pick up involves the use of small trailers, typically as a 28-foot dry van left with clients to enable them to preload the trailers with their loads. This allows a driver to move two PUP trailers at a time without exceeding the federal legal length restriction. PUP delivery and pickup typically involve customers who are regular shipper and who can generally fill the trailer themselves. Often, the freight terminal will release two PUP trailers for delivery to two customers that also have PUP trailers ready for pickup.

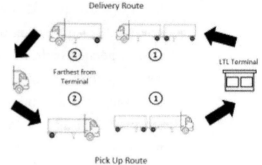

Figure 27. PUP Delivery and Pickup

- The driver will go to the customer closest to the terminal and deliver their trailer and then to the next. Once the trailers are delivered, the driver will then run a pickup route where it will pick up PUP two PUP trailers on the way back to the terminal. Figure 27 shows this process. PUP trailer operations differ from normal LTL PUD operations in that the drivers work directly with full PUP trailers. If a customer cannot fill a PUP trailer then they will use the normal PUD operations.

- Other Operations – LTL service providers are also branching into other kinds of operations that may involve local PUD centric operations or the full use of the LTL network. These include cold-chain operations for refrigerated and frozen goods that may be brought to the PUD terminal as FTL and then delivered to multiple customers. Some LTL companies are also providing contract based home delivery services. These contracts involve working with a larger chain store with durable goods like appliance and furniture that need to be delivered to individual homes. These are picked up at the chain's distribution center on the day of delivery and then teams deliver the goods to individual homes using a similar route approach.

  o Break-bulk Terminals – Where PUD terminals enable intake and delivery of mixed freight throughout the network, Break-bulk Terminals enable freight to move seamlessly throughout the network between service areas. It does this by bringing freight from PUD terminals and other Break-bulk Terminals and then sorting that freight based on the PUD terminal that will be the destination for the freight. If the break-bulk facility isn't connected directly to a PUD terminal it will send it to another break-bulk facility, and so on, until it reaches the destination PUD terminal. Figure 28 shows the flow of a Break-bulk terminal and we'll use Figure 28 to help understand the flow of freight through these terminals.

You'll notice in Figure 28 there are five numbers on the left of the diagram. The numbers signify the inbound freight to outbound freight and the internal sortation that occurs to make this happen:

- Step 1 – First, freight comes into the Break- bulk terminal in Toledo, Ohio. (1) This freight will come either from a PUD terminal that uses the Break-bulk terminal for mixing freight it does not deliver within its own service area or from another Break-bulk terminal in the network that has freight that needs to move through one or more other Break-bulk Terminals to get to its final PUD terminal destination. When the driver arrives at the facility they check in

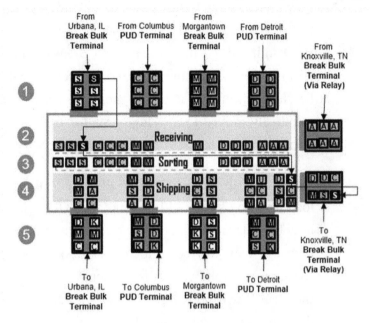

Figure 28. Breakbulk Terminal Operations

with the receiving team and turn the load over for processing. In the diagram there is a "pallet" that is all black and has a white "S" in the middle. We'll use this pallet to trace the break-bulk process. In our case, the pallet originated in the St. Louis, Missouri as denoted by the "S". The order with the pallet, not pictured, indicates the pallet needs to be delivered through the Atlanta PUD terminal. Because of this, the pallet has moved from the St. Louis PUD through the Urbana, IL Break-bulk terminal and is now coming into the Toledo Break-bulk terminal.

- Step 2 - As it arrives in the receiving area (2) the load is received and checked to ensure it is in good order. Then it will be moved to the center of the terminal into the sorting center. While this happens, the terminal is also unloading four other trucks. Two of the trucks are from the Detroit and Columbus PUD Terminals. The Toledo Break-bulk terminal serves these two specific PUD Terminals so any freight from outside the service area bound for either terminal must pass through the Toledo Break-bulk terminal. In addition, two other trucks are inbounding from Morgantown, WV and Knoxville, TN from Break-bulk Terminals that use this facility to move through to other locations. The distance between the Knoxville Break-bulk terminal and the Toledo terminal is so the company uses a relay terminal to ensure the freight can get there quickly. Once the trailers are emptied they will likely be put aside in a parking spot until needed next. Empty trailers have been put in the outbound dock, but these inbound trailers will ultimately become outbound trailers over the next day.

- Step 3 – Once the freight is unloaded and moved to the sorting area (3), it is then sorted based on its outbound destination. With our St. Louis pallet, it is bound for the Atlanta PUD so it will go from the Toledo Break- bulk Terminal to the Knoxville Break-bulk terminal next. The same is true for all freight as it is moved through the sorting center to be staged near the outbound freight docks. Like the others, the St. Louis pallets is eventually moved to the stage area for the outbound truck that will take it to it's next terminal.

- Step 4 – With the pallets now all staged to be loaded into their respective trucks, the loading process begins (4). Unlike the PUD terminal, there is no specific requirement for how the trucks are loaded because when they get to their next destination, even a PUD terminal, they will be offloaded and sorted again. With a Break-bulk terminal, that sortation will follow what is happening in the Toledo terminal. If it is a PUD terminal, the freight will be received and then staged to the route where it will ultimately be delivered to the customer. With the freight staged, forklift drivers now begin loading them into trucks for departure.

- Step 5 – With the trucks loaded, the shipping department provides all the drivers with their packing lists and bills of lading for their respective trips (5). Depending on the velocity of the freight movement, i.e. the number of trips done in a day between facilities, the drivers might wait for this process to come to completion and then pick up their truck to return to their home base. More likely, the freight volume is significant enough that the drivers in step 1 have left for their home base and by the time we get to step 5, a new set of drivers will have brought their load to be processed by the facility (the new step 1). As soon as they drop their loads, they will then be dispatched to return to their home base with a load from the facility they will be leaving. With our pallet of goods from St. Louis, they are now loaded on the Knoxville, TN truck and the drivers is heading toward the relay point to transfer the load to another driver that will return with it to Knoxville TN.

o Freight Relay terminals – Our last type of terminal is the Freight Relay Terminal. These terminals can differ greatly from one another. The primary purpose of a Freight Relay Terminal is to enable drivers to meet, swap trucks, and then return to their home base with the other load. Some companies will have gated parking lots for drivers to meet while others may simply use interstate truck stops. Sometimes, companies may actually work with a local company, like a diner, and work a deal where they can use the parking lot to coordinate the transfer and have a meal in the diner solving two issues simultaneously. Regardless of the approach, the true value of this terminal is to enable the load to move much farther in a 24-hour period in the direction of the delivery than it could with just one driver. If we go back to our load from St. Louis bound for the Atlanta terminal, we can see more clearly how this works. In our case, our load made it to the Toledo Ohio Break-bulk terminal where it was loaded on a truck bound for the Knoxville Break-bulk terminal. At about the same time our Toledo based driver was getting to the interstate, a driver was leaving the Knoxville break-bulk facility heading north. Both drivers will continue for about 5 to 6 hours to a truck stop off I-75 near Lexington, KY. This location is known to both because they meet there at least twice a week to swap loads. When the other driver arrives, they simply swap keys and each driver goes back to their home base with the other's truck (and load), or they may drop and swap trailers and keep the same truck tractor.

Regardless of the approach, both drivers take the other person's load and then drivers back to their home base. With our pallet from St. Louis, it was driven from Toledo to Lexington, KY by the driver out of Toledo and then the driver from Knoxville took the trailer from Lexington KY to Knoxville TN. Each driver will drive from their home base about 5 – 6 hours and then return back to their home base that night. The load in Toledo, however, will have travelled from Toledo all the way to Knoxville, or about twelve total hours.

EMERGING MOTOR CARRIER OPPORTUNITIES

As we have seen, the motor carrier segment is very diverse and the processes and approaches to doing business are well known. The industry continues to experience significant growth due to the general growth of freight needs in retail, distribution and manufacturing.

Emerging Business Models

Emerging business models, like expediting and final mile delivery are adding to the opportunities for trucking companies across the country. It is also bringing new entrants into the market that previously were not a major part of the industry. For instance, as home and final mile delivery has taken hold in the market, traditional LTL companies are working with major retailers and direct to consumer manufacturers to provide them contract delivery rates for all their home deliveries. A large home goods store may contract with a single trucking company to provide all its home deliveries. To do this, the company must build a new network that will include a mix of traditional trucks like the LTL pickup and delivery terminal operations along with box trucks in the same area for smaller delivery. Most of these networks involve both company assets and subcontractor drivers.

In a similar way, parcel networks have the potential for being disrupted from the traditional large parcel carriers to LTL and regional final mile delivery networks. Online retailers like Amazon are building regional distribution centers throughout the country to meet more aggressive delivery schedules. Regional delivery companies may enable these online retailers to bypass the parcel networks.

Line-haul companies will likely continue to clash with LTL business models as both groups seek to take on a larger market share in the areas, they have not traditionally supported. Likewise, LTL companies may see loss of business to TL companies beginning to accept loads that are smaller than normal as TL when it makes sense.

Fuel Efficiency and Greenhouse Gas Production

The trucking industry has created more pollution than any other mode of transportation because of the sheer number of trucks on the road and their use of diesel fuel. Fuel is one of the largest variable expenses in the motor carrier mode. There are a few experiments and pilots being done to look at new sources of fuel like bio-fuel and Liquid Natural Gas. To date, none of these have surfaced a large commercial scale operation as an alternative to diesel. Truck efficiency is also a priority and many trucks have improved their aerodynamics using kits that create a side skirts under the truck and scoops that sit on the top of the tractor pushing air more efficiently over the truck along with a back "wing kit" that creates an aerodynamic screen at the back of the truck. Most of these methods can yield one to two more miles per gallon.

There are also several new inventions beginning tested or coming to market to help drive much greater fuel efficiency including:

- Hybrid Axles[23] – A startup from a group at Carnegie Mellon University have created a hybrid axle for tractor-trailers that claims to improve fuel efficiency by up to 30% using the kinetic energy stored in the axle to reduce the amount fuel needed to run the tractor-trailer.

- Pneumatics to Manage Truck Airflow – Georgia Institute of Technology is developing a pneumatic air system that helps regulate the air flow from installed aerodynamic systems to ensure the air flow is smooth and optimized. Early testing claims that, when combined with the aerodynamic equipment, fuel efficiency improvements of up to a 12% can be achieved.

Shortage of Experienced Drivers

Another opportunity for the motor carrier industry is to develop new approaches to managing labor to improve retention of drivers, especially during the early years. At any time in the motor carrier industry, there's a shortage of at least 50,000 experienced truck drivers which could grow to almost 150,000 by 2024 [24]. Average industry turnover for OTR / TL drivers has grown from about

60% in 2011 to over 90% currently[25]. Compare this with LTL driver turnover closer to 10%. Most recognize the primary difference between the quality of life in a TL situation versus LTL is the frequency by which drivers are at home. LTL pays less than TL but still has dramatically lower turnover. The industry has been considering many approaches to reduce TL driver turnover including:

Reducing the time a TL driver is on the road – 20 years ago, it was not unusual for a driver to be on the road for up 6 weeks. Today, that is dropping and can be as little as two weeks with an average of 3 to 4 weeks on the road. TL drivers with many years of experience are comfortable with longer times on the road. For some, the time on the road was part of the reason they entered into the life[26]. For newer employees, however, this is not a draw but a liability. Giving drivers the option of being home more is one way the industry is looking at retaining TL drivers.

- Recruiting husband and wife teams – There has been a push in recent years to recruit "family" teams of drivers that include husband/wife teams. Recruiting family members for dual drivers keeps the money in the truck going to one family so it rarely is seen as "splitting wages". There's been stronger push to hire people that want to do work in a "semi-retirement" approach and younger couples. While it is too early to tell how this will affect the industry, the approach seems solid because the couple can stay on the road longer because they are together.

  Develop Talent Earlier – Another approach that's needed is developing talent early, especially from high school students. While the minimum age requirement for CDL drivers to do cross-state driving is 21, most states have a provision for an 18 year old to get their CDL license with the restriction of driving only within one state, provided they got their general motor vehicle license at sixteen. Trucking companies that run in-state and out- of-state driving can recruit students while in high school looking for an alternative to college and help them get their CDL at eighteen. They then can work for the company as an in-state driver for three years and then decide if they also want to do TL driving cross- state at twenty-one. The pay would be higher for multi-state drivers and the 21-year-old driver will already have three years of experience as a CDL driver. Allowing drivers to slowly adapt to the industry could well both improve the safety of operations for young drivers and also provide a viable career opportunity.

---

[23] https://gas2.org/2016/03/15/hybrid-axle-for-semi-trailers-could-improve-fuel-economy-30/

[24] *Truck Driver Shortage Analysis*. Bob Costello. 2015. ATA.org.

[25] Ibid.

[26] .*Findings from Interviews with Drivers*. March 2019. Heartland Professional Services

- <u>Driverless Vehicles</u> – Driverless vehicles came onto the scene several years ago as a technological concept. The technology to do this is very complex and early in its lifecycle. Recently, the concept of driverless vehicles has reached near the top of the "hype cycle" as many pilots have been launched with many early failures, including auto accidents. It is difficult to say when driverless technology will come of age. If this technology follows other kinds of innovations, we are probably be about 10 years before we could see any effective driverless vehicle at any significant commercial level. The technology, however, is yielding very significant improvements in driver operations safety with capabilities of advanced braking technology, cruise control monitoring, and more. While we may not see driverless trucks soon, the technology could evolve to where there could be tests related to truck "trains". In this scenario, a driver mans the first of four tractor-trailers. The two behind the front driver are managed by the telemetry of the lead truck and follow the lead trucks movements with a specific safe following distance. A tractor-trailer at the rear of the convoy creates the fourth truck. The trailing driver visually observes the operations of the two "driverless" tractors and can also monitor all telemetry from the lead vehicle. The result is the movement of four tractor-trailers with two active drivers which virtually doubles the capacity of effective drivers.

- <u>Expansion of LCV Operations</u> - Another opportunity dependent on regulatory change is the expansion of Longer Combination Vehicle (LCV) operations. The Federal Government froze LCV operations in 1980 when they deregulated transportation. LCV operations are very prominent in the Northwest of the US and have been very successful. If the government can see these as proof points of best practices, it could be possible to expand LCV operations throughout the country where it makes the most sense. Doing this would effective double, or more, the capacity that one driver could carry. For every 35,000 to 40,000 pounds of additional freight a driver can carry, it reduces the need for an additional driver. This ultimately reduced the number of tractor-trailers on the road, could cause less congestion and in the need for fewer drivers, i.e. a reduction in the shortage of drivers.

The motor carriers segment continues to be dynamic. For most, a truck is a truck and a load is a load. Each delivery model that requires the flexibility of trucking has its own dynamism and require carriers to be more creative and focused than ever before to take advantage of market changers. No matter the scenario, the motor carrier segment will continue to be the backbone of transportation into the foreseeable future. To change this would require re-thinking the entire supply chain model including developing ways to slow down the supply chain. Today, with consumer trends and preferences and the growth of eCommerce, there is little likelihood this could happen.

CHAPTER 7: RAILROADS

INTRODUCTION

Throughout its history, railroads have played a pivotal role in enabling commerce through freight. Rail was the earliest form of bulk freight movement in the US. Railroads trace their roots to early civilizations that moved freight using cars on tracks. The first breakthrough in what would lead to modern rail was the invention of the steam engine. Although not the first steam locomotive inventor, George Stephenson is credited with creating the first commercialized steam engines as part of England's development of their rail industry[27]. He invented over a dozen different engines, but it was the "rocket" that was designed in the 1820's and entered into a national contest in England that proved to be the first viable freight engine that could be used regularly in service. The design caught the world's attention and other countries bought these fledgling locomotives for their developing railroads. Ultimately, locomotive technology would be built throughout the world creating a dramatic increase in rail capacity throughout the 1800's. Rail is the best choice often the most prominent being:

- Very large bulk over long distances – rail has a high capacity for weight needed for many situations. Most of these involve raw or bulk materials that are dense and heavy, and shippers can schedule with enough time to use rail. This is a very dominant part of the rail industry making up over 70% of all carloads shipped in 2016[28]. The largest commodities in this category are coal and agricultural products

- Intermodal Goods – Consumer goods of all kinds are shipped using shipping containers. The link between ship for global locations, rail for port to inland movement, and truck for final delivery is one of the most optimized ways to move goods globally for cost and time

Steam and Steel

The two major components in early railroads were the track, often made from iron and then steel and the steam engine that would drive the industry's growth until diesel and electric engines. Steam locomotive engines were the backbone of rail from the early 1800's and were phased out in the US choice for railroads. While the first steam engines provide around two horsepower, the engine capacity grew rapidly through the 1800's as improved technology for boilers and more efficient engineering to transfer the power of the steam to engine's wheels were development. Steam engines were classified by their wheel configurations and around 1900 Frederick Whtye developed a set of wheel configuration standards that would become the Whyte Notation to classify steam engines.

between the 1930's and early 1950's when diesel engines and their increased power became the This notation distinguished between drive wheels (wheels connected to the steam engine and created drive) and the front (or bogie wheels) along with any trailing wheels that helped keep the train on the track. The notion looked at the wheel configuration and then classified them uniformly between engines (Figure 29). For instance, the first engine, 0-4-2 had no guide wheels up front (0) and then had four drive wheels (4) and two trailing wheels (2) creating the 0-4-2 configuration.

Another engine, the "American 4-4-0" was considered one of the most recognizable of the 4-4-0 engines from the mid-1800's until the early 1900's (Figure 30). One will notice the four guide wheels up front, the large four drive wheels behind and then a trailing tendering locomotive used to store the coal needed to feed the boilers. When a tendering locomotive was involved it was also considered a "0" in the configuration hence the 4-4-0.

Another factor in the development and growth of railroads was the railroad track itself. Early track was made of wood which proved to be unreliable and required regular replacement. Iron, which was relatively cheap became the primary material for rail in the early 1800's. Railroads wanted to use steel, but developing steel often took an entire day to produce three to five tons of the product. Railroads needed more steel and at a much cheaper price than the $100 per ton it cost in the mid-1800's. Henry

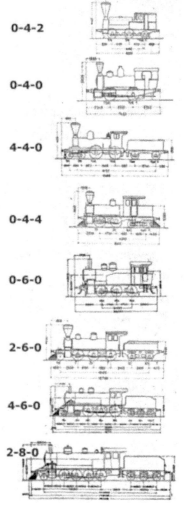

Figure 29. Steam Rail Whyte Notation

Bessemer, an English engineer developed a new process that enabled the use of pig iron with the ability to remove most impurities in a faster and cheaper way. Known as the Bessemer process, it revolutionized steel and with it the ability for railroads to expand. With the Bessemer process steel mills could produce the steel in about 30 minutes rather than an entire day. Also, the labor needed was lower and the cost fell from the $100

Figure 30. The American 4-4-0

per ton in the middle of the 1800's to around $18 per ton by the end of the century. This gave railroad companies all the steel it needed for greater expansion into the west and into the rural areas of the Midwest.

Rail Cars

Although much of developing railways involved the improvements and changes in engine and related technology, another major development that aided freight rail was the evolution of rail cars that went from general use to purpose built for specific kinds of freight. The first freight cars were basic flat cars on rail wheels. This general-purpose equipment had an axel at both ends and required shippers to conform to a basic flat surface for moving goods. As railroads grew, they also needed to provide more specialized services. In the early 1800's the Baltimore and Ohio (B&O) railroad develop a gondola car that had sides of iron and an open top to move heavy bulk items like coal, iron ore and scrap. Around 1820, the first covered gondola cars began to be developed to move goods like flour and other commodities to keep them from being wet or damaged by the elements. These helped to create box cars. These and flat cars became the true standard for rail for most commodities through the 1830's and are still heavily used today. Livestock cars would find their development somewhere in the middle of the 1850's as the need for and transportation of livestock became critical in the supply chain. Livestock haulers started as box cars with ventilation slots throughout to enable airflow for the animals. Hopper cars (the Jimmy) were developed around 1827.

These allowed for loads to be loaded via the top of the car and then delivered by gravity through doors on the bottom of the car. Using springs on cars began to be used around 1830 to provide both stability and less jostling of the car while it was underway[29].

Tanker cars became an important addition to the railcar inventory with the discovery of oil around 1860. Initially, existing cars were adapted to move liquid, but they proved difficult to manage and so using a horizontal tank on a spring bed became the choice to move liquids. Steel began to be used in the later part of the 1800's making them secure and very versatile. The use of steel over wood became more and more common in the last 1800's as steel became more affordable and was valued for its strength and diversity[30].

The refrigerated car, or Reefer, took longer to develop but its need was felt early in the 1800's. Because of the layout of the country and the value of the Midwest and its agriculture, Chicago became a major location for agricultural of all kinds including grains, fruits and vegetables, and livestock. It was very difficult moving these products long distances because of spoilage and the lack of processing plants closer to the centers of population.

---

[29] https://www.american-rails.com/freight-cars.html

With boxcars, ice was added where possible to create a colder environment, but this was difficult to do and had mixed success. Around 1890, Edward Tobias Earl built the first practical refrigerated car to move his produce from the south throughout the country. He later would sell his car to others and become a millionaire[31]. Other cars, like the intermodal car, automotive carrier and more would come in the modern era as business further drove specialization.

Today's Rail System

Regulating railroads began in the late 1800's and throughout its regulated history, the industry struggled due to regulatory issues, lack of approved new railroads, etc. With the Staggers Act of 1980. The rail industry became deregulated. There were thirty-one Class I railroads. A class I railroad is the largest railroad by revenue. The FRA / Surface Transportation Board (STB) has approval authority acquisitions that would cause a new class I. Because railroads were financially unstable often, the government through the Staggers Act had these policies going into deregulation:

- Changed the regulatory policy from strict to deregulated

- Assumes access to competition and no expected regulation between the railroads and their customers

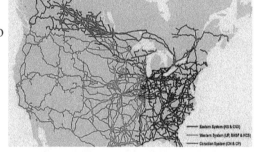

- Provide for antitrust protection especially related to stations served by only one railroad

- No prior approval or requirement to post railroad rates. Railroads can charge what the market will bear (whatever the customer will pay).

Figure 32. US and Canada Class I Railroad System

These Class I railroads operate generally in three regions and experience reduce competition among each other. The US and Canada National rail System is in Figure 32. The seven are spread out in several ways:

- The eastern System includes CSX and NS Railroads. Their territory is the eastern US east of the Mississippi river and they may not operate west of the Mississippi.

- The Western System includes Burlington Northern Santa Fe and Union Pacific railroads. Their territory is the Western US west of the Mississippi river. Likewise, these railroads cannot operate east of the Mississippi.

---

[30] Ibid.

[31] https://en.wikipedia.org/wiki/Refrigerator_car

[32] https://www.american-rails.com/common-carrier.html

- Kansas City Southern Railroad operates between the Western and eastern region but in a narrow corridor that spans Chicago, Kansas City, Houston and Dallas TX as major hubs. It is also the only railroad designated to ship in and out of Mexico. They also cannot operate outside of their specific corridor.

- Canada Pacific operates in the Northern Region along the Canadian Border to all major Canadian cities and Chicago, and with track rights to Kansas City, Detroit and New York City. They cannot operate in any other part of the US unless approved to do so.

- Canada National railroad operates in the Northern Region along the Canadian Border and throughout the interior of Canada. In 1998, it merged with the Illinois Central railroad giving it national track rights throughout Wisconsin and Illinois and directly with Memphis and New Orleans providing a southern port for the company. Likewise, other than their Illinois Central holdings, they cannot operate in the US with approval.

Besides Class I railroads, there are two other classes of railroads (Table 8). Each class of railroad requires specific regulatory reporting with class I having the most reporting requirements of all. The most common way we look at the class of railroad is by revenue as follows in Table 8 (numbers have been rounded)[33]:

Class of Railroad	Examples	Min Annual Revenue	Max Annual Revenue
Class I	BNSF, UP, CSX, NS, KCS, CN, CP	$ 433 M	No Max
Class II	Regional Railroads (Wisconsin Central)	$ 37 M	$ 433 M
Class III	Short-Line Railroads (Ashland Railway)	$ 1	$ 37 M

Table 8. Definitions of Railroad Classes

Between 1980 and today, primarily through acquisition, the number of Class I railroads has dropped from thirty-one to seven including Canada. There are over 28,000 rail stations for freight in the US. 78% are served by one railroad. This can be a misleading number however because many railroads use Short-Line (class I) and regional (Class II) railroads to serve a specific client in the system. No terminal would exist if the company didn't have a relationship with that customer. In addition, some railroads create "tying" agreements (an antitrust violation) by working with Short-Line railroads that will only move their company's freight. Concerns about these have been countered in that many of these Short-Line railroads are purpose built based on the class I railroad's need to access a railroad station to pick up freight. Class I railroads will often outsource the initial freight pickup and move to the mainline to Class II and Class I railroads.

Concerns arise occasionally about the potential of anti-competitive behavior. In 2007, The Railroad Antitrust Enforcement Act of 20017, Senate Bill 772, was put forth to remove the pre-Staggers Act antitrust exemptions. The bill did not pass. In 2015 another bill was introduced and did not proceed out of committee.

Railroad Building Standards

Railroads do not receive public promotion as a rule unlike other modes of transportation. Because of this, railroads average about 15% of revenue annually on track maintenances and expansion. About 85% of this goes to maintenance and 15% to track expansion and growth.[34] This amounts to around $1.5B per year in capital expansion among the Class I railroads.

The FRA recognizes railroads as private entities and the bulk of its regulation is related to safety operations in rail and in railway crossing. The FRA developed a National Transportation Plan[35] started in 2008 and completed and approved by the US Congress in 2010. The report covered the growing need for additional rail capacity for freight, an analysis of population and freight growth trends as part of evaluating capacity and focused on developing mega- regions in the US that ultimately drove the need for both passenger and freight rail. Both passenger and freight rail were also evaluated in terms of current speeds based on track classes (see track classes in this section) and the needs to create high speed rail for both passenger and freight rail. One of the most aggressive part of the plan is the goal to position rail to attract new intermodal shipment from freight that could be classed as intermodal for shipments over 500 miles. The report found value in reduced cost of shipping for these loads, less greenhouse gas emissions (GHG) that from other modes and an overall higher safety rate by using intermodal rail over traditional trucking. In addition, the plan addressed the Department of Transportation's (DOT) Strategic Plan that include these strategic goals:

- Safety – The FRA's response to the DOT safety goal is to continue to focus on safety and the strong track record of safety in rail. In recent years this has included focused areas like hazardous materials protection, highway rail grade crossings, close call reporting, research and development in cooperation with Class I railroads on car designs for high speed rail and a significant safety measure using Positive Train Control (PTC). PTC is a set of command center and other technologies that include electronic train management, collision avoidance, adaptive braking, enhanced and expanded communication networks and much more.

---

[33] https://www.aar.org/railroad-101/

- State of Good Repair – This includes the ongoing maintenance and expansion of the entire rail network and the quality and maintainability of the rail infrastructure, railway crossings, Signals, dispatch centers, and more.

- Economic Competitiveness – The rail industry has become more competitive for intermodal freight over the last decade. This is important because many of rails baselines commodities, especially coal, have the potential to be threatened as new technologies come into the market and older coal-fired plants are retired. Rail will always have a strong baseline business, but the rates are lower, and railroads must drive efficiencies to maintain their gross profitability for these commodities. Intermodal rail represents one of the greatest opportunities for rail since deregulation. Rail has historically not been a major freight provider for consumer finished goods.

- With intermodal this changes and opens many new avenues for growth. Intermodal has been steadily growing and now makes up about 8% of all rail carloads and about 10% of revenue. There is strong growth potential in intermodal and using rail with intermodal carries a very good value proposition for shippers in that revenue per ton-mile for rail intermodal runs about 12 cents per ton-mile where the same load in trucking is closer to 22 cents per ton-mile. A unit-train of intermodal would carry 200 containers (double stacked). The average length of haul for intermodal is about 1,000 miles. The average freight weight of a container is about 20 tons (40,000 pounds). For truck to move these will require 200 trucks each going 1,000 miles at about 22 cents per ton-mile. The cost to move 200 containers by truck would be roughly.

  Total Truck Cost = ((20 tons * 200 containers) * 1,000 miles) = 4,000,000 ton-miles at 22 centers per ton mile = $880,000

  Total Rail Cost = ((20 tons *200 containers) * 1,200 miles) = 4,800,000 ton miles at 12 cents per ton mile = $576,000 or 65% of the truck cost.

- Livable Communities – rail access for both freight and passenger rail can help with economic development and revitalization of communities. Access to rail for manufacturers can be critical for manufacturing that has the planning time to use rail. Make-to-Stock manufacturers and even some just-in-time manufacturing can do this. A city that has good rail access for freight is in a strong position to bring industry to its town. Similarly, if passenger rail is available this can bring additional tourism and other services to the city

---

[34] https://www.fra.dot.gov/Page/P0362 - Federal Railroad Administration

[35] https://www.fra.dot.gov/eLib/Details/L02696

- Environmental Sustainability – rail is already recognized as the most environmentally friendly mode of transportation primarily because of its ability to haul so much weight at once with engines and other technology developed to be greener. One of the more interesting developments in intermodal infrastructure by rail is the concept of Port-on-Rail. With Port-on-Rail, a global shipping port can unload container ships directly to intermodal rail cars for double stack operations. The cranes used for these loading is, more and more, electric and non-polluting. Modern rail engines average about 900 ton-miles per gallon with emissions dropping over the last decade. More work is needed but rail has achieved more environmental sustainability than most other modes although ship is also building a strong track record.

The American Railway Engineering and Maintenance-of-Way organization (AREMA) is an industry body that defines all rail building standards for all aspects of rail infrastructure. There are six committees and full members can apply to the following[36]:

- Communications and Signals – This committee works with much communications and signaling technology including sales, highway rail grade road crossing warning systems, signal systems, information, defect detection, and energy systems, Positive Train Control (PTC) and signals maintenance.

- Engineering Services – This committee handles building and support facilities, environmental, yards and terminals, economic of railway engineering and operations, light density and Short-Line rail, and education on engineering services.

- Maintenance-of-Way – This committee is focused on maintenance across the rail spectrum including track measurement and assessment systems, Maintenance-of-Way work equipment, engineering safety and track maintenance.

- Structures – This committee on specific approaches to building structures specific to timber, concrete and steel structures, seismic design, structures maintenance and construction, and rail clearances.

- Track – This committee defines all standards for building and maintaining all track sections in a rail system. It includes specifications related to roadway and ballast, rail, track, and rail ties.

- Passenger and Transit – This committee focuses on commuter and intercity rail systems, rail transit, high speed rail systems, and electric energy utilization.

The results from these committees may drive updates to the core publications of AREMA used extensively throughout the rail system and include the Manual of Railway Engineering, the Communications and Signals manual, the Practical Guide to Railway Engineering, and the bridge inspection handbook. AREMA is unique among the transportation modes and exists primarily because the FRA did not regulate the infrastructure of rail post the Staggers Act unless it dealt specifically with railway crossings or safety.

Track Rights and Sharing

As part of the Stagger's Act railroads must expand and maintain their own assets on their own with no public promotion. Typically, about 15% of a class I railroad's annual revenue is attributed to this cost. Railroads cannot operate outside of their regional or corridor territories. Does this imply that if Union Pacific, operating in the western region, has a load of coal that needs to go to a power plant in southern Georgia it cannot deliver the coal? In a matter of speaking, yes, that is exactly the case. However, the government does allow for track rights between rail companies if they reach a decision and the Surface Transportation Board (STB) approves it.

How does this work in practice? Let's start by thinking again about the Mississippi border. Chicago is the largest volume transshipment point in North America. Goods coming from the east to the west will have their shipments transferred (transship) from, say CSX railroad to BNSF because the delivery point is at or near of BNSF terminal. Similarly, if NS had a load that needed to go west, they would also transship from Chicago to the railroad that can deliver to the location. Sometimes both railroads can, other time only one railroad services the area. Similarly, Kansas City Southern will have loads from the east transshipped to them and they will transship any load to any carrier outside of their area. Each class I railroad has transshipment sharing agreements to transship out of Chicago and a few others but not to the level of Chicago.

Rail Track Classes

A final area of exploration in our introduction is the concept of classifications of track laid in the rail system. As interest in high speed rail has grown over the last decade so has the interest in high speed freight. The Federal Railroad Administration maintains a classification on all track segments in the US. A classification determines the maximum speed a freight rail train can use on the track, whether passenger trains are allowed on the track and how often it must be inspected. The classifications are in Table 9.

---

[36] http://www.AREMA.org – Section on Committees

Track Category	Max Freight Speed	Max Passenger Speed	Track Inspection Frequency	Track Inspection
Excepted	10 MPH	Not Allowed	Weekly	N/A
Class 1 Track	10 MPH	15 MPH	Weekly / 2x Weekly	Monthly
Class 2 Track	25 MPH	30 MPH	Weekly / 2x Weekly	Monthly
Class 3 Track	40 MPH	60 MPH	Weekly / 2x Weekly	Monthly
Class 4 Track*	60 MPH	80 MPH	2x Weekly	2x Weekly
Class 5 Track	80 MPH	90 MPH	2x Weekly	2x Weekly
Class 6 Track	110 MPH	110 MPH	2x Weekly	2x Weekly
Class 7 Track^	125 MPH	125 MPH	2x Weekly	2x Weekly
Class 8 Track	150 MPH	150 MPH	2x Weekly	2x Weekly
Class 9 Track	200 MPH	200 MPH	3x Weekly	3x Weekly

* Most tracking in the US is Class 4, ^Amtrak's NE Corridor is Class 7

Table 9. Track Classification in the US

The US rail system is generally characterized by its limited competition among railroads. Not that there is no competition. There is competition between at least two companies in every region. The rail companies have a natural tendency to expand its tracks to where it can be the most profitable and that leaves many locations with a single railroad company. Optimizing both the market and profit is a fundamental core discipline of any corporation. With the Staggers Act, the government wanted to limit the competition to enable railroads to regain stability and profitability. In any estimation, this has been achieved and has consolidated the market to a more optimal level. It has also created a rail system with artificial barriers, little incentive to pursue competition and has allowed rail companies to increasingly specialize. Whether the regulatory environment remains the same or changes, railroads are poised to be continuing to be a vital part of the heartbeat of freight commerce and serves a critical role in national transportation.

DEFINING THE RAIL SEGMENT

The post Staggers Railroad Act environment has seen significant change, growth, and challenges for railroads. The rail industry has seen a reduction from thirty- one Class I railroads to seven over about 30 years. The resulting railroads are large, profitable, and flexible and can afford to make the strategic investments needed to remain relevant. Between 1980 and 2004 rail rates consistently went down with most savings passed on to the shippers. Between 2004 and 2018 rail rates grew about 36% or about 2.5% per year.

As one would imagine, the Class I railroads drive the market. They represent about 90% of railroad workers and about 70% of all miles travelled. Class I railroads combined created $82.07 billion in revenue. All other classes of railroads (Short-Line and Regional) combined made up about $37 billion in 2017. Between the rate increases and robust revenue, railroads have been able to make several strategic investments to support ongoing operations and become more relevant in today's market. The industry has averaged a total market investment of around $25B over the last decade enabling them to upgrade track, build new terminals and stations, and create an intermodal rail infrastructure to support global goods from port to pocketbook. This has enabled manufactures and retailers to reduce their total cost of transportation per unit by leveraging rails bulk movement capabilities with the motor carrier's flexibility for the final mile deliveries.

Revenue and Ton-Mile Generation: What Does Rail Move the Most?

Freight railroads identify their freight using the Standard Transportation Commodity Code (STCC) which starts with two letters that define the industry. To where rail is used most, we can look at data published by the Federal Railroad Administration (FRA) to get a better sense of the rail market for freight. We will start by looking at the total carloads moved by two-digit STCC code (Table 10). There are 35 2-digit STCC codes that represents the total of unit-trains (Trains with 100 cars of the same commodity going from one point of origination to one point of destination) and

1	Misc Mixed Shipments Exc Forward.	46	27%
2	Coal	11	15%
3	Chemicals And Allied Products	28	9%
4	Transportation Equipment	37	8%
5	Food And Kindred Products	20	6%
6	Farm Products	01	5%
7	Nonmetallic Minerals	14	5%
8	Containers, Shipping, Rtd Empty	42	4%

Table 10. Top Rail Carloads by Commodity (2016)

Mixed Trains or trains with 100 cars of different commodities that originate in many places and are to be delivered too many places. The rail industry averages about 27% mixed trains and 73%-unit-trains as part of its operations. In Table 11, we see these 8 commodities make up 80% of all carloads used, about 24% of all STCC codes. Item 1 shows the category related to mixed freight. Mixed freight will carry many commodities but is counted in this category.

Another important way to look at the rail segment is via revenue by STCC code. When comparing the revenue within a specific 2-digit STCC code we see the areas with both high demand and strong rates. Table 11 shows the top 9 (80% of all revenue) STCC codes that drive the market's revenue. While there is a little bit of shift, chemicals and Allied Products are the highest area of revenue, for instance, the nine STCC segments here are all nine are also the top carload producers. This makes sense because there is generally a positive correlation between the number of total carloads and the revenue. That correlation is not perfect most likely due to prevailing market rates that are lower for some commodities than others. It'a important to remember that revenue comes from the rate per mile and the distance travelled. We know that density plays a role in rate making. Most often commodities with the highest density have a lower cost per mile than those with less density. Ton-Miles can help us understand this at the most basic level.

			REVENUE
1	Chemicals And Allied Products	28	$10,355
2	Coal	11	$9,111
3	Misc Mixed Shipments Exc Forward.	46	$8,970
4	Transportation Equipment	37	$6,557
5	Farm Products	01	$6,073
6	Food And Kindred Products	20	$5,734
7	Petroleum And Coal Products	29	$2,956
8	Nonmetallic Minerals	14	$2,948
9	Pulp, Paper And Allied Products	26	$2,434

Table 11. Revenue by 2 Digit STCC Code (2016)

			TON-MILE	REV/T-MILE
1	Coal	11	447,218	$0.02
2	Misc Mixed Shipments Exc Forward.	46	226,735	$0.04
3	Food And Kindred Products	20	194,453	$0.03
4	Chemicals And Allied Products	28	192,355	$0.05
5	Farm Products	01	149,868	$0.04
6	Petroleum And Coal Products	29	73,304	$0.04
7	Waste And Scrap Materials	40	56,446	$0.02
8	Pulp, Paper And Allied Products	26	55,769	$0.04
9	Transportation Equipment	37	55,075	$0.12
10	Lumber & Wood Products, Exc Furn	24	49,334	$0.05
11	Metallic Ores	10	48,216	$0.01
12	Crude Petro, Nat Gas & Gsln	13	40,782	$0.03

Table 12. Revenue Per Ton Miles (2016)

Rail accounts for about 40% of all ton-miles of freight moved in the US. Table 12 shows the 80% of ton-miles by STCC commodity. Coal has the largest number of total ton-miles in the industry. This makes sense since much of the coal used in coal-fired power plants today all over the country. Coal typically travels only about 761 miles slightly below the industry average ton-miles of almost 900. To achieve the highest number of ton-miles in the industry suggests that coal must carry many carloads which must be true because coal moves the second most carloads and, if eliminating mixed rail, it moves the most in the industry. We also see the revenue per ton-mile which tells a different story. Coal has, by far, the most-ton-miles but the rates for coal appear to be the lowest of any STCC commodity in Table 12 because the revenue per ton-mile is about $0.02. Compare this to the transportation equipment commodity which basically represents intermodal transportation. Here we see a revenue per ton-mile of $0.12 or about six times that of coal. As intermodal carries lower density and much higher value (fashion, electronics, etc.) the rates to move these commodities are higher.

EQUIPMENT IN THE RAIL MODE [37]

In rail, using specialized equipment is needed to create efficiency and effectiveness for bulk goods movement. In this section, we'll cover some of the major equipment available in rail and discuss the use of equipment for bulk hauling and intermodal. We'll do this using some these categories: Flats, Boxes, Tanks, Open Tops, and Specialized.

Flats

Our first category are trailers that have a wide and flat surface for moving freight. These flatcars provide little protection from the elements and rarely are configured to carry palleted items.

- <u>The Rail Flatcar (Figure 33)</u> – The flatcar is more specialized than one would think at first glance. It's difficult to notice the differences of the different specialized flat cars. There are generally four kinds of flat cars that serve specific purposes. Table 13 summarizes these different flat railcar configurations:

Figure 33. Rail Flat Car

Car Type	Specialization	Size Ranges	Weight Ranges
Plain Flatcar	None	60, 89 Feet	147 – 202k lbs.
Pipe Flatcar	Pipes	89 Feet	147 – 202k lbs.
Specialized Flatcar	Steel Beams and plates, Military Vehicles, tractors	60, 89 Feet	145 – 160k lbs.
Bulkhead Flatcar	Steel Plate, Pipe, Lumber	60, 62 Feet	142 – 210k lbs.

Table 13. Variations of Rail Flat Cars

---

[37] https://www.up.com/customers/all/equipment/descriptions/index.htm

Boxes

The second category of rail cars are boxes. These are enclosed steel rail cars built to primarily carry palleted freight or crated freight and freight that must be protected from the elements. Figure 34 pictures these trailers.

- The Rail Box Car – The Box Car is one of the most common rail cars and has been romanticized due to the temporary homes it used to provide to men moving from job to job during the depression. It is a enclosed car used to move primarily palleted or crated goods. The most common sizes range from 50 to 60 feet in length and can also provide a high cube model 13 feet in height. Some boxcars also come insulated to protect goods from extreme weather. The largest boxcar is the 60-foot-high cube which can carry 60 total pallets when loading the box car using standard pallets loaded 48" wide and 40" in length. The maximum freight weight is about 206,000 pounds or about five full truckloads in weight.

Boxcar

Refrigerated car (Reefer)

- Rail Refrigerated Boxcar (Reefer) – The Reefer is boxcar that includes a refrigeration / freezer unit to keeps palleted goods refrigerated or frozen throughout the transportation movement. Typical sizes are 50, 64, and 72 feet in length with the 50-foot Reefer car having both a 70- and 90-ton capacity. The maximum weight of the 72-foot Reefer car is 181,000 pounds which is less than the largest box car, but it can take up to seventy-two pallets of freight.

Side Beam Car

Figure 34. Rail "Box-Based" Cars

Rail Center Beam Car – The final car in this category is more of an outline of a boxcar than the enclosed cars we normally think about when thinking about boxes. The center beam car has a strong center beam running the length of the car used to secure freight to it to create a secure load. Construction materials are typically moved with center beam cars. Center Beam cars are typically around 72 feet and with their overall lighter car weight can often carry up to 225,000+ pounds.

Tanks

Rail cars that use tanks are diversified in the rail industry. When thinking about a "tank", we look at the equipment and the loading and unloading of what it carries. The traditional tanker car is an obvious choice for its design and purpose. Perhaps not as intuitive, are the hopper cars that are top loaded and unloaded through doors in the bottom of the car. These cars act as "holding tanks" for the goods it moves. Figure 35 shows these cars.

- Rail Tanker Car – The tanker car is one of the most recognizable rail cars today. Tankers carry liquids of all kinds from food grade chemicals to oils to dangerous hazardous materials. They also carry gases under pressure virtually which is categorized as a hazardous material. Tanker cars are measured in cubit feet or gallon capacities in the ranges of 6,500 to 31,500 gallons with a weight capacity well over 250,000 pounds.

Tanker Car

Covered Hopper Car

Open Top Hopper Car

- Rail Covered Hopper Car – This tank carries primarily agricultural dry bulk goods like rice, corn, flour, sugar and more. The car has a broad long top "door" that opens to accept bulk goods and then has a feeder bay shape with doors at the bottom of the car that open to allow the goods to flow via gravity into a container for storage. Many covered hopper cars are unified into 100 car unit-trains to move bulk agriculture throughout the country and the world. Hopper cars are typically sized by what they carry and general size. Small hopper cars are between 2,900 – 3,300 cubic feet and can carry up to 286,000 pounds. These usually have two gates, or doors, at the bottom of the car and are often used to move things like cement or sand. Large hopper cars are between 4,600 – 5,200 cubic feet and have three gates, or doors, at the bottom of the car.

Gondola Car

Figure 35. Rail "Tank-Based Cars

These cars carry bulk agricultural and industrial commodities (wheat, barley, soda ash, fertilizers etc.) and can carry up to 224,000 pounds. The third type of covered hopper car is used for food grade bulk materials like sugar, rice, and flour. These cars are also large at 4,600 – 5,200 cubic feet and can carry up to 286,000 pounds.

- Open Top Hopper Car – This tank like a closed hopper car with the exception that the open hopper car has no top and the contents will be exposed to weather. This kind of car carries coal, coke, sand, and rock. It is top loaded typically through a conveyer system or through loading machinery like front end loaders or bucket cranes. Small Open Top Hopper cars run about 37 to 45 feet on the outside and can carry between 2,300 and 2,800 cubic feet at a total weight up to 230,000+ pounds. Smaller cars typically have two to three bays for rapid unloading. The larger cars run 51 to 57 feet in length on the outside and can carry between 3,800 – 4,600 cubic feet with a total weight of over 243,000 pounds. Open Top Hopper cars are like gondola cars in terms of what it carries.

- Rail Gondola Cars – The Gondola Car is named after the gondola boats used to carry coal down the Potomac when the B&O railroad was being formed near Harper's Ferry, West Virginia, is an open tank like the Open Top Hoper Car, but the similarities end there. For one, they are not gravity delivered and there are no doors on the bottom of the car. They also have high sides and a flat interior that make them an excellent choice for hauling coal. Gondola delivery their freight through a special process called "car- tipping" also known as a rotary-car dumper machine. Individual rail cars are brought into housing the machine and then the machine decouples the car and rotates it to dump out its contents. It then returns the car to its natural position and re- couples the car for movement. In some operations, the car is also sprayed with water as it leaves the machine to enable cleanup and removal of coal left behind. There are also various cranes and front-end loader used and some even specially modified to take the contents out of the car by digging it out from top to bottom. Typical Gondola cars run 52 and 62 feet. The 52-foot car has sidewalls around five feet and can carry up to 267,000 pounds which is the highest weight capacity of all tank based cars. The 65-foot also has a side height between five and six feet tall and can carry a maximum of 214,000 pounds.

Specialized

The final category of cars are specialized cars. Over time, rail has created several unique rail cars for specialized purposes. In this section we'll discuss the Automotive Rack, the Coil Car, and intermodal cars for carrying containers and truck trailers. Figure 36 shows these specialized cars.

- The Rail Automotive Rack – The Automotive Rack is purpose build for carrying vehicles in bulk through rail. There are several configurations of Automotive Racks to accommodate the different needs for vehicle haulage. The four typical configurations are:

o The Automax – The Automax is the largest of the automotive racks and carries automobiles of all kinds including SUVs and minivans. It can carry between 18 and 26 cars depending on what it hauled. The Automax allows for adjustments in the deck height to create bi-level or tri-level configurations.

Automotive Rack

o The Bi-Level – The Bi-level is a smaller Automotive Rack that with two decks for holding vehicles. It typically carries between 8 and 10 vehicles total.

Coil Car   **Open Coil Car**

o The Tri-Level – Like the name implies, the Tri-Level has three levels on which to store vehicles. Its capacity is smaller than the Automax but larger than the Bi-level. It typically carries 14 to 15 vehicles.

Container on Flat Car (COFC)   **Trailer on Flat Car (TOFC)**

o Uni-Level – The Uni-Level Automotive Rack is more specialized to carry oversized

Figure 36. Specialized Rail Cars

vehicles that include Recreational vehicles, farm vehicles, truck tractors, emergency vehicles, delivery vans, farm implements and more. Its single level acts more like an enclosed flat trailer than a multi-level rack. It typically can carry 2-4 vehicles depending on size.

o Rail Coil Cars – Coil Cars are specialized rail cars that move various kind of rolled and coiled steel. Rolled strip steel, for instance is used in many automotive applications among others. These cars ensure rolls and coils do not lose their shape during transportation. There are two major these cars, the Covered Transverse Trough car (Center-Left Picture) and the Open Coil car (Center-Right Picture). The Transverse Trough car has troughs or channels throughout the car that allow coals of various diameter to be secured in the troughs. The 6-trough configuration holds 30 to 72-inch diameter coils where the 10-trough configuration holds 20 to 48-inch diameter coils. These cars can carry a maximum of 221,100 pounds. The Open Coil car is typically used for hot or cold rolled steel coils and the open nature of the car makes it easy to load and unload. These cars range in length from 48 to 53-feet and can carry a maximum load of about 186,000 pounds.

- o Intermodal Rail Cars– Our last kind of specialized equipment exists to enable intermodal rail movement which has become a critical part of current and long term rail operations. Purpose built equipment enables the ability to double stack containers using the Container on Flat Car Chassis (COFC) / intermodal Chassis (pictured bottom left in Figure 36) which uses a pin system to integrate the two containers into the chassis. Based on regulation, each lower corner of a container must have an integrated locking device to enable the ability to secure the load into an integrated whole. Containers lock together through either a twisting locking device or a pin-based locking device. These are generally at the corners of 20- and 40-foot containers with locking mechanisms at 20-foot increments for oversize containers above 40 feet besides the end of the container.

Shipping truck trailers for intermodal operations uses a traditional flatcar was the first intermodal transit and is generally referred to piggybacking (bottom right picture in Figure 36). Truck trailers cannot be double stacked and use a flat car as the chassis to secure the trailer. The largest flat cars are 89 feet meaning that trailers up to 40-feet in length can be doubled up on a standard flat car. Trailers above 40-feet however travel alone. Where Container on Flat Car (COFC) enables double stacking of containers effectively create a max load of around 90,000 – 100,000 pounds, trailers on flat cars are typically sent one per flat car with 53-foot trailers. Using Trailers on Flat Car (TOFC) are economical when the destination must be served by a truck and many trucks must move a long distance. Immediately driving on and off the flat car speeds up both the loading and unloading processes usually when compared to COFC. In addition, many trucking companies do not deal specifically in containerization, so the trailer is a ready commodity to be used, pooled, and returned. Regardless of the choice of COFC or TOFC, intermodal rail provides a significant benefit over long distances for containerize freight and trailer freight.

RAIL OPERATIONS

Operational Goals

Modern rail operations are complex requiring regular simulation to develop schedules that optimize rail capacity. Most rail operations focus on three goals used to help create and maintain operational disciplines[38]. The first is to minimize the trip times. Reducing the time, a train is on the mainline is a major consideration in capacity because trains must be spaced apart, higher priority passenger trains may need to overtake and pass slower freight trains and, if on a single track, trains must use passing rail sections to allow for each train to pass by the other. All these factors must be considered with the result being the most optimized time for one train given all the other traffic in designated route.

The second is to <u>respond to customer needs for flexibility and reliability.</u> If the railroad company does a good job of minimizing train times this is easier to do. Flexibility comes in several dimensions including the availability of rail equipment, the number of routes of available, flexibility in pickup times and more. Reliability is most often related to on-time operations.

The third is to <u>accommodate track and signaling maintenance.</u> In the classes of railroad track, rail infrastructure must be inspected regularly. Railroads lose capacity when the track inspections are going on if they are in a single track configuration or reduced capacity in a double track configuration. If heavy maintenance is required, like changing out rail ties or replacing track, the section of the track involved will be closed at least eight hours reducing capacity even more.

Railroads must manage their infrastructure and capacity to enable them to manage and balance these three goals.

Largest Variable Costs

Within the rail industry, there is high capital investment and a few variable costs that go into every shipment. Labor, and fuel are the largest of the variable costs and drives about 45% of the cost of the shipment.

Rail Capacity [39]

When we think about rail capacity we need to differentiate between physical and practical rail capacity. <u>Physical capacity</u> is defined as the maximum number of trains that could fit on a route regardless of other factors. Practical capacity is defined as the maximum number of trains that could fit on a route assuming a reasonable transit time. Transit time becomes a very important factor in both rail scheduling and capacity management. Transit time is the time one train on its own can reasonably be expected to transit over a specific route that includes these factors: `

- <u>Type of train</u> – Different trains have different priorities on mainline tracks. For freight trains the freight rail and their priority are below:

  - <u>Local Freight Rail</u> – these trains typically move between industrial areas with an average speed of 10 miles per hour and have the lowest priority trains.

---

[38] FRA Webinar on rail operations - https://www.youtube.com/watch?v=gFkHHzbsPBw

[39] Ibid.

- o Tonnage Trains (Unit-trains) – A Tonnage train is most often configured as a unit- train and has one point of origin and one point of destination with no requirements for changes or switching. Railroad scheduling allows for the slowdowns these trains will have while enroute to their destination. Given the distance and time travelled, these trains may end up a few hours late, but this still allows the rail company to meet client delivery schedules as these delays get factored into the transit time quotes to customers. They typically travel 20 – 30 mph. These trains have the second lowest priority.

- o Manifest Trains (Mixed Trains) – The Manifest train is a mixed train that picks up grouping of cars at distribution points including switching yards. They tend have. Their speed is typically in the 30 – 40 mph range and due to their need to meet deadlines at various rail points (switching yards, terminals, etc.). They have the second highest priority.

- o Intermodal Trains – Intermodal trains are unit-trains double stacked with intermodal containers or with TOFCs. They have the highest speed for freight because of the lighter consumer-based cargo they carry enabling them to travel around 50 mph. Intermodal based trains are the highest priority of freight trains.

Regardless of the freight train, all passenger trains have priority higher than freight and travel much faster.

- • Minimum Running time – The minimum running time is the least time it will take for a train to transit the route it has assigned.

- • Stopping distances – Stopping distances is the minimum distance it takes the train to come to a full stop if it is operating at maximum speed. This is an important factor when considering trains that must us passing track to allow other trains to go by or overtake them.

- • Slowing and speed restrictions – In a rail district urban areas and other areas designated for increased safety will impose speed restrictions. These impacts must be considered when looking at capacity. Slowing occurs due to congestion most often so known areas of congestion are important to know.

- • Known or expected delays – Some routes have unavoidable delays due to several factors including rail construction, limited infrastructure, maintenance, and more.

For a rail corridor with many trains, all the factors of the individual train defined above are considered along with added factors like:

- The number and Kinds of Trains and speeds – Trains in a corridor have different priorities and speeds. These must be well understood to manage scheduling and smooth operations.

- Stopping Patterns – The number of stops, the dwell time at each stop, and whether the stops impact the mainline track where other trains are operating all affect capacity. Figure 37 shows a good example of excepted stopping patterns for various kinds of trains.

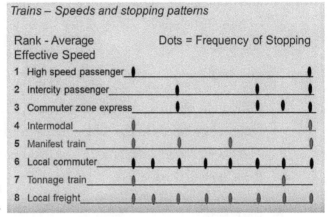

- Train Priorities – different trains have different priorities based on their schedule and operating mission. Capacity planning helps ensure lower priority

Figure 37. Train Speed and Stopping Times

trains have a track passing lane they can use to allow other trains to pass or overtake them and must be scheduled to be in the passing zone at the right time to avoid delays.

- Uniform / Non-Uniform Schedules – Commuter trains have very uniform schedules as do most passenger trains. Freight, however, works off of non-uniform schedules where the timing is more flexible. Mixing passenger and freight rail requires careful planning due to the different schedules.

- Train Densities – 100-car long unit freight trains mover slower and take up more capacity than high speed commuter rail. The density of the trains in the schedule must be carefully ensured train size doesn't create issues in passing or overtaking by higher priority trains.

- Headways – Headways are the spacing defined between trains reducing no train's speed. In a perfect world, all trains would move at the same speed and be spaced just a small distance from each other, but the world of railroads is never perfect. A given route could have many trains of varying speeds. The headways allow the train schedulers and operators to evaluate routes to create headways that ensure all trains meet their schedules and do not overtake each other.

- Overtakes – Do you remember the math question that starts with "A train leaves the station at 6:00 pm"? With many trains on a corridor, a higher speed train overtaking a lower speed train is inevitable. Likewise, on a single-track rail system, trains must pass each other by using specific passing track sections that may exist every 10 or 20 miles. A key part of managing rail capacity is managing the timing of overtakes to keep disruption of any rail route to a minimum. Higher priority trains have the right of way but if a passing operation is already in progress, its timetable will be disrupted. Managing overtakes basically solves a very complex version of the "train leaves the station" question. With railroads, they do it with simulation tools. There are two basic simulations used to understand the impacts of scheduling on capacity. These are:

- Train Performance Calculator (TPC) – The train performance calculator is used to evaluation one train based on its own performance criteria but assumes no other traffic or factors beyond this. The TPC creates a 'perfect' schedule for the train but it's too perfect. The FRA requires that any TPC schedule add 7% as a 'padding' to the schedule to consider these potential variables.

- Rail Traffic Control Calculator (RTC) – The rail traffic control calculator considers all factors involved in schedules and capacity discussed to this point. It provides a graphical output that shows all trains in the corridor and potential conflicts or areas where additional infrastructure is needed to manage the total capacity of the volume required in the rail network.

Rail Freight Terminals

Unlike other modes, railroads must share a very limited infrastructure that is has constant traffic and movement. For freight, all origins and destination are freight terminals. Rail freight terminals are a generic name for any place in a rail network where freight can be taken and moved. People who drive through the heartland of the US will often see large structures in the distance surround farms or in small towns near farming. Many will think of these as grain elevators and farming cooperatives and they are that. They are also freight terminals where trains can come and load various grains and soybeans in covered hopper cars and move them to another kinds of freight terminal, a processor with a rail siding where the train rolls over the top of large storage tanks. They load from the top at the grain elevator using a grain chute and drop their loads from the bottom into the storage tanks. Manufacturing facilities, distribution centers and more are rail freight terminals.

Rail freight terminal loading and unloading operations are on a scale much larger than tracking or air but not as intensive as water. Let's go back to that grain elevator in a farming community. In our case, we're in Livingston Iowa (intended to be a fictitious town) and the rail company has sent an engine to pick up a unit-train of 100 covered hopper cars full of soybeans from the Livingston Grain CO-OP (LGC) (also fictitious). They dispatched the engine about an hour ago, but the operation has its roots as much as 9 months ago. LGC is a cooperative of over 100 farms in and around the Livingston Iowa area. About 18 months ago, LGC went to the Chicago Board of Exchange (CBOE) after estimating this upcoming year crop would likely yield around 7 – 8 million bushels of soybeans. LGC had been watching soybean futures and as the price trends up toward $10 per bushel, they decided it was time to go sell some soybean futures. It's March and LGC sells contracts to six manufacturing companies that would require them to deliver eighteen unit-trains of soybeans or about 7 million bushels. The total value of the contracts came in at $10.22 cents per bushel and LGC's timing paid off with an expected revenue of about $71.5m.

It's now October and the yields have proven true and the soybeans are in the grain elevator waiting for orders to ship. This will be the fourth shipment they have made since the harvest. Each covered hopper car can hold around 4,000 bushels of soybeans. It takes about 18 hours to load all the cars. As they pass through the grain elevator one by one, each car is inspected to ensure it is in good working order and then a technician opens the top of the hopper. A vertical grain chute lines up with the car and pours in soybeans as it slowly moves forward the length of the car. After about 10 minutes, it's full. The technician then closes the cover and ensures it's secured. They then put LGC tamper evident tags on the bottom doors of the hopper cars so if something happens during shipment, they know to contact LGC to make any claims. This is done 100 times over about 18 hours. They can't miss their deadline because the rail engine is coming to pick them up at a specified time.

They provide incentives to the employees loading the soybeans and moving the equipment around. If they have no safety issues and meet the 18 hour deadline, each can get up to a $200 bonus for that load. For the year, that's about an additional $4,000 in potential bonus money and it has its affect. LGC has met is requirements for over the last five years on ninety total shipments and its safety record is perfect.

It's labor intensive and time consuming the team gets done moving the empties from one side of the CO-OP through the elevator and then to the siding on the other side where they are coupled together as unit-train. The rail engine shows up on-time. The engineer and the CO-OP trade waybills and shipping documentation and after short inspection of the cars, the train moves out headed from the Port of Savannah where the soybeans are being shipped to China.

This operation, whether grain, or auto or manufactured goods happens thousands of times every day throughout the country. The ability for a single unit-train, a "grain-train" if you will, to move over 400,000 bushels of soybeans at a time is a critical link to keeping the transportation cost low while also moving a great amount of freight long distances.

At the Port of Savannah, this train will be joined by another six trains that, together, will fill the elf- trimming bulk carrier ship that will move 100,000 cubic meters of soybeans to China. A port is another rail freight terminal. Freight terminals area critical link in the rail supply chain. They act as origin and destination and are the locations that create or consume the freight rail moves.

Classification Yards

Unit-trains are relatively straight forward. They go from one origination location to one destination. Mixed trains, also referred to previously as manifest trains, take goods from many originating locations and deliver them to many destinations. Moving them through the rail network requires a version of break-bulk where we use classification yards to separate, sort, and reconfigure trains toward the ultimate destination. Figure 38 show an aerial view of a classification yard. Classification yards are the general term for this facility but there are others that include switching yards, shunting yards, and even hump yards. The role of a classification yard is to receive trains, decouple the cars and then run them through tracks split out into section, called Ladders, with the final goal of having each car configured to a new train going toward or two the car's ultimate destination.

The People

There are many roles involved in running rail operations and they must work in harmony. The main operational functions are:

- Transportation – Transportation roles are involved directly in the operations and movement of trains. Example roles includes the engineer who operates the train between points, the conductor who manages the train and its loads (consist) and the yardmaster that manages the rail yards throughout the route.

- Mechanical – Mechanical functions take care of the engine and rail cars and ensure they are serviceable. Example roles include carman who maintains the rail cars, the mechanic that fixes engines and all things mechanical, and the boilermaker who focuses on the power plants of the engines.

- Labor / Engineering – This function focuses on the people that support the rail infrastructure for track, signaling and crossings. Example roles include track workers, welders, signal worker and roadway mechanic.

- Clerical – This function handles the shipping paperwork flow and other administrative functions including crew planning and dispatching.

- Telecommunications – This role deals with all

  communications involved in signaling, telemetry, and radio communications.
  Example roles include electronic and installation technicians

- Management - Throughout the organizational functions, there is management at all levels.
  Most management stays in their area of operations, engineering, and mechanical and rise
  in those specialized areas

EMERGING RAIL OPPORTUNITIES

The rail industry has been the traditional mode of choice for large bulk movement of goods and it is still the best mode for domestic bulk. Bulk materials like coal, petroleum, iron ore, and agricultural products are commoditized raw materials and there is little growth in these areas.

Demand for shipping these commodities, especially coal and petroleum has been dropping over the last decade and rail has looked to intermodal both replace the revenue and enter the

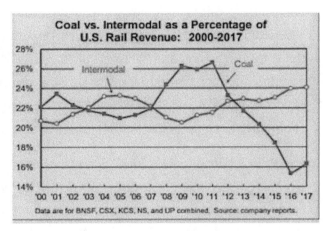

Figure 39. Intermodal Rail versus Coal

more lucrative consumer goods market. Figure 39 [40] shows the impact intermodal has had while coal demand has been dropping. To get to this point has required billions of dollars of investments among the Class I railroads and will continue to require substantial investment into the future.

Intermodal Capacity Growth

Intermodal capacity growth, improved automation for Intermodal Yard equipment, and driving both speed and efficiency in intermodal rail is key to future revenue growth. To go further, reducing transit times may be a key to finding new growth. There are very few scenarios where rail is more expensive than truck but if time based constraints are an issue, motor carriers have a distinct edge for both speed and flexibility. Can intermodal rail bridge the speed and flexibility gap? This is difficult to answer in today's market. Speed appears to be king as many online and traditional retailers look to same day and last mile delivery. These new models of delivery are expensive and product margins are tight as it is. Rail could be one way to reduce the cost before the final mile delivery. Distribution centers are being built closer to consumer markets to support final mile delivery. If planned well and collaboratively, intermodal rail could play a key role in moving consumer goods thousands of miles either directly to these centers or through strategically placed intermodal yards.

Positive Train Control

Positive Train Control (PTC) was mandated by the US Congress in 2008 to create a system to prevent rail accidents due to human error before they occur. The deadline for completing this for all Class I railroads is 2020 and according to the Association of American Railroads [41], PTC is in operation across over 80% of class I and Amtrak rail lines. The cost of implementing PTC is expected to be offset by the reduction of rail accidents and their costs.

Sustainability in Rail

Sustainability is gaining momentum throughout the world and from a transportation perspective, rail is the most sustainable domestic option available. As companies adopt a sustainability agenda, rail may have new opportunities to serve clients if they are prepared with the right infrastructure and technology to support this. One of the biggest potential needs in sustainability for transportation is slowing down the supply chain without disrupting consumer expectations. To date, few solutions have emerged. Rail can be a leader in this space and help companies learn how to use rail to be more sustainable.

Rail is critical core of the US transportation system. Moving bulk commodities at a low price has helped keep manufacturing costs down. Intermodal rail provides new flexibility for consumer-based companies as they look at their distribution needs. Rail infrastructure and improvements in technology may ultimately be the key to rails growth.

CHAPTER 8: MARITIME CARRIERS

INTRODUCTION

Nothing did more to spread trade and culture in the early world than did the knowledge of sailing and boat building. The Phoenicians are generally credited with starting commercial shipping in the 1300's by building ships that could cross the Mediterranean Sea. The generally growth of the maritime shipping grew as technology created bigger boats and lead to the exploration of the world, development of global trade routes and ultimately globalization. The Suez Canal came into operation in late 1869 and reduced the transit time from Asia to Europe by water by almost 1/3 while also reducing the danger of the journey by not having to travel under Africa. Similarly, the Panama Canal was built by the US and Panama between 1904 and 1914 which dramatically reduced the transit time from the Asia and Australia to the East Cost of the US and South America. These two canals continue to be major thoroughfares for global shipping today. Today, maritime shipping is more than just rivers and lakes and oceans. Each segment provides different kinds of value for shipping both domestically and globally. Regardless of segment, the maritime industry is usually the best choice for these kinds of freight:

Very large bulk over long distances – maritime assets have a high capacity for weight needed for many situations. Most of these involve raw or bulk materials that are dense and heavy, and shippers can schedule with enough time to use the water mode. This includes goods like coal and scrap iron being moved up and down rivers to power plants and processing facilities. It includes the Great Lakes and the movement of coal and large volumes of agricultural products to power and food and feed plants. It also includes the large bulk shipments that

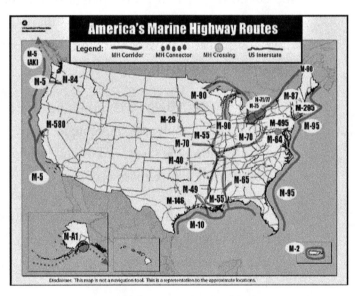

Figure 40. The Maritime Highway

leaves ports by the hundreds every day moving oil, coal, agricultural products, metals and more between countries and oi between Alaska and the US mainland.

<u>Coastal movements, shuttles and repositioning of assets</u> – Another important but small in overall percentage of shipments involves coastal shipping where smaller capacity ships move between ports to reposition assets. The Marine Highway Project (Figure 40) was done for The Maritime Administration (MARAD) [42] in 2011 and defines shipping corridors around the US coasts and seaways that use costal carriers, among others to move goods between US locations to help reduce congestion from trucking and rail.

<u>Intermodal Goods</u> – Intermodal goods are a high value commodity for global shipping. Containerization has had a dramatic impact on shipping since it began in the 1950's. Container shipping needs have grown since then and container shipping became a critical link between manufacturing and consumer markets as companies went to offshore production facilities throughout the 80's, 90' and today. Likewise, the size of container ships has also steadily grown throughout this period to absorb the freight growth. Container goods are economically sensitive and so there is an ongoing issue in maritime shipping of building to overcapacity when global economic growth is strong and a contraction of the same as markets soften and enter recessions.

<u>Freight on rivers</u> – In its hey-day, river carriers moved most of the coal in the US from coal sources to river based power plants across the Illinois, Mississippi, Ohio, and Tennessee rivers. With EPA changes from high Sulphur to low Sulphur coal, much of the coal for coal-fired power plants now come from the Rocky Mountains reducing this one very popular transportation approach.

<u>Great Lakes</u> – The Great Lakes continue to be a major artery for goods movement, especially bulk agricultural and coal movement. Many power plants and food and feed processing centers are within the Great Lakes and specialized bulk ship carriers move goods from rail and other port points to these producers.

As we look at the maritime industry, there are several general topics we need to discuss to create a baseline of understanding and terminology for the rest of the chapter. We'll put forward these topics in the introduction and continue to discuss some throughout the chapter.

---

[43] https://en.wikipedia.org/wiki/Twenty-foot_equivalent_unit

[44] https://www.maritimemanual.com/ship-sizes-classification-of-ships-by-sizes/

The concept of TEU (Twenty Foot Equivalent Unit)

Just as we have covered the concept of the ton-mile previously and use this measure to understand relative costs between modes, there is a maritime concept for containers called the Twenty-Foot Equivalent Unit, or TEU. The TEU is an inexact unit of capacity and its primary purpose is to help understand the capacity of container ships. A standard single TEU container is 20 feet long by 8 feet wide and over various heights although the most normal height is 8 feet 6 inches. A two TEU container is generally 40 feet long. The challenge with the TEU as an Inexact measure stems from a 26

Length	Width	Height	Volume
20 ft (6.1 m)	8 ft (2.44 m)	8 ft 6 in (2.59 m)	1,172 cu ft (33.2 m³)
40 ft (12.2 m)	8 ft (2.44 m)	8 ft 6 in (2.59 m)	2,377 cu ft (67 m³)
45 ft (13.7 m)	8 ft (2.44 m)	8 ft 6 in (2.59 m)	3,060 cu ft (86.6 m³)
48 ft (14.6 m)	8 ft (2.44 m)	8 ft 6 in (2.59 m)	3,264 cu ft (92.4 m³)
53 ft (16.2 m)	8 ft (2.44 m)	8 ft 6 in (2.59 m)	3,604 cu ft (102.1 m³)
High cube			
20 ft (6.1 m)	8 ft (2.44 m)	9 ft 6 in (2.90 m)	1,520 cu ft (43 m³)
Half height			
20 ft (6.1 m)	8 ft (2.44 m)	4 ft 3 in (1.30 m)	680 cu ft (19.3 m³)

Table 14. TEU Capacities of Common Shipping Containers

foot container being also considered a TEU and a 48 ft. container is considered a 2 TEU container. Table 14 [43] shows the standard dimensions of most widely used containers.

Ship Size

Another important element of the maritime mode is ship size. There are many designations of ship sizes in the maritime mode. Many have very specific meanings in their names that designate their capacity for certain geographic locations. Other names are more generic to the actual size and use of the vessel. We'll explore these designations in this section by first discussion the "names" with specific meanings and then the other designations.

- Names [44] – In many maritime applications, ships must be of a certain size to use a canal or something else geographic. We use names to designate those that can and cannot use these geographic or port water ways. Below, we'll discuss the name designation and the ships are affected within that name.

  o Seawaymax – These are the largest ships that can pass through the locks of the St. Lawrence Seaway into the Great Lakes. They average 740 Feet long, 78 feet wide and draft no more than 26 feet.

  o Handysize – Handsize ships are smaller bulk carriers with DWT in the 15,000 – 35,000 ton range. They are smallest of the modern bulk, ships and work in coastal carriage and service secondary and tertiary ports worldwide.

o Handymax – Handymax ships are smaller bulk carriers with DWT in the 40,000 – 60,000 ton range. They serve major and secondary ports throughout the world.

o Panamax – Panamax is the name given to any vessel, especially container ships that can use the original modified locks of the Panama Canal. For container ships, these are ships under 4,500 TEU.

o New Panamax – New Panamax ships are those that can go through the Panama Canal completed in 2016.

o Post New Panamax – Post New Panamax ships cannot go through the Panama Canal due to size restrictions and typically must go through the Suez Canal to get to the eastern seaboard of the US.

o Suezmax – Suezmax ships go through the Suez Canal with ease and can serve all major ports in the world. They average 120,000 – 200,000 DWT.

o Aframax – Aframax comes from a term developed by Shell Corporation called the Average Freight Rate Assessment schematic for oil tankers. They typically represent ships with a dead weight tonnage (DWT) of 120,000 tons and can carry up to 7 million crude oil casks.

o Chinamax – Chinamax vessels are also designated as VLOC (Very Large Ocean Carriers; see below under other designations) and are among the largest bulk carriers in the world with a DWT of around 400,000 tons.

o Capesize – Capesize are a very large and ultra large vessels with 150,000 DWT and above. Some can be as large as 400,000 DWT. They require the largest of deep-water ports and the name derives from the fact these vessels cannot use the Suez Canal but must go under Africa using the Cape of Good Hope.

o Malaccamax – Malaccamax are the largest ships that can pass through the Malacca straits which enables access to Malaysia and Singapore.

o Q-Max – The Q-Max is the largest Liquefied Natural Gas tanker in the world and the name standards for vessels that are services at the port of Ras Laffan in Qatar.

---

[43] https://en.wikipedia.org/wiki/Twenty-foot_equivalent_unit

[44] https://www.maritimemanual.com/ship-sizes-classification-of-ships-by-sizes/

- Other Designations – There are two other major designations that describe the largest ships typically in the Aframax, Chinamax, and Capesize classifications. These are specific to crude carriers, i.e. oil tankers:

    o VLCC – Very Large Crude Carriers – VLCC ships range between 180,000 – 320,000 DWT and can operate in virtually any oil port in the world, especially around the North Sea, Mediterranean, and West Africa.

    o ULCC – Ultra Large Crude Carriers – ULCC ships are ships over 320,000 DWT. These are the largest of all crude vessels are used for long haul crude lanes.

    o ULVC – Ultra Large container Vessels – ULVC ships are containers ships rated for over 15,000 TEUs. About 200 ULVCs operate in global shipping today.

The Role of the Maritime Administration (MARAD) [45]

The Maritime Administration (MARAD) is the regulating agency for the maritime industry. Unlike other regulators, MARAD has other missions beyond just regulation. These other missions help maintain a robust US maritime environment and provides services to support the maritime mission. There are three main areas where MARAD serves the maritime industry as more than just a regulator

- International Agreements – MARAD negotiates international treaties and agreements with countries to help ease trade restrictions and other port access issues. Agreements negotiated on behalf of US merchant marine operators include bi-lateral agreements with such countries as Brazil, Japan, China, Panama, Korea, and Vietnam.

- Merchant Marine Academy – MARAD operates the US Merchant Marine Academies across the US including the Merchant Marine Academy at King's Point New York which is on par with the US military academies. Besides the primary Merchant Marine Academy, MARAD also support six state academies that lead to licensure as mariners and in shore-side careers.

- Mariner Fleet – Part of MARAD's mission is to ensure there are enough US flagged ships and US merchant mariners to enable the effective movement of military goods and troops during a time of national security. Most do not know that MARAD has a wartime mission that dates to WWII. Much of the material and personnel movements of the military are done by civilian merchant mariners who work under contract for the government. MARAD itself manages a large fleet of vessels that support rapid deployment during times of national security and emergency. This includes the concept of Cargo Preference maintained as part of the MARAD Office of Cargo and Sealift. Cargo Preference requires all government based cargo to be moved only by US flagged ships creating an economic opportunity for US ships and mariners to move US goods to ensure an adequate revenue stream to maintain a US merchant marine inventory. The office has three areas of focus: agricultural cargos, civilian agencies, and military cargos.

- The following are the cargo requirements for US Flag carriage:

  o Military Cargo – 100% of all cargo moved must done by US flagged vessels.

  o Export-Import Bank – All cargo related to any customer of the EXIM Bank (Export-Import Bank) including exporters, importers and others must use a US flagged vessel to move any cargo related to the relationship.

  o Civilian Agencies – Government agencies that ship goods must ensure 50% of all goods shipped are done via US flagged vessels.

  o Agricultural Cargos – Similarly, 50% of all agricultural cargos leaving the US must be transported by US flagged vessels.

DEFINING THE MARITIME SEGMENT

92% of all consumer goods in the US are shipped via the maritime industry. Most of this is in bulk and containerized freight from all over the world imported into the US. Long haul global shipping, or intercontinental shipping costs about one cent per ton-mile making it an efficient method for global shipping. Most people think of global shipping when hey think of the maritime industry but there are actual four segments in the industry based primarily on the waterways that are used in transportation:

- International / Intercontinental Shipping – The largest segment of the maritime industry is global shipping, or intercontinental shipping. The ships that carry goods globally are the largest ships in the industry. They include bulk carriers, tankers, and container ships with capacities that enable them to move very large cargos with ease. These ships are global port to global port with some ships using traditional ports and the new and largest ships requiring deep water ports. Traditional ports are about 20 feet deep- and deep-water ports are at least 30 feet allowing for larger ships to dock there. There are about 5,150 ports worldwide and of these 178 are deep water ports. The US has thirty-six deep water ports or about 20% of the total. International Shipping includes virtually every good and raw material known today.

- Great Lakes Shipping – The second segment is the shippers and ships that operate on the Great Lakes. Most of these are built to operate in the Great Lakes and St. Lawrence Seaway. These ships include mainly bulk carriers and tanker ships although there are a few container ships from ports like Montreal, Toronto and Cleveland, Ohio with international long-haul lanes. Great Lakes carriers carry bulk agricultural, metals, and coal from rail and other ports to processes throughout the Great Lakes.

- Coastal Carriers – Costal Carriers are typically smaller versions of the international ships. Most are earlier models that are no longer relevant for international shipping but have good capacity and can move goods between northern US and Gulf of Mexico ports. They also provide shuttles of goods between ports or within the Gulf of Mexico. They also provide repositioning of containers when containers get out of balance between ports.

- River Carriers – The last segment of carriers are the river carriers. Rivers use tub boats and barges exclusively to move bulk cargo up and down rivers between ports. Barges are generally open steel flat barges that sit low in the water and carry much bulk goods that do not need protection. Their principal cargo has been coal through their history along with scrap metals. Today, this segment is slowly going away as coal has been diverted to the Rocky Mountains and demand for river carriers is dropping every year.

EQUIPMENT IN THE MARITIME MODE

In the maritime industry, ship types define the equipment available to shippers to use to move their goods domestically and internationally. In this section, we'll cover the major equipment available and used for movement of goods. We'll cover general freight ships, bulk good ships, tanker ships, Roll-on / roll-off ships, the container ships and the tugs and barges. Figure 41 provides pictures of these ships.

Figure 41. Ship Types in Maritime

General Cargo Freighters – Freighters were the backbone of the maritime industry for centuries. Modern freighters have large holds within the ship and can store cargo on top of the deck of the ship. Freighters are most notable for the cranes integrated into the ship enabling them to move cargo from virtually any location onto the ship. General freighter ships can virtually anything, but they specialize more in very large equipment that won't fit in any other ship. This could include generators for power plants over a hundred feet high and weigh thousands of tons to heavy machinery, and more. When looking for parallels across other modes one might consider the General Cargo Freighter like a rail flat car or a flat trailer in the motor carrier mode.

- Bulk Goods Ships – Bulk goods ships carry grains, iron ore, wood chips, coal and more. These items are typically loaded onto the ship from rail equipment at the port. Even the most basic Handymax bulk carrier can transport about five unit-trains of grain and a Chinamax can handle over 35 unit-trains of grain or other bulk. Bulk ships specialize in specific commodities like agricultural, metals and ores, or coal. Ships that transport in these commodity categories need basic cleaning to move goods within that commodity but would need to be sanitized to cross commodities.

- Tanker Ships – Tanker ships carry oil and oil products throughout the world. There are also Liquefied Natural Gas tankers that move gas under pressure in this same class. Tankers also move chemicals and food grade chemicals. Like bulk good ships, tankers specialize in their cargo and move the same things with the same tanker to avoid extensive and timely sanitation processes to move different goods.

- Roll-on / Roll-off Ships – Roll-on / Roll-off ships, or "RO-RO" ships carry automotive vehicles throughout the world. These ships are loaded by having vehicles driven onto the decks of the ship. Cars are parked within a few inches of each other and are loaded left to right or right to left depending on the where the steering wheel is located. When delivered they are then offloaded in the same way with drivers driving the vehicles off to holding areas where they will be transferred to auto carriers via rail or truck.

- Containers Ships – Container ships have steadily involved since the beginning of containerization in the 1950's. Container ships are rated within the Panamax, Post Panamax, New Panamax, and Suezmax sizes of ships. Within the industry, the average size of a container ship is around 8,000 – 11,000 TEU although the largest ships are now well over 18,000 or more. Container ships are vital link for consumer goods shipping because the containerization process of loading once and unloading at the destination enables millions of individual items to be moved without being loaded individually.

- Tugs and Barges – The Tug and Barge are the domain of river transportation in the US. Rivers around and connected to the Mississippi river have formed vital artery for transportation over the US history. The primary role of the Tug and Barge has been the movement of coal to river-based power plants along with Midwest of the US. Metals, ore, and scrap metal are also common cargos moved over rivers. There has been some experimentation with "container on barge" with moving shipping containers via Tug and Barge to get containers from the interior of the Midwest to ports like New Orleans. To date, there has not been a large demand for this and it's not clear whether container on barge will be a success. If not, this method of transportation will continue to be reduced as much of the coal these carriers once moved are now shipped via train from areas like Wyoming.

MARITIME OPERATIONS

When thinking about maritime operations for shipping, we think about ports, ships, and other structures that enable goods to be loaded, transported, and unloaded. Maritime operations is port to port with supporting modes of transportation delivering goods for loading to the originating port and the same at the destination port. We covered the concept of Incoterms in Chapter 3 and Incoterm drives the terms under which shipments are done in the maritime industry. One area of focus in maritime trade is trade flows in terms of loaded and unloaded freight across regions of the world. Figure 42 shows the breakdown trade flows between various regions of the world. Goods loaded are specific to exports and goods unloaded are imports.

When looking at the world, it's interesting how most regions of the world have more goods loaded than unloaded except for Europe and China. This is a significant change for China from their traditional position of being the largest exporter in the world. As one can see, they are still the largest exporter in the world, but they are now also the largest importer. This is an example of the evolution that has occurred since the late 1970's. Companies looked to China in the late 1970's and early 1980's as a strong market for offshoring production to reduce production costs.

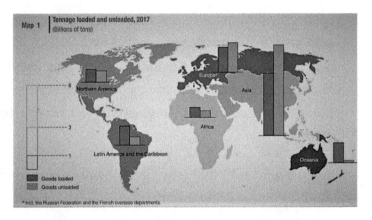

Figure 42. Global Trade Flows in Billions of Tons

In 1960, Walt Rostow, an economist developed a model of economic development that applies in China. Rostow posited that every economy goes through a maturity process where opportunities exist as it moves beyond a traditional hunter/gather or agricultural society. He suggests that developing a manufacturing economy based on the needs for raw materials and the value added of production will eventually allow a company to "take off" toward a more complex service-based economy.

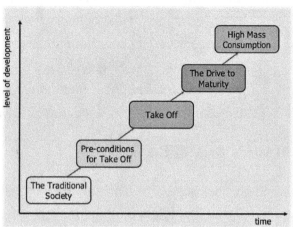

Figure 43. Dr. Rostow's Economic Theory of Development

He suggests that as countries become manufacturing centric, it builds a middle class that demands services and ultimately becomes its own market for the products it manufactures for others (Figure 43). Globalization has aided in this effort throughout the world enabling global supply chains to be built off international maritime shipping which enables the movement of goods all over the world at a very economical pricing.

The maritime industry is considered an increasingly environmentally friendly mode of transportation. While maritime moves over 90% of all consumer goods worldwide, it only represents 3% of Greenhouse Gas Emissions (GHG) [46]. The IMO of the UN uses the SOLAS, Safety of Life at Sea, convention to drive environmental efficiency in the industry. Please refer to Chapter Two, regulation, section *Critical International Regulatory Agencies (Safety, Security and Environment),* for more information.

In the remainder of this section we will discuss the two major operations related to the maritime industry: Ports and ship operations.

Ports

Port operations enable the loading and delivering of cargo for shipments. They include both ports that accept container based freight and port terminals used to load and offload goods like grain, coal, oil, and other bulk cargos. Modern large ports have automation and integration from data and integration to the management of loading / unloading operations. Ports also have space and leasing opportunities for companies like freight forwarders and others to manage and store freight as part of their commercial operations. Ports are also the home of customs clearance and cargo is managed through the customs process to be loaded and cleared to be released to domestic carriers.

Port placement is an important factor in trade flows for a country and its use in transshipment operations. Port placement is based on several factors including:

- Geographic Location – A primary consideration in developing a port is its location. Ports are generally best when there is natural geographic protection to enable smooth operations. A bay or inlet can be an excellent starting point with additional improvements through dredging and natural barrier construction creating a good area for port calls.

- Capacity and Operations – a second consideration is the capacity and type of operations achieved using the port. The number of berths created to allow for multiple simultaneous port calls defines much of the capacity of the port. The superstructure to support the berths including cranes, yard equipment, rail infrastructure for Port-on-Rail all add to the efficiency and capacity of the port.

- Administrative Capabilities – The creation of the port authority and its regulatory and administrative capabilities also create efficiency and effectiveness for processing freight including providing for efficient customs, effective scheduling and administrative processing.

- Value Chain – Co-locating industry and industry terminals in ports create a broader value chain enabling more specific commodity based efficiencies in shipping. The more diverse the industries in a port area the more operational processes and terminals are needed so most ports do not have a high diversity of industry favoring instead to be more focused on, say, a grain terminal or a specific heavy industry or two. This helps avoid congestion due to too much diversity while providing high value chain value.

- Ports using scheduling to receive and dispatch ships as part of the loading and unloading operations. Ports also integrated with other ports as part of a way to aggregate smaller port operations to very large operations. We can consider several missions for ports including:

- Hub or Master Ports – These ports are the major ports that form the bulk of the major shipping lanes across the world. These ports service hundreds of port calls per year and are generally set up to accept most cargos. Ports in this class include ports like the Port of Shanghai, Rotterdam, Singapore, New York, Long Beach / LA, Newport News Virginia and more. Some ports will also be more specialized like the Baltimore or Jacksonville Ports in the US focused on Roll-on / Roll-off vehicle operations but can also accept other kinds of freight. The Port of Houston, TX is similar for oil and LNG operations.

---

46 https://www.newsdeeply.com/oceans/articles/2018/01/02/in-2018-keep-an-eye-on-these-big-ocean-issues-and- trends

- Domestic Ports and Terminals – These ports are smaller and more specialized receiving goods distributed within the broader area around the port. They also include freight terminals for things like grain, metals, and others. Domestic ports are an important part of the maritime industry because they allow traffic to be diverted to them for goods used in the area instead of having to go through Hubs or Master Ports. Domestic ports include secondary ports around the world including ports like the Port of Miami, Boston, Seattle, Mobile, Alabama, and others.

- Feeder Ports – Feeder ports are smaller ports with feeder ships (smaller ships than the traditional "mother vessels") that move cargo from that port to a hub or major port. This uses feeder ports to provide domestic cargo capacity that can be used for loading and receiving goods. These ports have feeder ships that then move that cargo to a major port as part of aggregating capacity for large and ultra large capacity ships. Feeder ships are also used for repositioning of containers and other materials that build up in one port and need to be distributed to others.

- Transshipment Ports and Styles – Transshipment is moving freight between vessels to have goods get to similar ports from ships not originally bound for those ports. There are seven regions in the world that use transshipment as part of the regional logistics strategy enabling global equatorial routes to intersect with north south water routes to reach more ports from major ships without those ships having to make a port call into smaller ports Transshipment can occur between two vessels or using ports. Transshipment ports are similar in some ways to feeder ports but are specifically used is in various regions across the world. There are several reasons a company would use transshipment in their global shipping processes.

Large vessels will often carry goods for multiple ports to fill their capacity. Then as they go through a region setup for transshipment, they can use a transshipment method to distribute the cargo to other ports using smaller feeder ships as backhauls.

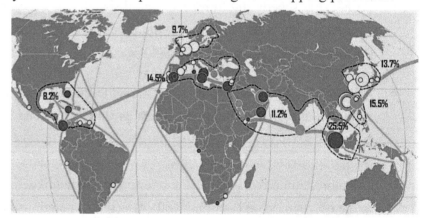

Figure 44. Main Transshipment Routes in the World

[47] https://www.porteconomics.eu/2015/09/17/transshipment-hubs-connecting-global-and-regional-maritime-shipping-networks/

There's also a concept of Less than Container (LTC) which is like LTL. In these instances, ships will offload LTC in ports to be consolidated with others to move to secondary or tertiary ports. There are different transshipment styles used throughout the world including:

Direct Transshipment – Direct Transshipment occurs when two ships anchor besides each other and transfer cargo between them. This practice is less frequent than using ports and typically occurs when using ports is not a feasible option.

  o Indirect Transshipment [47] – Indirect Transshipment uses ports as the means to move goods between ships. There are several types including:

   ▪ Hub and Spoke – Hub and Spoke transshipment uses multiple feeder ports in a region and links these to regional and global sea lanes. This creates an efficient system that can leverage the major port (hub) to regional and domestic ports. Capacity can be managed by aggregating the capacity of regional and domestic ports as part of major port shipment planning. Hub transshipment accounts for about 85% of all transshipment using hubs.

   ▪ Intersection Transshipment – In Intersection Transshipment, the transshipment hub acts as a point of transfer between multiple long-distance shipping routes. This can allow for a a ship based "break-bulk" where offloaded cargo can be loaded on ships going on different routes to enable more efficient deep-sea routes across the world.

  ▪ Relay Transshipment – Relay transshipment involves transshipment hubs connect regional routes to other ports that use smaller ships rather than have the larger ships go to multiple port calls.

Largest Variable Costs

Within the maritime industry, there is high capital investment and a few variable costs that go into every shipment. Labor, fuel and port fees are the highest variable costs but among these fuel and port fees are, by far, the largest variable costs.

Safety, Security, and Piracy

Safety and Security drills are also a regular part of a commercial ship operations. SOLAS (Safety of Life at Sea) has a set of protocols for fire drills and ship egress with emergencies that must be reported and documents on every voyage. Generally, the Second Mate oversees there operations along with testing all safety and fire equipment. The security mission and role on a ship varies primarily with where the ship's route will take it. Throughout parts of the world there are different security threats from unannounced inspections when in territorial waters to the threat of piracy.

Piracy operations are common throughout different parts of the world. The area most known for piracy today is off the north eastern coasts of Africa near Somalia and other countries, but this is not the only hotbed of piracy. The International Chamber of Commerce published piracy statistics in 2018 found in Figure 45 [48]). The largest areas of piracy in the world are within Nigeria, Somalia, Indonesia, Malaysia, and the Philippines. Different countries are handling these issues in different ways. For instance, the US will now provide armed guards on the commercial vessels when going through high risk areas. The navies of the world, especially the US and UK navies also patrol these waters to help support interdiction efforts. Most corporations also have policies related to vessels captured by pirates in terms of negotiation of ransom etc.

EMERGING MARITIME OPPORTUNITIES

Because of Maritime's role of shipping about 90% of goods across the world is very sensitive to economic conditions. The capacity of the industry is related to port and ship sizes and both involve significant capital spending to increase capacity. Historically, the industry has been characterized as building to meet capacity and then finding a recession or turn down reduce the demand for capacity resulting in lower rates pressuring the major shipping companies to be profitable. Sometimes this has resulted in consolidation within the industry or for key players to go bankrupt during difficult economic periods. When the period is over, the industry meets capacity and then moving to being under capacity due to the renewed high demand for global shipping. Companies then add capacity only to find there's a new downturn. In addition, containerization is a major factor in global shipping but also very sensitive to economic cycles. Other segments, most the river carriers, are under continued threat due to the lack of strong demand for loads on the rivers.

Some of this volatility is endemic to the industry and won't change. Maritime is resilient because of the collaboration within the industry and because of its ability to adapt to new technologies and shipping approaches. There are several opportunities for the maritime industry to improve and innovate as they continue to experience a baseline of demand along with seasonal and economic cycles. This section discusses several opportunities.

---

[48] MARAD

Bunker Fuel: The Dirty Fuel of Maritime

Bunker Fuel is one of the most polluting fuels. Figure 46 shows a comparison between diesel fuel (left) and bunker fuel (right). The diesel is a light brown and has flows easily whereas the bunker fuel is the bottom of the barrel, tarry, black fuel. It is the lowest grade of fuel available and most global shipping is based on its use.

Figure 46. Diesel versus Bunker Fuel

The IMO within the United Nations has an environmental mandate for all bunker fuel to be low Sulphur based by 2020 [49]. This is creating a scramble for refiners to create this new bunker fuel and will also see significant compliance costs from ships. Bunker fuel has become more controversial since the focus on global Green House Gas (GHG) production. The maritime industry is generally seen as becoming "greener" based on its policies for water filtration, improvements in managing bilge water and returning this water back to a level of purity that cleans the ocean water as the ship uses it for cooling engines and its management of solid waste. Bunker Fuel is the one area that hasn't been addressed. Longer term, ships will need to have alternative fuels that are cleaner, including the use of Liquid Natural Gas. Most of these alternatives are in an early stage so the first step of reducing the Sulphur content will be a good one, if only incrementally, for the industry. Improvements in this area would have a direct positive impact on pollution and potentially in other environmental areas.

Growth of Shipping from Developing Nations

A second opportunity will come from developing nations as they become larger producers of consumer goods throughout the world. Today, many raw materials come from these countries but over time, as their manufacturing economy and middle class grow, they will also become major markets for export and import of consumer goods. Development of ports and technology to support this growth must take place over the next 10 to 15 years to avoid new dimensions of port congestion. New dimensions of shipping demand as they grow may also help manage some of the economic turmoil experienced in shipping due to more consistent demand but it's not clear if it will help or add to the problem.

---

[49] *Refining and Shipping Industries Will Scramble to Meet the 2020 IMO Bunker Fuel Rules*. IMO, 2017

Soothing Port Congestion

Port congestion continues to be a major issue as the top 50 ports in the US drive over 80% of all traffic worldwide. There are several reasons we experience the level of congestion we do including:

- Infrastructure – Port infrastructure has been going through an evolution as new deep water ports handled bigger vessels. Automation is playing a role, but the level of automation needed to reduce port congestion isn't available to enable high degrees of automated loading and unloading, etc. The largest ports in the world have now set themselves apart from all others in their ability to service the most port calls with the largest ships. The challenge is in expansion. These parts are often seen as the only effective ports to use in their respective countries which causes them to be over-subscribed schedule wise. This leads to delays simply due to the need to service so man ports of call for inbound and outbound shipping.

- Vessel Size – Vessel size also plays a large role in port congestion. As we have built larger and larger vessels the general belief has been that we would see a reduction in the number of port calls due to high capacity ships. In reality, the demand for shipping continues to grow steadily taking up much of the capacity additions of these new ships leading to just as many, if not more, port calls. Port calls for these ships can lead to offloading times that used to be 2 to 3 days are now approaching 5 to 7 days if there is no delay. Without a lower number of ports of calls, these larger vessels now add to the existing congestion creating new bottlenecks that weren't before.

- Human Error – Human navigation error or maintenance issues that stops ships on their routes is another major factor in port congestion. These errors lead to delays in getting to the port disrupting liner ship schedules and often causing docking delays that can be days to weeks. Because of infrastructure limitations and lack of automation in scheduling management of inbound ships, delays due to human errors often have ripple effects to the port that can last for days or weeks.

- Weather – Weather will always play a factor in ship delivery times and their result on port congestion. Generally, delays due to weather are low when compared to the other factors listed above.

As global shipping continues to grow, the need for added port automation and effective growth in infrastructure will be critical to help the most popular ports manage capacity and congestion. The rise of new ports and increased transshipment may also help to ease congestion. Ports have become a victim of their success and congestion will likely be a reality for a long time.

Collaborating for Capacity

Shipping Alliances have been used to help manage capacity and drive route efficiency. These alliances act like airline code sharing arrangements for passenger traffic allowing the shipping companies to co-mingle and consolidate shipments to one partner from many to reduce the need for multiple ports of call and to enable better efficiency in shipping. Today there are three major alliances focused on container shipping capacity. Figure 47 [50] shows these alliances along with their capacities along with the largest independent shipping operations.

1. **2M Alliance** (MSC, Maersk, Hamburg Sud, Hyundai)
2. **Ocean Alliance** (CMA CGM, APL, COSCO, China Shipping, OOCL, Evergreen)
3. **The Alliance** (NYK Group, "K" Line, MOL, Yang Ming, Hapag-Lloyd, UASC)

Having alliances that can manage capacity across multiple carrier's enables better capacity management and sharing that may lead to more stability especially during economic downturns. Instead of every line trying to build greater capacity, capacity sharing, and consolidation can help manage load growth to better indicate when more capacity is needed. The primary purpose of this is to help manage capacity against global economic shifts. The three major alliances of 2M, Ocean Alliance and The Alliance make up over 1,155 ships representing almost 30% of all container ship assets in the world and the largest of the shipping lines. These alliances will give way to new alliances as the market continues to evolve.

As we have seen, the maritime industry is a highly diverse industry with very strong global reach. With over 90% of goods being moved in this mode, it is critical the industry continues to evolve and grow in efficiency and capacity to handle the growing freight trends. The ability for maritime companies to respond rather than react to economic changes, trade flow changes, and industry changes will have a profound impact on worldwide economics moving forward.

---

[50] https://www.logisticsplus.net/understanding-the-new-ocean-carrier-alliances/

CHAPTER 9: AIR CARGO CARRIERS

INTRODUCTION

The airline industry is a specialized industry for cargo in transportation. Air cargo via airline companies only about 2% of all cargo in the world but about 25% of all value of goods moved. Air is best at high value goods moved internationally and is much less indicated for heavy, lower value goods and air cargo domestically. Most domestic air cargo is related to expediting goods, typically components or spare parts. Air cargo is best indicated for these situations [51]:

- <u>eCommerce Parcel Shipments</u> – Over 95% of all eCommerce is shipped via parcel with air involved at some point. For international shipments, the number approaches 99% for air parcel. UPS, Fedex, and DHL are all major players in global parcel for eCommerce. Air will benefit the most from the change to eCommerce from traditional store based distribution. The growth of eCommerce will be a major factor in the growth of global air freight for at least the next decade. Parcel growth has been substantial and while there is much growth in the domestic parcel market there is an equal growth in international parcel and cross-border eCommerce that is fueling air cargo growth. Figure 48 [52] shows the general growth of the global parcel market from 2012 -2017.

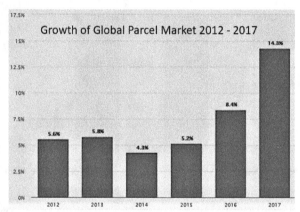

Figure 48. Global Growth of Parcel

<u>Perishable Goods and Food and Beverage</u> – This includes most fruits and vegetables in grocery stores during the off-season in the destination country. This also includes other meat items, like lamb and fish from specific regions of the world. Perishable food items are one of the largest segments of goods moved by air because without it, the goods would spoil before reaching their destinations. This is also true for smaller shipments of food and beverage products when the timing related to international maritime shipping doesn't support the demand for goods.

---

[51] https://www.mrrse.com/air-cargo-market

- <u>Consumer Electronics and other "High Value" goods</u> – Consumer electronics and similarly high value items are often shipped via air to global locations unless the One reason manufacturers ship via air is the overall value of the items and the potential for theft. Because of the value of the item, the cost for air shipments are more easily absorbed into the product price. By using air, the product is in-transit hours rather than weeks reducing the risk of damage, theft, and the opportunity costs of not having the products available to be sold.

- <u>Pharmaceuticals and Healthcare</u> – Another segment of growth is healthcare and especially pharmaceuticals. Like consumer electronics, moving pharmaceuticals by air reduces the potential for theft and counterfeiting and ensures the goods are well protected from temperature while being in the transit phase for a short a time as possible.

- <u>Retail "Drop Ins"</u> – While most non-perishable retail and consumer goods are moved by container ships worldwide there are still times when we need to rapidly move consumer goods between international markets. One of the most common examples is in higher end items like those in the fashion industry. Fashion is seasonal and buyers buy six to nine months ahead of the season. Goods are moved by container ship in mass to global markets for shelf and distribution stocking at the beginning of the season. Once the goods sell, buyers may find some SKUs (Stock Keeping Units) are selling faster than projected. In those situations, they will put in additional orders for goods and have them shipped via air cargo to reduce the time it takes for those goods to get to market. These "drop ins" help keep goods from being out of stock when their selling profile exceeds the buyers plan.

- <u>Just-in-Time manufacturing / expediting</u> – JIT manufacturing is typically done with suppliers close to the factory locations. For some items, manufacturing is done on a different continent and goods are shipped via container and rail. For some, that timing won't work and so air cargo is used to rapidly get the component into the JIT cycle. Expediting is the process where goods must be moved out of the normal order cycle and time is critical. Spare parts are expedited globally and sometimes domestically to fix manufacturing machinery or other equipment that is affecting normal operations. By getting spares to the site faster, operations can resume quicker reducing the impact and exposure of the failure.

Freight Ton Kilometers and Ton-Miles

In the air cargo mode, ton-mile does apply but the Air Mode using a metric that works across the global called freight ton kilometers which is a measure like the ton-mile that applies the global metric system. Like ton-mile, Freight Ton per Kilometer (FTK) measures one ton of freight moved one kilometer as a measure of both weight and distance but also of revenue. This is the purest measure of air cargo freight. Another measure that includes cargo, unaccompanied baggage and mail is Cargo Ton Kilometer (CTK). For our purposes we will use FTK to eliminate the non-freight data part of CTK. In addition, some data may be provided in the traditional ton-mile configuration when looking at US Statistics.

Hubs and air cargo Flows

Most modes of transportation rates are driven by the lanes, or city-pairs, that are used for transportation. Higher demand lanes typically cost less on a ton-mile basis than lower demand lanes due to the need for backhauls and other factors. In the air cargo market rates are also partially driven by city-pairs. Another factor involving rates are the absolute volumes of a airport or region both in terms of the airports that are origination points for freight, destination points of freight, and those airports involved in transshipment. The air cargo market was about $69 billion in ton-mile revenue in 2016. Figure 49 [53] shows the breakdown by month and between the domestic air cargos versus international air cargo on a global basis.

2016 Air Cargo Revenue Ton-Miles ($B)			
Month	Region		Total
	Domestic	International	
January	1,032.31	4,066.45	5,098.76
February	952.297	3,720.60	4,672.90
March	1,138.15	4,523.61	5,661.75
April	1,092.55	4,464.49	5,557.04
May	1,076.07	4,438.34	5,514.41
June	1,145.57	4,486.01	5,631.57
July	1,106.08	4,535.88	5,641.96
August	1,166.54	4,425.90	5,592.44
September	1,182.53	4,560.21	5,742.75
October	1,209.49	5,058.21	6,267.70
November	1,263.54	4,971.50	6,235.05
December	1,392.91	4,904.67	6,297.58
Totals	13,758.03	54,155.87	67,913.90
% of Total	20.00%	80.00%	100%

Figure 49. Ton-Mile Revenue of Global Air Cargo

---

[53] https://transtats.bts.gov/freight.asp

Over 80% of all air cargo is international and related to the six situations mentioned earlier in the chapter. When thinking of international air cargos, the immediate question is related to how these international ton-miles are distributed? Are there well-known cargo hubs throughout the world much like in the maritime industry, the takes the lion's share of cargo and moves it around in transshipment? Are there strong city-pairs that move manufactured goods directly to the market? Are there global "Import" cities that take on air cargo in an intermodal model that then distributes the cargo throughout a country? To understand this better, we need to understand the volumes of the major airport hubs, if there are any, and their role in air cargo specifically. If we can understand the airports involved and their

RANK 2017	RANK 2016	AIRPORT CITY / COUNTRY / CODE	CARGO (Metric tonnes)	
			(Loaded and unloaded)	Percent change
1	1	HONG KONG, HK (HKG)	5 049 898	9.4
2	2	MEMPHIS TN, US (MEM)	4 336 752	0.3
3	3	SHANGHAI, CN (PVG)	3 824 280	11.2
4	4	INCHEON, KR (ICN)	2 921 691	7.6
5	6	ANCHORAGE AK, US (ANC)*	2 713 230	6.7
6	5	DUBAI, AE (DXB)	2 654 494	2.4
7	7	LOUISVILLE KY, US (SDF)	2 602 695	6.8
8	8	TOKYO, JP (NRT)	2 336 427	7.9
9	11	TAIPEI, TW (TPE)	2 269 585	8.2
10	9	PARIS, FR (CDG)	2 195 229	2.8
11	10	FRANKFURT, DE (FRA)	2 194 056	3.8
12	13	SINGAPORE, SG (SIN)	2 164 700	7.9
13	14	LOS ANGELES CA, US (LAX)	2 158 324	8.1
14	12	MIAMI FL, US (MIA)	2 071 722	2.9
15	15	BEIJING, CN (PEK)	2 029 584	4.5
16	16	DOHA, QA (DOH)	2 020 942	15.0
17	19	LONDON, GB (LHR)	1 794 276	9.4
18	18	GUANGZHOU, CN (CAN)	1 780 423	7.8
19	17	AMSTERDAM, NL (AMS)	1 778 382	4.9
20	20	CHICAGO IL, US (ORD)	1 721 807	12.6
TOP 20 FOR 2017			50 618 497	6.8

*includes transit freight

Figure 50. Ton-Mile Revenue of Global Airports of Entry

missions, we can infer their role as either an origination point, a transshipment point, or a destination point. Figure 50 [54] shows the airports with the largest air cargo trade flows in 2016 along with their year over year growth rates.

By analyzing the flow of air cargo through these hubs we can better characterize how air cargo works. In analyzing the data initially, we find that among the rankings there are multiple airports in some regions that creates capacity to handle freight through these lanes compared to others. To get an accurate view of trade flows we need to combine these. Examples in Figure 50 include airport hubs like Louisville KY and Indianapolis IN. Both airports serve as hubs for UPS break-bulk and are points of origin for global eCommerce parcels and similar goods. Another is Dubai which has both the Dubai and Maktoum airports and have distributed volume between the two to provide improved and increased service levels. These airports primary mission is solely transshipment as they receive goods from all over the world and provide a transshipment capability for the goods to go within the middle-east region but also across all other regions of the world. When looking at the Biayun- Huada / Bao'an airports in the Guangdong province of China, these airports are used primarily as points of origin for goods moving throughout the world. They, like Shanghai with a similar point of origin mission, also are major points of destination for goods coming into China and serve a dual capacity. Honk Kong is similar but with more slightly more imports than exports. Tokyo and Narita airports in Japan are true hybrids with a strong export and import mission. Dubai isn't the only major transshipment hub in the world either. Hamad airport in Doha, also provides this service.

Qatar is the fastest growing transshipment hub in the world and home to Qatar airlines which has won the Global Air Cargo Airline of the Year from STAT Trade Times in both 2016 and 2017 for its air cargo services to Africa. Doha acts primarily as a transshipment hub for Qatar airlines and others. As we look deeper at these top ports we find that air cargo volumes are generally split evenly between points of origin of goods for movement, points of destination for those goods, and transshipment hubs across the world to enable a break-bulk and sortation function to drive efficiencies. The other area of significant interest is that of the 67,813,000,000 ton-miles of goods, 57,915,138,000 are attributed to these 30 airports (including the combined airports) which is over 85% of all air freight movement worldwide in 2016.

Global Cargo Characteristics: Revenue and Flight Styles

A second factor to consider in the role of air cargo worldwide is both the total volume and the revenue represented within the average airline that is a major hauler of freight. As we mentioned before air freight moves about 25% of the global value of goods but only represents about 2% of global freight movement. Figure 51 [55] shows the percentage of revenue by type for a global commercial airline. Air freight revenue (except for UPS and Fedex), averages about 7% of their revenue.

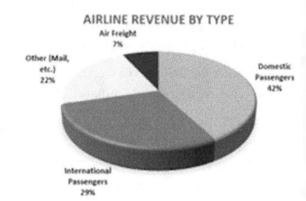

Figure 51. Airline Revenue by Type

Another factor in looking at the air cargo market is the use of scheduled flights versus charter flights and postal based mail. Mail is a global commodity that moves both domestic and internationally. Some postal services have their own fleets or outsource to freight carriers. Some also use commercial carriers for movement. As we see in Figure 52[56], the percentage of mail in terms of the total of all air cargo is small and the majority of air cargo is scheduled. Scheduled air cargo includes regularly scheduled dedicated air freighters and using commercial aircraft to move freight. Chartered freight is freight specifically coordinated as a onetime shipment usually due to the need to expedite. Most air freight is moved by contract carriage with either a commercial airline or dedicated air freight company.

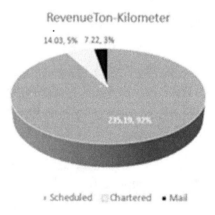

Figure 52. Air Cargo by Type of Flight

---

[55] Airfacts.com

The air cargo industry plays an important role in global freight trade by providing a global speed and flexibility that the maritime industry is not intended to provide. As we've seen, transshipment also plays a critical role similar to other modes. The ability to consolidate and de-consolidate global air freight as it moves through the supply chain is a key factor in flexibility.

DEFINING THE AIR CARGO SEGMENT

We've discussed the market in terms of sizing, types of cargo and the flights that are used to move the cargo along with the major hubs in the world. In this section, we'll discuss the different approaches used to move air cargo globally. We'll principally focus on two very different methods of air cargo freight movement: Dedicated Air

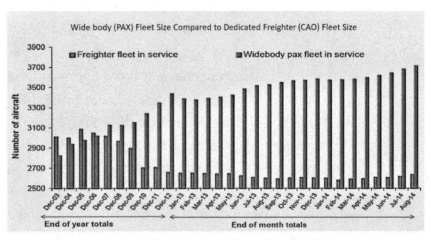

Figure 53. Change in Dedicated Airfreights

Freighters and Belly Freight. Whether air cargo is scheduled, chartered or is postal based, they are moved using either a dedicated air freighter or through commercial airlines in the "belly" of their cargo hold below the passenger deck. Let's explore this in more detail as the airline industry has been in a transition process since around 2008 in increasing the use of belly freight for flexibility and lower volume shipping.

> Dedicated Air Freighters versus Belly Freight (Figure 53) – To begin, there are two approaches to moving air cargo worldwide. The first is the dedicated air freighter which is built and configured to move freight only. The major freight carriers, UPS, Fedex, amounts of freight worldwide. Most of the dedicated air freighters are involved in scheduled flights. These flights are one way as opposed to passenger flights and so only lanes that can be profitable with a one way, or with a back haul that can create a round trip revenue source are developed. Dedicated air freighters are also used in consolidating less than air cargo (LAC) loads going to the same destination which can be competitively priced when comparing Belly freight.

[56] ibid

<u>Belly Freight Approach</u> - Belly freight uses commercial wide-body jets to move freight within their cargo holds. This has become a very popular way to move freight due to its flexibility but also because it enables loads to be moved at a competitive price. Belly freight is also considered scheduled freight because the passenger airline schedules are used to carry freight. Like passengers connecting flights, belly freight also has connecting flights to get to their ultimate destinations if a direct flight does not get the cargo where it needs to be. With the last "great" recession in 2008 – 2009, the airlines began a more aggressive shift from dedicated air cargo to belly freight. Part of that transition was charging passengers for storing bags in the cargo hold. So, if you ever wondered why you had to pay for your bags, it was primarily because the airlines wanted to discourage people from using the cargo hold so it could be reserved for more belly fright. Figure 53 shows this transition of reducing dedicated air freighters while increase wide-body passenger aircraft. Because of this shift, there inventory of dedicated freighters in the world has dropped from a high of 3,100 in 2005 to about 1,800 in 2017. Assuming an average of 70 tons per freighter this is a drop in dedicated air cargo capacity of over 91,000 tons or about 40%of total capacity. The wide-body passenger fleet has grown from 3,100 plans in 2005 to about 5,320 planes as of 2017. With an average payload capacity of around 30,000 pounds, this represents an increase in cargo capacity through wide-body planes of about 33,300 tons. This has effectively shifted the dedicated freighter capacity to commercial wide-body planes. Today, about 52% of all air freight capacity is in wide-body passenger airplanes and 48% is in dedicated air freighters. Long term projections see this dropping much further by 2025 to 61% from wide-body passenger planes and 39% for dedicated air freighters[57].

<u>Dedicated Air Freighters</u> – Dedicated Air Freighters are in a category called Cargo only Aviation (CAO) and use planes built to carry only cargo. These planes have varying capacity from as small as 15-20 tons up to the largest freighter, the Boeing 747-8F at almost 150 tons. Perspective is important here. The smaller end of the market has a capacity of about 40,000 pounds equivalent to a one truck dry van. The bulk of the dedicated freighter offerings   are around 60 tons, or about 120,000 tons about one-half a rail car or 2+ truck dry vans. The 747-8F, the only offering of its kind, can carry up to about 300,000 tons which is more than one rail car. While the weights are smaller than one might think, the cargo itself is light and very valuable which creates the right weight situation to make the economics work. The Boeing Company has been in the dedicated air freighter business longer than its main competitor, Airbus.

---

[57] IATA

[58] Boeing Company / Airbus Freighter Offerings

It has a larger span of offerings than does Airbus. Boeing has air cargo capacities in the middle tier (60 – 130 tons) which is not as popular as. Both companies have announced in the past that their new planes, the Boeing 787 and the Airbus 380, would also have new high capacity (for air cargo) offerings.

<u>Wide-body Passenger Aircraft (PAX)</u> – Wide-body Passenger Airplanes, also called PAX, are passenger planes with the capacity to carry containerized or palletized freight. The PAX fleet that can carry cargo represents about 19% of all commercial passenger aircraft. Traditionally, regional jets, turboprop aircraft, and narrow body jets do not carry freight. The only Boeing narrow body jet in production is the Boeing 737 which is a 3x3 set cabin configuration. Among Airbus, the only narrow body planes in production are the Airbus A220 which is a 3x2 seat cabin configuration. All other narrow body planes are made by companies like Tupolev (Russia), Comac (China), Irkut (Russia), Antonov (Ukraine), Sukoi (Russia), Bombadier (Canada), Embraer (Brazil), Mitsubishi (Japan), and ATR (France). Wide-body PAX planes are made primarily by Boeing (B747, B767, B777, B787) and Airbus (A330, A350, and the A380). In addition, ILC from Russia has the IL-96 and China, through a joint venture called CRAIC is expected to launch a wide-body PAX aircraft called the CR929 by 2023. Today, all major airports in the world service PAX aircraft create a global network for freight cargo. In addition, most secondary airports, like Manchester UK, Columbus, out of Harrisburg (OH) USA, Hamburg Germany, Osaka Japan, and others also have at least one flight per day from a PAX plane to enable them to be feeders for belly freight to the major airports. Belly freight is a very effective operation for airlines and allows them to provide options for thousands of different air route combinations a day. This has changed the landscape for air cargo operations worldwide and appears to be the preferred method moving into the future.

EQUIPMENT IN THE AIR CARGO MODE

Our next topic is to understand the equipment in the air cargo mode. Unlike other modes, the PAX and Dedicated freighters do not specialize in specific cargo so the plane itself, while a piece of equipment is a general-purpose hauler. This is also true of the containers and the pallet load configurations used to create the loads for the aircraft. Each individual aircraft has a specific load plan for that craft. It defines the pallet configurations, or the specific equipment used for containerization. However, the only thing different between these pieces of equipment or pallet configurations is the size and dimensions which are purpose built to fit the exact aircraft being loaded. So, unlike other modes, the equipment used in air cargo is not specialized beyond the equipment specifications to fit in the cargo hold of the aircraft.

Figure 56 shows an example of a container and a pallet configuration to better underline this. The container on the right is specifically built for a right or left side of the cargo hold and the cut-ins is specific to an aircraft that requires that to fit in the curved fuselage. Similarly, you'll notice the pallet is built to have a gap on the top right (or left) side of the pallet to enable it fit in the side of the fuselage along the curve

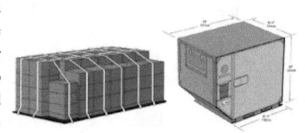

Figure 56. Pallets and Containers in Air Freight

of the airplane. There is no other specification of equipment but it's important to understand that to load cargo efficiently every model of aircraft has a specific load plan and example of a pallet or container configuration that must be used for the right, the left, and the center of the aircraft.

AIR CARGO OPERATIONS

Air cargo is driven the airway bill like other bills of lading and specific to the airline industry. In addition, the same international paperwork (Commercial Invoice, Certification or Origin, etc. discussed in Chapter 3) is required for air cargo as for any other international cargo.

Air cargo operations work very similar whether the cargo is shipped via a dedicated air freighter (CAO) or through belly freight via PAX. All air cargo operations is airport to airport. Because of this, airlines partner with third Party logistics providers, especially freight forwarders who can manage freight on behalf of clients. Often, these partners will pick up the freight on behalf of their clients and then delivery them to the airport into the freight cargo terminal. Similarly, on the other end, they will have the freight picked up and delivered to the customer's end destination. Air cargo clients can also do this themselves but often using an expert like a freight forwarder who focused on air cargo in specific lanes works well because the forwarders also know all the paperwork and other activities, including how the freight must be configured, to create a successful shipment. Sometimes, the freight forwarders will also store the goods for a time at the airport until the scheduled flight is open to receive freight. This allows the customer to ensure they have their freight in the forwarder's hands well ahead of the actual flight.

Regardless of the source, the freight intake process is also similar between PAX and CAO providers. Based on US and international regulations all cargo must be screened before being accepted into the secure area of the airport. This is done usually by using large x-ray machines to scan the cargo similar to passenger baggage and carry-on bags.

With international shipments, the cargo is received in an unsecure area and then the documentation is checked and approved, the cargo is scanned and then put into the bonded area of the airport which includes customs operations. At this point the customs office takes over and inspects the cargo using the country's custom procedures and then releases the cargo into the secure area of the airport for loading on the aircraft. This also means that if customs does not clear the freight, it will stay in the bonded area until the issues are resolved, or customs will deny the cargo requiring the customer to remove it from the airport. This is another reason using third Party providers like freight forwarders can be an advantage. Forwarders and others are adept at working with customs and can often correct errors on the spot to ensure the cargo passes inspection and meets the deadline for the aircraft loading.

While dedicated air freighter cargos go through the same process, they also can provide consolidation services for clients with smaller loads. Working with multiple customers, they can take partial loads from multiple customers to fill the freighter as part of its regular scheduled flight operations. This can be an important factor when the lane involved does not traverse through major airports. For instance, Rickenbacker airport (LCK) in Columbus out of Harrisburg (OH) is one of the largest dedicated freight hubs in the US and is a good example of airports focused on freight management versus passenger movement, although Rickenbacker does have one passenger carrier, an ultra-low cost carrier Allegiant Airlines. Rickenbacker has nineteen weekly air freight schedules and foreign trade zone and customs operations for international shipments and is within one day's truck drive of 50% of the US population and 1/3 of Canada's population. The destinations have been developed based on client needs and flexibility for multiple destinations and provide direct access via Airbridge Cargo to Moscow Russia and Liege Belgium (A large origination and transshipment point for Europe), Luxemburg and Hong Kong (Another large transshipment point for China) via Cargo Lux, Direct to and from Hong Kong via Cathay Pacific, to Taipei Taiwan via China Airlines, to and from Dubai (another major transshipment point) with access to Brussels via Emirates air cargo, Hanoi Viet Nam to Rickenbacker and return through Amsterdam and East Midlands in the England (a transshipment hub in the UK) and Al Hoceima Morocco through Etihad Cargo. The John Glenn international airport, a Tier II passenger airport is nearby but Rickenbacker provides the flexibility and access needed for dedicated freight operations.

Because most major airports have large freight cargo operations, airports like Rickenbacker are not necessarily as well-known but these secondary cargo hubs are vital to freight commerce as other alternatives, especially for developing dedicated lanes for secondary markets. Other freight airports like Rickenbacker include Portland international airport, Chicago/Rockford airport in Illinois, Ft. Worth Alliance airport in Ft. Worth Texas, Bradley international airport in Windsor Locks, CT, and Laredo international airport in Laredo, TX. These dedicated freight airports play a key role in global cargo movement.

Air cargo is the most expensive mode of transportation in logistics. Using air, in the right circumstances, can be a very valuable approach to freight movement. Using airline partners and belly freight or moving cargo through secondary dedicated airports can be some of the most economical ways to move goods when air is the indicated mode.

Largest Variable Costs in Air Cargo

Like the motor carrier and rail modes, air cargo's largest variable costs are fuel and labor. Fuel costs are the dominant driver today of air cargo for dedicated fleets and for belly freight and represents about 45% of the total cost of an airplane.

EMERGING AIR CARGO OPPORTUNITIES

According to Hexa Research, the global air cargo market is expected to grow from around 105 billion FTK to over 135 FTK by 2025[60] representing about a 3.2% per year growth and 23% growth total between 2017 and 2025. Most of this growth is predicated on the continued double digit growth of the digital economy and global eCommerce. Because the airline industry is very sensitive to economic changes, it is difficult to know if this prediction will be close or far off the target. There are a few opportunities that the airline industry needs to take advantage of over the next six years to be ready for this growth should it occur. These include:

- Continued Conversion of the Freight Fleet to PAX – New airplane orders are one source of growth for the PAX fleet and its associated belly freight. Converting dedicated freights to PAX aircraft is another major need for the industry. The industry has been doing this having already converted about 800 aircraft per year and this is expected to continue through 2025. Creating new belly freight capacity will be an important factor in managing this growth.

- Managing the disruption of traditional parcel carriers through new entrants – The largest new entrant into the parcel delivery business is Amazon.com. They have been steadily leasing 767 freighters to enable them to bypass traditional parcel carriers and manage the entire end to end delivery through disruptive models. As Amazon becomes more dominant in the market, its unclear how other carriers will react to meet the growing parcel need or if the parcel need will be curtailed by these developments. While Amazon is a major force in eCommerce, there are other channels being developed worldwide including traditional big-box retailers like Walmart, Costco, Auchan and Carrefour in France, Tesco in the UK, CRC in Hong Kong and many others. In addition, companies Alibaba who dominate the market in China has yet to begin any aggressive growth out of China, but this is also inevitable. It may be these other retail sources will continue to fair well overall and create their own markets for parcel and eCommerce goods movement with Amazon.

It's important to remember that, today, eCommerce globally represents about 9% of the total retail market. Amazon is being attributed with about 45% of the US market share while Alibaba has an82% market share in China. With eCommerce poised to continue its growth, all retailers are adapting to the eCommerce market with capabilities like Omni-Channel Commerce, and global eCommerce sales to locations where they don't have a retail presence. It's easy to get excited about Amazon.com and its vision to become the "World's Largest Store", but it's also important to remember that for over 110 years, there actually was a company at one point the World's Largest Store. That company was Sears now almost an afterthought in retail. It's critical to remember that the eCommerce wars are just beginning and will likely be shaped over the next 10 to 20 years. Parcel growth will clearly benefit from the global attention and will add to the growth of parcel worldwide which will have a positive effect on air cargo.

- <u>Greater Efficiency and Aircraft Range</u> - The airline industry is experimenting with Liquid Natural Gas (LNG) as an alternative fuel to its traditional fuel JP4. Fuel management is a key part of the long term profitability and viability of the air industry. Finding other technology to improve the fuel efficiency of aircraft is another key to air cargo's future.

A World without Air Cargo: Would it Work?

The airlines and air cargo mode is a highly dynamic mode for freight movement. On the one hand, air cargo accounts for a small portion of all freight movement while representing a large amount of the total value of goods shipped. Without air cargo as an efficient mode of transportation, the entire parcel industry would be paralyzed in today's rapidly growing eCommerce market. Similarly, without the ability to rapidly move perishable foods to grocery stores all over the world, many countries would not have the choices and varieties they now enjoy and the countries that grow the product would have overproduction and spoilage. From a supply chain perspective, retailers would have to have perfect forecasting to avoid out of stock. As this is all but impossible, it would mean that many industries would have much higher rates of out of stocks, or much higher carrying costs due to overproduction and much high levels of customer dissatisfaction. In addition, factories and field operations all over the world would bleed cash as they sit idle waiting for that "one-off" spare part holding up operations, or the manufacturing industry would suffer a dramatic loss of profit because of the massive requirement for forward stocking of spares. This from 2% of the global volume of shipping.

When thinking about air cargo, we must forget the small impact of goods movement in the industry and instead reflect on the time criticality that air provides in keeping the supply chain working well with many choices, many options, and the effective management of contingencies.

CHAPTER 10: PIPELINES

INTRODUCTION

The pipeline mode is a very specialized mode in transportation. It is also a small industry, employment wise, when compared to all other transportation mode. The US pipeline distribution segment, the transporters of pipeline goods, has less than 100,000 employees. Unlike other modes, pipeline is almost exclusively a private carrier. We can test this notion with a simple example. Let's say I have a barrel of kerosene I want to ship to my mother in St. Louis, Missouri. I am in El Paso Texas within three miles of a major pipeline. If I go into that company with my barrel of kerosene and ask them to "please pour it into your pipeline and ship it to my mom", they are likely to call the police! Pipelines simply don't work that way. The move the goods of the companies that built them and that run them.

Because of this, we need a cursory understanding of the role of pipelines and their value in meeting the needs of oil & gas and chemical industries. Almost everything that is moved by pipelines is considered a hazardous material. The Pipeline and Hazardous Material Administration (PHMA) oversees the pipeline industry which is logical given the goods it moves. PHMA also handles all hazardous materials for all modes besides pipeline.

The primary pipelines that drive the oil, gas, and chemical industry in the world are oil pipelines (petroleum products) and the Liquid Natural Gas. Pipelines are used throughout the world and pipelines continue to get larger and longer as we evolve our techniques and capabilities for moving goods through them. The five largest pipelines and pipeline projects in the world are:

- West-East pipeline (China) – This pipeline is 5,410 miles and crosses China from the west to the east travelling through over 70 cities bringing electricity and natural gas to power plants, industry, and households

- GASUN pipeline (Brazil) – This 3,100 mile long pipeline in Brazil moving from its rich gas field near Sao Paulo and Rio and will travel through the Amazon basin to northern Brazil to bring them gas to enable more industry and gas to cities

- Yamal-Europe pipeline (Russia and Europe) – This 2,607 mile pipeline starts in the Yamal Fields in Northern Russia and travels through multiple locations in Russia, Belarus, Poland and Germany

- Trans-Saharan pipeline (Nigeria to Southern Europe) – This pipeline is 2,607 miles long and starts in the southern part of Nigeria progressing up to Hassi R'Mel in Algeria and then splits into multiple pipelines serving Morocco, Spain, Tunisia, Libya, and throughout Italy

- TransCanada Pipeline – The TransCanada pipeline is 2,005 miles and runs from the western part of Canada through Calgary, Edmonton, Thunder Bay, Toronto, and Quebec City to Halifax on the far eastern side of the country

Pipelines are a mainstay throughout the world and are used extensively to move oil and oil products (gas, fuels, etc.) and natural gas. They are very capital intensive with such a small variable cost it does not significant impact the profit economics of pipelines.

Pipelines are the most efficient way to move oil and oil products and natural gas when compared to other modes. Pipelines are very capital intensive and the pipeline industry does not receive public promotion from the US Government and must manage its own capital and operating costs including the designing building of new pipelines and pipeline segments along with the ongoing maintenance of the pipelines themselves. The industry uses significant automation to inspect and maintain the pipelines and for operations.

Scope of Pipelines

Different pipelines have different purposes beyond just the goods they move. In the United States, the entire pipeline industry revenue was about $93 billion in 2016. Of that, the oil pipelines accounted for 25% of this revenue and the LNG pipeline was 75% of the total. This reflects the use of these pipelines when compared to each other.

- Oil Pipelines - Oil pipelines act as a conduit from the point of extraction to the point of refinement and then other methods are used to ship the goods after refining to their ultimate destinations. Some of the oil pipelines have feeder networks to chemical plants and power plants but do not reach to consumer points of use, i.e. gas stations. In the US the oil pipeline network is about 160,000 miles in total length (Figure 57) [61].

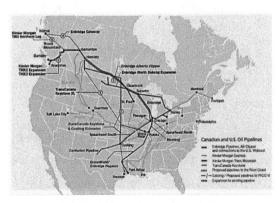

Figure 57. US and Canadian Pipelines

[61] https://www.bts.gov/content/us-oil-and-gas-pipeline-mileage

- Natural Gas Pipelines - Natural Gas pipelines provide both an upstream pipeline network from extraction to refining and a downstream pipeline distribution network that reaches to power plants, industry, and directly to consumer homes for gas cooking and heating. The LNG pipeline's network is about 1.4 million miles long or about nine times as big as the Oil Pipeline (Figure 58)[62].

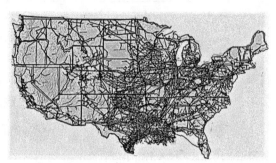

Figure 58. US LNG Pipeline

Products and Pipeline Movement

While oil products and natural gas products are the norm and represent over 90% of all pipeline goods movement, two other materials are moved in more specialized pipelines. We won't include water among these only because the commercial nature of water pipelines is governed by utilities and governments. These include:

- Hydrogen – Hydrogen is moved via pipelines in some parts of the world. These are generally small pipelines within 50 – 100 miles of an industrial site.

- Organic Chemicals □ Products made from chemicals often arrive via chemical feedstocks directly from chemical producers.

- Coal – Slurry pipelines are used to transport coal through a pipeline to a power point or holding tank. Some of these holding tanks can be in port areas where the coal is moved from a coal mining area within a few hundred miles of the port or power plant. To move coal by pipelines, the coal is mined and then pulverized and mixed with water. The pipelines then move the slurry under pressure between the origination and destination.

PIPELINE OPERATIONS

Pipeline operations vary based on the pipeline and covers both an upstream network for both oil and gas and a centralized downstream network for gas with a downstream distribution network for oil. Oil products in pipelines move about 5 miles per hour and generally the pipeline is full creating a warehousing effect. LNG products move at about 18 – 20 miles per hour based on large compressors that force the gas through the pipeline at a uniform speed. As the goods in the pipelines are used they are replaced with raw materials to move to refining to replenish the pipeline. In this section we'll explore these approaches and the key functions involved in these operations.

---

[62] Ibid.

- The Upstream Network – The upstream, or supply network in pipelines is based on the extraction of raw materials at their source. While oil, gas and chemical exploration are done to find these sources, the pipeline industry doesn't get involved until those sources have been secured and are functionally ready to move raw materials. The key functions in the upstream network include:

  o Platforms for Delivery of Raw Materials – The supplier source is connected to the pipeline networks via their delivery platforms and well heads.

    - For oil, this includes the oil rig, the oil pump sites and the offshore platforms that pull oil from the ground and then send it into small feeder pipelines then sent to terminals where the raw material is stored and merged into large transmissions lines that can move the goods 100s to 1,000s of miles. The terminals act as a storage point enabling the pipeline to be fed as goods are used.

    - For Liquid Natural Gas, the gas is collected in similar feeder lines but then are sent directly to gas processing facilities. Liquid Natural Gas is a highly compressed form of natural gas that only takes up $1/600^{th}$ of the space that natural gas does. It is a highly efficient method for development of natural gas based fuels. At processing facilities, the gases collected are separated and some are sent to other refineries for process. The processing facility adds methanethiol for safety as LNG is odorless and colorless. Once the gas is processed it will then enter the downstream network.

- Oil Refining Operations – Oil refineries are built to refine specific crude products for industrial and consumer markets. The upstream pipeline provides these specific products to storage tanks at the refinery and then the products are refined into finished goods that includes chemicals, refined oil products, gasoline, diesel, JP4 jet fuel and other fuels.

- LNG Downstream Network – Unlike oil refining, LNG is refined by removing impurities as part of the upstream network. So, when the LNG is released it goes directly into the downstream distribution network. This is done through Compressor stations. Compressor stations use large compressors like jet engines to create the compression needed to move the gas through the pipelines. The gas will pass through compression stations and is routed to wherever it is needed in the LNG pipeline.

- Oil and oil Products Downstream Network – The oil downstream network comprises some pipelines that act as feeder lines to chemical factors and other industrial factors that use the refined products. Similarly, it has feeder lines that go directly to oil based power plants. It also feeds ports for bunker fuel and bunkers for airplane JP4 fuel. Beyond that, the oil and oil products are stored in large storage fields where they are then distributed by either rail via tanker cars or truck via tanker trucks. Trucks are mainly used for consumer products for gasoline, oil deliveries etc. Rail may be used when bulk products are being delivered and for international shipments to ports.

EMERGING PIPELINE OPPORTUNITIES

Pipelines will continue to be the preferred method of movement for oil and oil products and LNG products into the foreseeable future. As the US energy market ebbs and flows so will the need for pipeline capacity. Pipelines already carry over 95% of all raw materials for crude oil and natural gas so its expansion will be directly related to developing new capacity. The XL Keystone pipeline which is a pipeline venture between Canada and the US is being built. This pipeline should carry tar sand oil from Western Canada to Houston Texas which has refineries specifically built for this oil.

General expansion of the pipelines will likely be incremental as will the maintenance needed to replace old infrastructure with updated and new infrastructure. Barring any significant new discoveries of oil and gas, new opportunities for pipelines will come, most likely from oil products considered less desirable, like fracking and tar sand oil. Given this, and the nature of these products, new developments in monitoring, inspecting and maintaining pipelines will be very important to combat the higher corrosive levels of these products.

Pipelines are generally considered the safest way to transport these goods when compared to all other modes for domestic distribution. Liking pipelines to oil tankers for international shipments is highly efficient and is also considered the safest way to move these products. Safety will continue to be a key driver in the industry. While the number of incidents and fatalities related to pipelines is low when compared to other forms of transportation, pipelines, like airlines, have the potential to have accidents with disastrous results when things go wrong. So, the level of safety, inspection and maintenance is critical. There are a few opportunities for pipelines to continue to focus and grow in safety. New developments include:

- Advanced Inspection Robots – Oil and gas already use robots in some of their operations, especially mainlines, to inspect corrosion and look for weaknesses in welds and other potential issues. Feeder lines have traditionally been more of a challenge due to their smaller size. A few companies, like Honeybee Robotics[63], are developing small robots (hand size) to allow robot inspections to occur where they were cost prohibitive. As robotic technology improves, there will be new opportunities to use it to improve the inspection levels and early detection of issues in the pipeline distribution networks.

- Increased used of advanced sensors – Measuring pressure, flow, and vibration are important factors in understanding pipeline health. Sensors have traditionally been an expensive approach for pipelines that, while viable, have had limited ability to evaluate and inspect the entire pipeline network. A team at the University of California at Berkeley, have been experimenting with developing low-cost sensor modules that can be added to inspection robots, used as inspection agents at various points in the pipeline and using ultrasonic lasers to be measure defects in the pipelines [64]. Lab testing suggests these approaches are viable and can be produced at a lower price than. Similar projects and pilots like these will continue until a commercially viable approach is found.

- Improving oil Spill Clean Up – The pipeline system is a very safe system but when something does go wrong the results can be disastrous. During the BP Gulf oil spill in 2010, scientist found a bacterium called *Alcanivorax borkumensis* that thrives uses hydrocarbons in oil as food [65]. The bacterium has had their DNA sequenced and work is underway to develop an approach to cleaning oil spills using these naturally occurring bacteria. This is one example of work going on but there will continue to be more work done leading to new ways to manage the results of a spill.

The pipeline mode is a very specialized mode focused on moving oil and oil products and natural gas and its products. Pipelines are used extensively throughout the world more as private carriers for the energy companies who come together to build them. They are an important backbone of transportation because moving goods without pipelines would be much more complex and would lead to significant new issues in congestion and capacity. As we continue forward, developing new methods of streamlining operations, improving inspection and maintenance, and developing effective ways to counter accidents will be critical to the long-term health of this mode.

---

[63] http://www.honeybeerobotics.com/portfolio/pipe-inspection-robot/
[64] https://www.energy.ca.gov/2014publications/CEC-500-2014-104/CEC-500-2014-104.pdf
[65] https://www.businessinsider.com/oil-eating-bacteria-could-help-clean-up-the-next-oil-spill-2018-4

CHAPTER 11: LOGISTICS SERVICE PROVIDERS

INTRODUCTION

During the period of regulated transportation in the US, shippers would use the available carriers for shipments based on their needs and the modes of transportation available to them. Some companies could help shippers manage freight for overseas shipments but generally the only transportation assets available to third Party shippers were carriers.

With the deregulation of transportation in 1980, we began a new era. We have not only seen dramatic growth in transportation assets, capacities, and capabilities, we have also seen new choices in how basic logistics and transportation functions can be done. In this chapter we will discuss the role outsourcing plays in transportation and logistics. We'll explore the options that companies have available to them to outsource services off all kinds beyond just transportation to carriers. We'll also see the evolution of outsourcing as a market including the evolution of services available to companies from the largest multi-national conglomerates to small companies. Finally, we'll discuss how these services are changing as the market both matures and finds new avenues of growth and innovation.

The term we will use for the entire class of companies that offer transportation and logistics services as an outsourced option is <u>Transportation Services Providers (TSP)</u>. TSPs are businesses that help shippers meet their transportation requirements either by taking on the actual transportation or logistics function on behalf of the company or, by representing the company in the market to help them find the specific services to meet a specific transportation challenge. While some TSPs can do much more than manage transportation, and we'll discuss these briefly, our focus on TSPs will in their ability to meet client's transportation challenges.

DEFINING THE LOGISTICS SERVICE PROVIDER SEGMENT

In Chapter one we provided a general overview of the transportation services market noting that about half of the market is related to carriers and the other half to service providers. To put a finer point on this, let's look at Table 15[66]. In this table take the two broad categories and break them down into the specific companies, or roles involved in the market. One

---

[66] Heartland Professional Services. *Analysis of the Transportation Services Market*. April 2019.

of the immediate things that should stand out is the impact that trucking (52% of the entire carrier market) and 3PLs (56% of all service providers) have on the totals. We've discussed the use of trucking in last mile delivery along with its role in intermodal which contributes significantly to its size. In this chapter, we'll see a similar role that Third Party Logistics Providers (3PLs) play as a general contractor of sorts for all transportation services. This is a change from even a decade ago where most

All Transportation Services		
Carriers	$ 404,430,000,000	55%
Trucking	$ 208,320,000,000	52%
Rail	$ 75,810,000,000	19%
Pipeline	$ 49,400,000,000	12%
Water	$ 38,400,000,000	9%
Air	$ 32,500,000,000	8%
Service Providers	$ 332,498,500,000	45%
3rd Party Logistics Providers (3PL)	$ 187,400,000,000	56%
Freight Forwarders	$ 72,744,300,000	22%
Freight Brokers	$ 65,554,200,000	20%
4PL	$ 6,800,000,000	2%
Total:	$ 736,928,500,000	100%

Table 15. Transportation Services Market by Segment

transportation Services outside of carriers were based on companies with little overlap between each other. It is that overlap that 3PLs have added to become one full-service provider for all outsourcing services in the industry.

Why do companies outsource services? What services do customers prefer to outsource? How is the industry evolving? These are the key questions to answer to understand the value and implications of TSPs on the broader market. There are typically three reasons a company will outsource services to a third party firm, regardless of the industry. These are:

1. Services are Not Strategic or Core to the Business – One of the primary reasons companies look for third parties to do specific corporate functions is because the company wants to focus on its core business and doesn't want to invest in the people, process, and technology needed to build the function internally. The ability for a company to build and operate strategic functions in the business and outsource tactical or more commoditized services is a set of decisions that vary by business based on their own unique markets and needs. Some areas of business, like travel, health plan management, and even help desk support for administrative computer users are very common for outsourcing since many companies are very effective at providing the service at a relatively low cost. By outsourcing the function, the company gains the expertise of an entire company and a cost lower than it would likely have if it had done the same level of service itself.

2. The Company has Competency Issues in the Function – Another reason a company may consider outsourcing is that their capabilities in doing the function are not very strong and, based on their own internal analysis, are not likely to get where they need to be without

significant investment or time. Some of these competencies may even be strategic but the company isn't able to rapidly improve the area. It looks to outsource the service to third Parties who can immediately provide more capability and quality of service than the company could provide on its own.

213

3. <u>The Company Cannot Find Enough Talent</u> - A growing reason companies outsource logistics functions is due to talent shortages. Issues with finding and retaining talent in logistics has been an ongoing issue for many years. Truck driver shortages, for instance, have been around for decades. As complexity and the need for automation and integration grows, it becomes more difficult to find all the specialized talent needed to operate a global logistics network. Companies are looking to third parties to help fill their talent gap issues, especially when the talent issues are outside of the core business functions of the business.

4. <u>The Company Values Partnership in the Outsourced Area</u> – While not a traditional reason, some companies are realizing they can outsource different functions either in whole or to add capabilities and capacities on an incremental level. By outsourcing, they may gain specific industry experts in planning, for instance, that can add to the company's capabilities without having to be developed. In today's transportation market, some changes are happening so quickly that companies need additional support and expertise to understand market changes and develop strategies to adapt to them. This is especially true of companies that plan to use outsourcing in their organizations and evaluate suppliers not only for the value they can provide but also for the value added they can bring to the organization.

While there are more reasons companies outsource the four above are the most common and tend to drive the evolution of services and capabilities in the industry. Like most industries, third Party Service Providers (TSPs) provide a large spectrum of services available for clients to outsource. For TSPs, many of these services are well known and are specific to a problem a company is trying to solve. One of the best ways to understand transportation outsourcing and its trends is to understand the problems companies are looking to solve. For most companies, there are five problems that tend to resolve into an outsourcing decision. The five problems are:

1. <u>The Company needs to have a regular set of carriers to move their goods</u> – The most common reason companies outsource is to secure freight carriers. While we may not think of it in these terms, using a third Party carrier is the most basic form of outsourcing in transportation. While a company may contemplate having a small fleet of trucks, depending on its business, it will not build railroads or ships for its own personal use. Using a carrier is so common that many forget that it is a outsourced service.

a. <u>What Function Solves this Problem</u>? For transportation, the transportation carrier within a mode will solve the problem for the customer. There's no magic here. <u>Transportation Carriers</u> have been used for outsourcing transportation moves since the first commercial shipping company went into business. The 2PL, a now archaic term for a carrier, is the most common form of outsourcing in the industry.

2. <u>A Company needs a carrier but can't find one</u> – Another common problem a company may have is their inability to find a carrier when they need one. Companies that are regular shippers establish carrier relationships and contracts. More causal shippers do not. Casual shippers may know of a carrier or two, but they might have availability when needed. Further, any company that needs to expedite a transportation move may not know which carriers can provide the most effective service. Finally, even with established carriers are in place, a company may need a specialized carrier or may be looking for new carriers in places they are not traditionally doing shipping operations.

   a. <u>What Function Solves this Problem</u>? In transportation there is both a function and a specific company business model that acts as a trusted third Party to help customers fulfill loads through carriers. We call this freight Brokerage. A <u>freight broker</u> function is one where a company maintains a large network of carriers and capacity solely to sell that capacity to regular and casual shippers who need to move freight. The operative word in this relationship is trust. The freight broker has specific rules by which it must operate to prove it has independence over carriers and are not sending companies to carriers it owns itself or a carrier that provides any other compensation to the broker beyond the spread between what the broker charges the company versus pays the carrier. Brokers are often invaluable when a carrier is needed for expediting, a hard to tender lane, or for general capacity growth needs. Brokers differ from other outsourcing functions in that they cannot, based on their business model, ever manage freight or be liable for freight. To do so would break the test of independence required to be a broker. It's important to remember that freight broking is both a function and a company type. There are Freight Brokerage companies that specialize in this work and their entire company is focused on brokerage operations. In addition, some freight forwarders may provide a function for brokerage to help their client manage capacity issues. Similarly, many 3PLs have begun independent brokerage operations to help solve more diverse issues for clients and provide support for capacity management when the market has capacity constraints.

3. <u>A company needs help to move goods between two specific locations, often including an international movement</u>. Another issue a company may face may be related to a specific point to point problem difficult to manage. For instance, a company involved in making organic food additives has many customers around the US. During their business, they have developed carrier relationships to move goods between all their domestic factories, distribution centers, and customers. They recently have won an opportunity for a new customer that is global conglomerate operating out of Switzerland. This customer is in Bern Switzerland and allows the company to expand. This is their first European customer and

the only problem is, they have no idea how to ship internationally. As the company looks at the problem, they realize that there's more involved in this transportation movement than in their normal domestic movements including specialized paperwork, documentation, and the timing of shipments. By finding a third Party, they can bridge their lack of knowledge along supported by a partner to enable the loads to move efficiently and consistently.

   a. <u>What Function Solves this Problem</u>? There is a <u>freight forwarding</u> function in outsourcing that is used to solve this problem. Companies that specialize solely on this are called Freight Forwarders and they many specific lanes for customers, virtually all being international. Companies that provide a freight forwarding service provide great flexibility in management a specific lane. Services include freight holding, documentation, customs clearance, and they will arrange for all modes of transportation and use them together to keep your costs low. Freight forwarders can be independent companies and 3PLs can provide these services independently or through outsourcing all logistics operations to them.

4. <u>A Company needs to outsource its entire logistics, including transportation, to a third Party</u>. This could be a company's primary operation, or it could be in a new operation it is growing elsewhere. Regardless of the approach, the company needs a provider than can perform every aspect of the logistics and transportation needed.

   a. <u>What Function Solves this Problem</u>? A 3PL can manage all logistics functions and leverage its existing capabilities in networks, storage, and movement to drive high degrees of efficiency to a company that needs to outsource all its functions. 3PLs are the most comprehensive service provider of all categories of logistics outsourcing. Some 3PL relationships with a client start with providing a comprehensive set of outsourcing services for all operations of the company. More often, however, the relationship doesn't start with a "big bang" but instead the 3PL provides other services, like managing a distribution center, or managing international transportation, or something that is more incremental. Once the company sees the value the 3PL provides they are then more open to outsourcing more services. This progressive nature has helped 3PLs evolve to become more of a "general contractor" for companies seeking to outsource as they can provide a myriad of services themselves and leverage their own partnerships for me reach and capacity when needed.

5. <u>Global Complexity of Logistics Operations Requires A New Dimension of Management</u> – This final area is a relatively new area of transportation and logistics and is still ill defined. Clients experience the need for this service in different ways. For instance, one company may have a few 3PLs that are managing freight operations in different regions of the world.

This would be a large multi-national corporation with global operations across the world. Their operations will be complex, and the company must rely on the 3PLs to work well together. Sometimes, when issues arise, the company can't understand how to solve the problem or even how to identify the accountability in the problem. When this happens, the company may opt to use the services of a third Party to help manage the large number of complex relationships involved in their global operations. The company, in this case would hire expertise in strategic and execution- oriented logistics management and then have that third Party manage all the other third parties. Another scenario that arises is from the small and medium business market. Sometimes, the companies may have regular shipping operations that become more complex than they intend. They need not outsource their logistics as much as have a relationship with an expert that can help advise them on the right relationships, processes, and metrics to use to manage the growing complexity. In this scenario, a company may hire a third party logistics consulting firm to be its expert in logistics planning, in setting up relationships, and in monitoring the performance of the company. This is likely not a full-time position but one that requires specific projects followed by period monitoring. A similar function to the large company issue is needed.

a. <u>What Function Solves this Problem</u>? For these highly complex and highly specialized needs, we look to the <u>4th Generation Logistics Provider, or 4PL</u>. 4PLs are also sometimes called Lead Logistics Providers (LLPs). 4PLs act as a mediator and manager between large complex operations involving many outsourcing parties and work to create a common operation, global transparency, and consistent metrics and hand off processes to eliminate bottlenecks and other issues. Similarly, in a down-market situation, the 4PL acts as a member of staff and as a consultant to provide specific expertise to the company to help augment and manage its existing small logistics staff.

Ultimately, companies outsource functions to third parties with high expectations of the value they will receive. Outsourcing of logistics services, including transportation, continues to be an important option for business. The Council on Supply Chain Management Professionals (CSCMP) conducts an annual third party logistics study that reviews the state of logistics outsourcing. While the study focuses on 3PLs, it captures the broader outsourcing market because 3PLs can provide the entire spectrum out logistics outsourcing functions including transportation carriage, brokerage, forwarding, and 3PL and 4PL services. In the 2019 report [67], 28% of shippers indicated they were looking to insource logistics services suggesting that most shippers continue to look to outsourcing as either a tactical or strategic alternative to doing it themselves.

Companies that outsource can also leverage third parties for their functional capabilities and their automation, visibility, and reporting capabilities. Outsourcing companies, especially

3PLs, will typically have an automation platform that is cloud-based and provides the customer with functional capabilities for areas like visibility and reporting without having to purchase and implement a separate system. This can improve a company's logistics capabilities beyond just functional planning and execution. Factors like these, functional expertise, system capabilities, visibility, reporting, and efficiency, all come together to create the value drivers' companies use to justify the business case for outsourcing.

LOGISTICS SERVICE PROVIDER OPERATIONS

Different transportation services require different approaches and different terms between the shipper and the outsourcing provider. The core of TSP operations is related to the relationship between the function that the outsourcer is providing and its use by the shipper. It also requires an understanding of how the transfer of liability is affected by the outsourcing relationship. Finally, it also is important to understand how the services are priced and how they are paid. Not all transportation services have the same approach. For each area of outsourcing, we will discuss these attributes to better understand the outsourced function:

- What is outsourced – The first things we'll explore is the specific category of need that is outsourced.

- Key Processes Management – We will look at what process or processes are managed by the outsourcer on behalf of the client. The processes we will look at specifically are the contract for carriage, identifying a carrier, the management of a transportation lane, the management of a transportation network, and the management of multiple networks.

- Scope of Services – We'll look at the specific scope of the outsourced service function involved in the outsourcing process. Some scopes are very narrow while other outsourcing functions involve entire lifecycles of the business.

- Liability Transfer – Another important aspect of outsourcing is to understand where liability is transferred as part of the outsourcing function. Liability determines who is accountable for any damage or loss in a shipment and, specifically, who is accountable for filing the insurance claims involved in a loss.

- Delivery Agent / Accountability – We will also look at who delivers the shipment to the destination along with who is specifically accountable to ensure it happens. Sometimes these are the same, other times they are different.

- Freight Audit and Pay – The last area analyzed involves the billing and payment processes. We will specifically look at who bills for the services and that billing. Typically, the billing will be done by the specific provider of the service, but it may also come from the outsourcer involved.

218

Outsourcing Functions and Analysis

In this section, we will discuss the operational aspects of the specific outsourcing function and its impact on the shipper, the outsourcer, and any other third parties involved. We'll cover contract for carrier, shipment brokerage, freight forwarding, 3PL outsourcing, and 4PL outsourcing from these perspectives.

- Contracting for Carriage (Carriers) – The first and most common method of outsourcing is arranging a shipment with a carrier. Regardless of mode, the process is virtually the same although rate structures and other specific aspects of shipping may be very different. Figure 59 shows the analysis of the functions involved in contracting with a carrier for shipments. Although contracting with a carrier directly is a very common practice, we rarely think about all that

What is Outsourced	Key Processes Managed	Scope of Services	Liability Transfer	Delivery Agent / Accountability	Freight Audit and Pay
Carriage	Shipment of Goods	Pickup and Deliver Freight	From Shipper to Carrier to Receiver	Carrier / Carrier	Carrier Bills Shipper

Figure 59. Key Elements of Contracting for Carriage

goes into outsourcing to a carrier. The primary purpose of this outsourcing arrangement is the movement of goods from a point of origin to destination. The scope is specific to the on-time pickup and delivery of the assigned load to the carrier. For the carrier, they will accept liability for the shipment when they receive and sign the bill of lading from the customer. This process makes the carrier responsible for the load while under management by them. As the carrier has the liability, they will also be both the delivery agent and the one accountable for any issues. To complete the process, the carrier bills the shipper directly and requires payment from the shipper.

- Finding a carrier (Brokerage) – A second outsourcing involves using a freight broker to help the shipper find the right carrier. This can be done for expediting, for casual shippers, and for regular shippers wishing to leverage a broker for capacity. Figure 60 shows the specific areas of function and accountability for this outsourcing. The key processes that are done on behalf of the client is the process of understanding the client's need for a shipping movement and then matching that load to an available carrier that is, most likely, close to the pickup location. Brokers are not

What is Outsourced	Key Processes Managed	Scope of Services	Liability Transfer	Delivery Agent / Accountability	Freight Audit and Pay
Brokering Freight	Identification and Acceptance of a Carrier for a Specific Load	Coordinate to secure a carrier on behalf of the client	From Shipper to Carrier to Receiver	Carrier / Carrier	Broker Bills Shipper and Pays Carrier

Figure 60. Key Elements of Brokering

allowed, by business model and regulation, to manage any freight or take on liability for the freight. Because of this, when the broker finds a carrier, they will then coordinate the shipment pickup time and other details. The carrier will then arrive on-time and transferring liability will occur between the shipper and the carrier rather than the broker. The carrier is the agent for the delivery and the broker monitors the delivery and is accountable for the customer satisfaction while the carrier is the accountable party for the shipment delivery. The broker bills the client and includes both the carrier and their fees.

- Managing a Specific Lane (Freight Forwarding) – The third kind of outsourcing involves using a third Party to manage a specific lane for the company. This is often a specialized lane and most often is an international lane. However, there are lanes that could include management of eCommerce orders through parcel that the company separates from their normal transportation lanes and this could be outsourced. Regardless, the critical element of this outsourcing situation is the shipper wanting a third Party to manage a specialized lane. Specialized companies focus solely on freight forwarding. 3PLs also can provide this service. Figure 11-3 shows the specific areas of function and accountability for this outsourcing. The key processes done on behalf of the client are the entire order to delivery lifecycle that includes receiving orders, picking, packing, and shipping

orders, monitoring delivery, and billing. It also usually include managing goods storage depending on the

What is Outsourced	Key Processes Managed	Scope of Services	Liability Transfer	Delivery Agent / Accountability	Freight Audit and Pay
Brokering Freight	Identification and Acceptance of a Carrier for a Specific Load	Coordinate to secure a carrier on behalf of the client	From Shipper to Carrier to Receiver	Carrier / Carrier	Broker Bills Shipper and Pays Carrier

Figure 61. Key Elements of Freight Forward Contracts

situation. The forwarding function is accountable to the shipper for all liability involved in the management and delivery of freight. The forwarder will hold the carrier accountability for delivery and the condition of goods under their management, but it DOES NOT relieve the forwarder of the liability responsibility to the shipper for the entire lifecycle.

- Outsourced Logistics (3PL) – The fourth level of outsourcing involves companies outsourcing their logistics operations to a third Party. Generally, outsourcing logistics to a 3PL involves outsourcing the entire logistics network to them. The level of outsourcing is often related to a specific geography, like Europe, or South America, but it can also cover global operations, or even a specific sub-geography. The critical element is that the outsourcer has full responsibility and accountability for the entire logistics lifecycle of the geography or channel being outsourced. The 3PL firm is the most comprehensive firm when thinking about processes able to be managed and the geographic reach the 3PL can achieve. Figure 62 shows the specific areas of function and accountability for this outsourcing.

The 3PL can provide all logistics services from forward to reverse logistics. Asset based 3PLs, like DB Schenker, will often have their own trucking assets and will manage this. Non-Asset based companies, like C.H. Robinson use third parties and will sub-contract and hold

What is Outsourced	Key Processes Managed	Scope of Services	Liability Transfer	Delivery Agent / Accountability	Freight Audit and Pay
All logistics functions	Entire logistics lifecycle	Order Management, Freight Management, Shipping, Storage, and Billing	Shipper to 3PL (3PL manages liability based on their business model)	3PL	3PL

Figure 62. Key Elements of Contracting for 3PL Services

those subcontractor's liability but, to the shipper, it is always the 3PL with full accountability f or both delivery and liability. It also usually includes managing goods storage depending on the situation. The forwarding function is accountable to the shipper for all liability involved in the management and delivery of freight. The forwarder will hold the carrier accountability for delivery and the condition of goods under their management, but it DOES NOT relieve the forwarder of the liability responsibility to the shipper for the entire lifecycle. They are a one-stop shop for all logistics functions and a single point of accountability for all services provided.

- Manage Multiple Logistics Outsourcers (4PL) – The last and newest form of outsourcing involves using a third Party firm to help manage complex logistical networks with many different outsourcing providers. The 4PL acts as the lead contractor (Lead Logistics Provider, LLP) and manages all contractors in their regular logistics functions. They help to resolve global issues and is the company's ultimate single point of contract for all contract, billing, and logistics discrepancies. This doesn't imply that other logistics providers, liked 3PL or broker functions, are not accessible to the company operationally. Each subcontractor has their operational role and engages with the company in their way. What it does say is for planning, billing, and issue resolution, the 4PL plays the critical role and both represents and drives all other subcontractors. Figure 63 shows the specific areas of function and accountability for this outsourcing. The 4PL has a slightly different role from other Outsourcing situations. We look at the 4PL as a staff function that then oversees the execution of logistics for the company. This makes the 4PL's role   principally planning, oversight of operations, and billing and freight audit. The 4PL doesn't touch the freight but is accountable for all planning, operations, and spend. To do this, they are accountable to the company in all ways and then they transfer the accountability to the execution elements of the logistics network. With claims and other situations, the 4PL will work with the accountable delivery part to ensure claims are put in etc. They will

What is Outsourced	Key Processes Managed	Scope of Services	Liability Transfer	Delivery Agent / Accountability	Freight Audit and Pay
All Logistics Contracting	Planning, Contract Mgt. Execution Oversight, Freight Audit and Pay	Logistics staff functions	From Shipper to 4PL who then delegates accountability to sub-contractors	Sub-Contractor / 4PL	4PL

Figure 63. Key Elements of Contracting for 4PL Services

pay whatever credit is required and then will subrogate to the accountable partner to be reimbursed for the claim they submitted. This is one example of how this firm can work but there are many variations because this form of outsource is relatively new and best practices have not been realized.

Regardless of the outsourcing, the execution and performance of these relations hinges on the understanding of the roles and functions provided by the outsourcer being so performance can be effectively measured and managed. In addition, transferring liability for various functions is important because it affects the ability to submit and have claims paid.

Finally, most outsourcing situations are very effective when the transportation roles are well defined, it is clear who to contact for issues, and the key performance management criteria are transparent and actively managed

LOGISTICS SERVICE PROVIDER OPPORTUNITIES

Outsourcing as an option for business will continue to grow as the advantage of the approach continues to be proven in the market. Overall, the industry is very effective and satisfaction with outsourcing service providers is high. In a recent study on the state of logistics by CSCMP, 91% of 3PL users report they have a successful relationship with their 3PL outsourced provider. Further, 89% indicated that using a 3PL had positively affected their ability to serve their customers [68]. Similar levels of satisfaction are generally found with other areas of outsourcing. There are many emerging opportunities for outsourcing in logistics and for the providers of services. In this section we will explore several of the largest opportunities and trends within the industry.

Generalists Versus Specialists: Where Is the Industry Going?

An important aspect of logistics outsourcing moving forward is the actual makeup of the industry. As little as 10 years ago, there was more distinction between the functions of outsourcing and the roles of those who provide it. Since around 2007, third Party Logistics Providers (3PL) have added capabilities and capacities to become much more functional rather than expecting a company to outsource their entire logistics network.

---

[68] 2019 third Party Logistics Study: The State of Logistics Outsourcing. CSCMP. 2019.

The result has been to pressure certain markets, like freight forwarding and brokerage, that have traditionally had only specialty companies that would offer these services. While this change has not had a significant impact on the industry yet, one would consider that if a 3PL could provide virtually any outsourcing function that, over time, they would become the most dominant outsourcing providers. 3PLs, today, are the key player in the industry but there are still many carriers, brokers, forwarders, etc. all over the world. Will this resolve itself as 3PL's becoming more a general contractor kind of firm or might it be that, twenty years from now, 80% of all outsourcing will be with 3PLs and the other functions will be served by niche players? While the direction is not clear today, we can take lessons from other industries that have gone through similar changes. Often, industries will gravitate overtime to larger and more diversified corporations rather than having a large de-centralized group of specialty companies. This has been true in manufacturing, retail, IT hardware and management, and healthcare. Even with this trend, industries will also have middle market and smaller companies. There is a macro-economic concept called "Barbell-Like" industries and it is likely outsourcing will follow this path. In a barbell-like industry, traditional business models and practices are disrupted by changes in consumer preferences and expectations, new technologies, or disruptive innovation. When this occurs, very large companies have enough leverage and brand to work through industry shift by slowly adapting to the shifts primarily through acquiring the technologies or companies driving the disruption. The enables them to weather the change effectively even though it may cause short term revenue and equity value loss. The adapting companies will ultimately respond to the change and see a return to their previous level and grow beyond. The behavior is like an economic downturn that initially creates a significant impact but, over time, returns to previous levels and grow from there.

Small companies are often the authors of the disruption whether through the develop of new technologies, or by focusing on a small set of practices that then experience innovation into new and more market valuable practices. The result is disruption with rapid market share growth as the new practice takes hold. Small companies can adapt quickly and innovate continuously. The best companies will find their rapid growth enough to sustain them while they capture a market share that grows them. Similarly, these companies will often become targets of strategic acquisitions by large companies that can afford the high multiple.

Many of these acquisitions by large companies become strategic plays where they pickup technology that enables the adaptation to the new model. An example of this was Amazon's purchase of Kiva Systems; a provider of robotic picking in March of 2012 [69]. Before the acquisition, Kiva Systems was the leading provider of robotic picking solutions for warehouses and distribution centers. After Amazon bought them, they took the Kiva products off the market and used them extensively within their own operations while denying other companies the ability to get the growing and expanding technology that was being built inside Amazon. This led to a significant advantage for Amazon in its distribution operations. Kiva systems was a relatively small company and the purchase price of $775M was considered and low price compared to the value it would provide Amazon. This is a normal practice when disruption occurs.

The challenge is the medium sized companies. The medium sized companies do not have the speed and innovative agility of small companies and are normally mainstream to late adopters of technology and innovation. They don't have the size and market brand quality of large companies making them more vulnerable to market shifts, especially related to disruptive market shifts. Because of this, they are squeezed between the speed of small company disruption on their client base and the power and draw of the large company that will take advantage of the disruption to adapt enough to eat into the market share of these companies. This is effectively what has happened to Sears, incorporated. Their size among big-box retailers and others has fallen over the last 20 years as they failed to meet and manage market disruption; especially Omni-Channel Commerce.

The result was a loss of market share, a bloated infrastructure of stores and other assets, and the inability to effectively manage customer expectations in an Omni-Channel Commerce environment. Sears had not had a profitable year since 2010 and in 2018 became insolvent. In January 2019, it received a bail-out offer that the company rejected leaving the company little to no option but to begin the liquidation process. Sears, once the world largest store, suffered from being a middle-sized company in a barbell-like industry. There is likely to be similar changes and disruptions in the outsourcing market over the next decade or two.

Tactical Versus Strategic Outsourcing

Another opportunity, especially for 3PLs involve the functions outsourced. In the 2019 3PL study by CSCMP, they found that the most common areas of outsourcing were Domestic Transportation (81%), International Transportation (71%), Warehousing (69%), Freight Forwarding (50%) and Freight Brokerage (40%). These functions are very common in logistics and transportation and are considered commoditized. So, it makes sense companies would be looking at outsourcing options because it's cheap, and it's common. These are all areas of tactical outsourcing.

Areas that are more strategic, like transportation planning, reverse logistics, service parts logistics, 4PL, and others are more strategic and therefore more valuable to the client than tactical services. When this occurs, we think of the resulting relationship as "stickier" than when a client outsources something that is tactical. As the market evolves, companies that show value through these more strategic outsourcing approaches will find their ability to gain market share and differentiate to be strong than those that do not. Some of these advanced services could disrupt the outsourcing industry because of the lack of others to provide them. This could cause accelerating the barbell-like industry concept discussed.

Leveraging and Expanding Logistics Technology

Technology is at the core of effective logistics management today. Today, supply chains have become both complex and fast to adapt to customer preferences. International shipping through eCommerce has become one of the fastest growing segments that also has its own level of complexities. The adoption of advanced technologies in Omni-Channel Commerce, transportation management, supply chain visibility and even warehouse management create new dimensions of efficiency and differentiation in logistics outsourcing services. Better integration layers within these application domains allow outsources to provide deep integration between their services and their customers. This enables better transparency for things like visibility, cost management, and performance. When executed well, increased visibility, improved cost management and performance demonstrate to the outsourcing client the value the outsourcer provides which also makes the relationship stickier. Further, companies that don't seek to effectively drive efficiencies into their offerings through technology will find their pricing to become more expensive than their competitors ultimately pricing themselves out of the market.

Technology adoption as a core competence of outsourced logistics services providers will become a strong potential differentiator for outsourcing companies especially when the outsourcer can provide value through their platform by adding capabilities themselves. Staying ahead of the client on technology creates a compelling business case to use outsourcing if for nothing else than the market lag of acquiring and implementing technology in their own environments. Logistics Services Providers that can differentiate on technology can provide their customers "leaps" without having to purchase that technology themselves rather than "steps" toward an effective solution.

Enabling Co-Opetition to Reduce Client Costs

Outsourcing services like transportation and warehousing also provides new opportunities to leverage consolidated volume, lanes, and other synergies to reduce the cost of services. To do this, outsourcers need to look at their total volume and capacity without a specific regard to the customer. From one perspective, freight is freight and if the outsourcer can reduce the total cost of the service by consolidating freight from multiple customers, it makes sense to do so because the cost savings will have a positive impact on the client's operational costs. From another, there is the question as to the impact of co-mingling freight among companies that would be competitors. Regardless of the perspective today, multi-vendor consolidation, or the mingling of volumes of freight from multiple outsourcing customers to reduce the total costs of transportation and warehousing service will have long term implications on the industry. Today, most of this related to warehouse movements and warehouse to distribution movements, but there is much more opportunity for outsourcing clients to leverage co-opetition. Consider these two additional examples:

- <u>Consolidated Freight Brokering</u> – As capacity for trucking continues to be constrained, there is natural competition for companies in terms of pricing and availability for load movement. Manufacturers that need to move product to intermediate distribution centers, or even to specific regional distribution centers often find they have assets or storage points in similar geographies. If these companies work together, they can leverage their combined volume with freight brokers to get better priority, better pricing, and better service.

- <u>Sharing Warehouse Space</u> – Some companies have a regular requirement for warehousing space that is volume specific. Other companies have needs that adjust due to seasonality, specific activities (like product end of life or returns) or other factors. Customers that use third Party warehousing for storage, inventory management and transportation do not have the visibility into the capacity and use of the warehouse environment. Outsources can evaluate client needs with leveraging seasonal client's lack of capacity needs to support other client's additional storage need. This virtual space management could provide new dimensions of value to both clients and cost savings.

The Logistics Outsourcing Industry is a large part of the entire logistics market. Outsourcing as an alternative to building a complex logistics function has strong potential to provide value from cost savings and superior service. When evaluating the industry, we find the outsourcing has a strong track record of success and efficacy for the industry. Managing disruption, expanding into new services and market, and leveraging new practices and approach to driving customer value and satisfaction are key drivers to the continued growth of the industry.

CHAPTER 12: TRANSPORTATION NETWORKS

INTRODUCTION

When we think about networks, we often think about the interconnectivity between many things that allow us to effectively go from any point to another. The Internet, for instance, is a global network that connects users to various organizations that include different entities based on their addresses, or type of organization. Any user can virtually go to any other site directly on their own if they know the address. This a network, called a mesh network, is excellent for some situations and inefficient in other situations.

As we look at transportation networks, one of the most important aspects of the design of the network is efficiency. Efficiency changes based on the situation and need within the network. In this chapter, we'll explore transportation networks, understand their components, and how we use the networks to meet load movement requirements. We'll also look at network optimization and areas where we can drive efficiency in the network through these optimization techniques.

TRANSPORTATION NETWORKS: COMPONENTS AND USAGE

We'll look at transportation networks by understanding the two key terms that drive their development. This includes the components and terminology of a typical transportation network. At the most basic level, a transportation network comprises two locations serviced by transportation assets. When we combine two locations and provide transit between them, we call this a transportation lane. A transportation lane is the foundation of a transportation network. In transportation networks, one node will belong to the shipper of goods and the other will be receiver of goods. Figure 64 shows an example of this construct. Location A is the shipper of goods. This could be a manufacturing facility, a distribution center, or even a warehouse. Location B is the receiver of the goods. This could also manufacture facility, a distribution center,

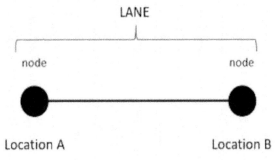

Figure 64. A Transportation Lane

or even a warehouse. In a transportation network, each lane has a purpose and stands alone. Transportation lanes are planning functions in networks. Once established, the execution of the network is governed by the transportation route. The transportation route (second term) is the actual driving directions used to move through the lane between Location A and Location B. The route is governed by compliance requirements that the carrier must observe or there will be penalties involved in the shipping costs. Typical compliance for trucking will include things like the requirement to use interstates when available, avoiding tolls, the time a carrier may wait at a node before they can charge time for the wait, and more.

Analyzing Network Requirements and Creating Transportation Networks

To develop an effective transportation network requires those developing the network to understand first the requirements and needs of various locations that may become part of the network and their associated destinations. Network analysis starts with understanding the demands and volumes for shipments from shipping nodes and the demand and volumes of from each shipping node to a destination node. To understand this, let's consider a hypothetical network. SunLove Soda is a soda manufacturer with a proprietary blend of soda that includes juices and carbonation along with other ingredients to create its products. Its first plant was in Jacksonville Florida and it has since expanded with a plant in Birmingham Alabama. The flagship product, SunUp soda became very popular in the south and the company used this popularity to build its company. It has since followed up with two additional soda offerings, Diet SunUp and SunDown; a new soda. Its most mature distribution is in the Southeast US and it has expanded into the Midwest with a plant in Dayton, Ohio and to the Atlantic Coast with a plant in Harrisburg Pennsylvania. Each plant have specific distribution clients that are grocery wholesalers who distribution to grocery chains that have picked up the company's products. Each plant is also occasionally will ship product to a peer plant in the network where there is shortage of product or a production problem that requires soda to be moved from another plant to cover capacity needs. In those instances, the other plants will increase production for a short time, and, in extreme circumstances, all the available plants will ship to the plant with the issue although it is more common for the closest plant to increase production to cover the problem. In these instances, the product is moved to the plant rather than the customer for continuity.

Figure 65 shows the current plant locations and the wholesale distribution customer locations and volumes. To build the network, we need to look at the shipper and receiver locations. We have volume captured as total pallets to be delivered per year. From this number, we then estimate the number of truckloads per week that need to be delivered. In terms of truckloads, any truckload of one or less is delivered once per week and those that are above 1, are delivered twice per week.

When looking at the data, we see, for instance, that the Jacksonville, FL plant will produce 27,500 pallets of soda per year and will distribute those to seven distributor locations. We also see in the last column which shows the number of truckloads we have per week that both Tampa and

City	State	Node Purpose	Node Type	Annual Pallet	Truckloads	Delivery Day(s)
Dayton	OH	Distribution	Shipping	12,500		
Columbus	OH	Customer Distribution	Receiving	2,500	1.00	Monday
Toledo	OH	Customer Distribution	Receiving	1,250	0.50	Tuesday
Richmond	IN	Customer Distribution	Receiving	1,250	0.50	Tuesday
Indianapolis	IN	Customer Distribution	Receiving	2,500	1.00	Monday
Cincinnati	OH	Customer Distribution	Receiving	2,500	1.00	Thursday
Cleveland	OH	Customer Distribution	Receiving	2,500	1.00	Thursday
Harrisburg	PA	Distribution	Shipping	12,500		
Pittsburgh	PA	Customer Distribution	Receiving	2,500	1.00	Monday
Buffalo	NY	Customer Distribution	Receiving	2,500	1.00	Tuesday
Philadelphia	PA	Customer Distribution	Receiving	5,000	2.00	Mon / Wed
Baltimore	MD	Customer Distribution	Receiving	1,250	0.50	Thursday
Arlington	VA	Customer Distribution	Receiving	1,250	0.50	Thursday
Birmingham	AL	Distribution	Shipping	22,500		
Mobile	AL	Customer Distribution	Receiving	1,250	0.50	Tuesday
Montgomery	AL	Customer Distribution	Receiving	1,250	0.50	Tuesday
Tuscaloosa	AL	Customer Distribution	Receiving	2,500	1.00	Monday
Altanta	GA	Customer Distribution	Receiving	5,000	2.00	Mon / Thur
Macon	GA	Customer Distribution	Receiving	2,500	1.00	Monday
Jackson	MS	Customer Distribution	Receiving	1,250	0.50	Thursday
Knoxville	TN	Customer Distribution	Receiving	2,500	1.00	Wednesday
Memphis	TN	Customer Distribution	Receiving	1,250	0.50	Thursday
Nashville	TN	Customer Distribution	Receiving	5,000	2.00	Wed / Fri
Jacksonville	FL	Distribution	Shipping	27,500		
Miami	FL	Customer Distribution	Receiving	5,000	2.00	Mon. / Thur
Tampa	FL	Customer Distribution	Receiving	3,750	1.50	Tues / Thur
Gainesville	FL	Customer Distribution	Receiving	3,750	1.50	Mon / Wed
Pensacola	FL	Customer Distribution	Receiving	2,500	1.00	Tuesday
Greenville	SC	Customer Distribution	Receiving	2,500	1.00	Friday
Charlotte	NC	Customer Distribution	Receiving	5,000	2.00	Monday
Raleigh-Durham	NC	Customer Distribution	Receiving	5,000	2.00	Thursday

Figure 65. Soda Plants, Destinations and Volumes

Gainesville have 1 and ½ trucks to be delivered per week. This means that one delivery will be a truckload and the second will be an LTL load. We don't want to send ¾ of a truckload twice because this will probably result in two LTL loads rather than one which would be more expensive. Let's build the Jacksonville node transportation network. To begin, we simply create the lands between Jacksonville and their delivery locations. Figure 12-3 shows the resulting network.

When looking at it what does it look like to you? Some will say a spider's web; others may say a spider with many legs. In terms of transportation networks, this is one of the most common constructs we have. We call is a Hub and Spoke construct. In a Hub and Spoke configuration, the network has a central hub from which all products flow to many destinations. This is a very efficient kind of network construct with one drawback.

With Figure 66, there is one hub with a direct connection to every spoke without regard for volume. That means any Hub and Spoke lane without a full truck running to the destination will cause an LTL load which will be more expensive than a TL load. This will mean that any lanes with LTL will have a higher unit cost per unit of soda than those that are not LTL. We'll talk more about this when we discuss optimization. Now that we have identified the transportation lanes, we need to consider capacity. We assume we can fit forty-eight pallets into a full truck. This would require 48 foot trucks which is good because they are normally easy to get. We could also look at 53 foot trucks, but this will add only four more pallets and it doesn't change our needs. 48 foot trailers would be optimal for our situation. Looking at Volumes, we see that the weekly requirement for total truckloads is ten truckloads which includes two LTL loads. How many trucks will that require to haul the goods? An obvious answer is ten and as that is the capacity requirements of the network.

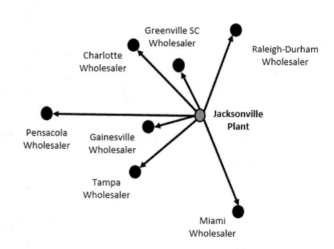

Figure 66. Jacksonville, FL Plant Soda Network

While carriers must maintain rolling assets to support any lane developed, these assets must be available for the expected delivery days. Given this, a carrier working with us for say the Jacksonville, to Miami lane must plan to allocate the required trucks to us for our delivery days. We see in Figure 67 under delivery days that means we require a truck to be available on Mondays and Thursdays to go from Jacksonville FL to Miami FL. We don't' care if there is a truck on other days for

City	M	T	W	TH	F	Total
Miami	1			1		2
Tampa		1		1		2
Gainesville	1		1			2
Pensacola		1				1
Greenville					1	1
Charlotte	1					1
Raleigh-Durham				1		1
Totals	3	2	1	3	1	10

Figure 67. Truck Requirements Based on Delivery Day

routine shipments meaning the carrier will have that rolling asset available for another customer as needed. Figure 67 displays the actual number of trucks per day required. The most trucks required on any given day is three rather than ten because of the way the deliveries are configured. Just by staggering the delivery days we can reduce the total required per day which makes it easier to manage the capacity. The one downside of this network is that both Tampa and Gainesville have one day a week where there is a need to deliver ½ of a truck. These routes will be LTL on their respective days and will add cost to the network.

Ultimately, we have four Hub and Spoke networks within the network (Figure 68). One out of Jacksonville that we've completed, one out of Birmingham, AL, one out of Dayton, OH PA. The only interaction we expect is between the manufacturing facilities for cross- leveling stock when needed. We can also look closer at the partial loads to see if there is a way to reduce the number of LTL loads by consolidating them to TL truckloads. In our case, we will concentrate on Toledo Ohio and Richmond Indiana in the Dayton plant's network, and Baltimore Maryland and Arlington, VA in the Harrisburg plant's network. In Birmingham's network we have two areas of LTL. The first is specific to Montgomery and Mobile Alabama which only require ½ truckload each per week. There is also Memphis, Tennessee and Jackson Mississippi that also require only ½ truckload per week. Finally, in the Jacksonville Florida network we have Tampa and Gainesville which have one full truckload delivery each and require ½ truckload to these cities in the later part of the week.

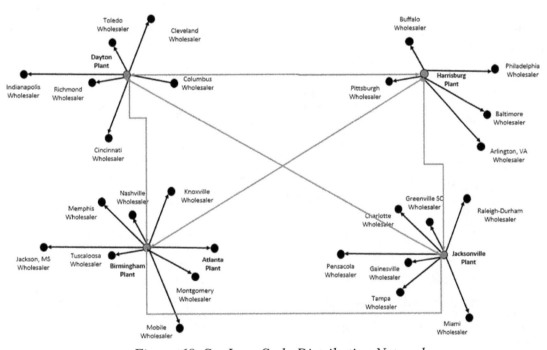

Figure 68. SunLove Soda Distribution Network

Our goal with these specific lanes is to look at the locations to determine if we could consolidate the loads into one coordinated transportation movement. If we can do this, then we can eliminate one lane by combining the two cities into a single lane. With Florida, there would be two lanes on one day per week when delivering full truckloads and a consolidated lane on the other that uses one truck to delivery both ½ loads in sequence. To do this, we need to ensure:

1. The loads we wish to consolidate are run on the same day

231

2. The consolidation of the loads will not exceed the maximum capacity of the trailer for both volume and weight. With our 48-foot trailer, we must ensure the loads do not exceed 48 pallets and 42,000 pounds. If they do, however, we can also increase our trailer size to a 53 foot trailer which will carry 54 pallets and 48,000 pounds based on the carrier information for that trailer and the expected weight of the tractor and trailer. If either the pallet count or weight is exceeded or if the loads are delivered on different days, then they cannot be consolidated. In addition, if any consolidated lane exceeds 10 hours of driving time exceeds 11 hours, it likely cannot be consolidated unless we recognize that the lane will take more than one day to accomplish. This is not a specific constraint but if there are delivery constraints that don't allow the transit time required the lane may not be consolidated.

Given this, let's analyze each lane to see if we can achieve this. Figure 69 shows the data for analysis of these lanes. For each lane, we have the pallet count and weight of the load at the count. We also show the days of delivery for the partial loads. As we can see, there are several opportunities to consolidate lanes and create more efficiency. In the Dayton, Ohio plant's network, when combined, the Toledo – Richmond Indiana lane is below the forty-eight pallet and 42,000 pound limits and the delivery days are aligned.

Lane Information		Location 1 Pallets, Weight, Delivery Day		Location 1 Pallets, Weight, Delivery Day		Final Analysis	
Primary Lane	Potential Lanes for Consolidation	Pallets	Weight	Pallets	Weight	Pallets < 48	Weight < 42,000
Dayton	Toledo - Richman	28	16,800	18	10,800	46	27,600
Harrisburg	Baltimore-Arlington	24	14,400	24	14,000	48	28,400
Birmingham	Montgomery-Mobile	24	14,400	24	14,000	48	28,400
Birmingham	Jackson - Memphis	32	19,200	22	13,200	54	32,400
Jacksonville	Gainesville-Tampa	32	19,200	28	16,800	60	36,000

Figure 69. Lane Analysis Results for Consolidation Potential

This enables us to consolidate the land by combining both locations into one lane and with a single truck delivery. As we look at Figure 69 this is also true for the Baltimore-Arlington, and the Montgomery-Mobile. In these situations, we can use the existing 48 foot trailer because we do not exceed the forty-eight pallets and 42,000 pounds. Notice that for the Jackson-Memphis lane, notice that the weight is below the 42,000 pound requirement but our pallet count has climbed to fifty-four. The good news here is that we can still consolidate the lane. To do so, we will need to increase the trailer size to a 53 foot trailer as this trailer allows us 54 pallets. Weight is not a concern.

In the last example, Gainesville to Tampa, they also have a potential to consolidate. When we look at it closely, we run into sixty pallets. The 53 foot trailer gives us 54 pallets, but no larger piece of equipment can accommodate sixty pallets.

In addition, the delivery days contradict Gainesville being delivered on Thursday and Tampa on Wednesday. If the pallet count and weight indicated we could consolidate the load, our next step would be to talk to each customer and see if we could move either Gainesville to Wednesday or Tampa to Thursday. Here, there's no reason to broach the subject as we couldn't create a consolidated lane even if we did have the delivery date. The result of this will be a higher cost for the Gainesville and Tampa lanes respectively.

The final network that results has several areas of lane consolidation that results in a more efficient transportation network for those lanes with LTLs now consolidated to full truckloads that will go to multiple destinations but still within the same day of driving. Figure 707 shows the final lane configuration (boxes are shown for the consolidated lanes). The network doesn't look that different from our original but there is new levels of value by making these changes.

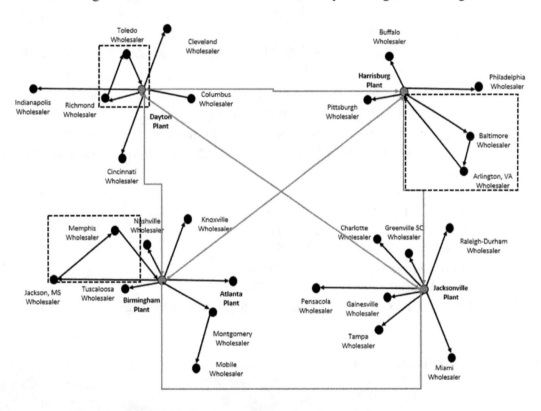

Figure 70. SunLove Soda after Consolidation

How much value do we derive from the lanes we can consolidate? This depends on the mechanics of each lane. Let's take the Dayton lanes (Dayton-Toledo and Dayton-Richmond, IN). In a consolidated lane, we will have one truck and one set of charges as a full truckload. At current contract rates this rate would be something on the order of about $2.00 per mile. Without consolidation, each lane would be an LTL lane that would include a higher fuel surcharge and a higher rate around $2.25 at a minimum. We can derive the results by computing the LTL costs for each lane at $2.25 per mile plus a 20% fuel surcharge. This must be applied to both the Toledo and the Richmond lanes individually and then added together to get the total transportation costs:

- LTL Costs for the Richmond IN and Toledo OH Lanes:
  - Dayton to Richmond Indiana:
    - *Richmond lane Cost = 96 Miles (Round Trip) * 2.25 per mile + 20% Fuel Surcharge = $259.20*
  - Dayton to Toledo Ohio:
    - *Toledo lane Cost = 300 Miles (Round Trip) * 2.25 per mile + 20% Fuel Surcharge = $810.00*
  - Total of All lane Costs:
    - *Total Cost for Both Lanes = 1,069.20*
- TL Costs for a Dayton to Richmond, IN to Toledo Ohio and Roundtrip lane:
  - Total lane Cost = *379 Miles (Round Trip) *2.00 per mile + 15% Fuel Surcharge = $921.71*
- Cost Comparison:
  - LTL Total Cost = $ 1,069.20; less
  - TL Total Cost = $ 817.71
  - Consolidate Savings: $ 197.50
  - **Annual Savings:**   **$ 10,2,70.00**
  - **Total Annual Cost**   **$47,929.00**
  - **Savings Percent:**   **18.42% transportation savings**

Upstream and Downstream Networks

In our example of SunLove Soda, we have analyzed the downstream network to say the network that goes from the manufacturing point to the consumer. This is half of a typical network for the supply chain. The other half, the upstream network goes from the raw material supplier to the manufacturer.

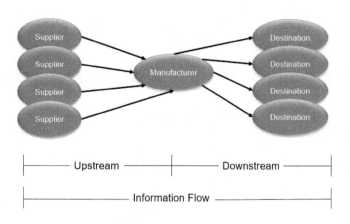

Figure 72. Up and Downstream Networks

234

One of the important elements of the modern transportation network is the flow of information and supply chain visibility (in-transit status, visual location on a map, adjusted estimated delivery time based on current location and speed, etc.). Figure 72 shows a simple example of this construct which shows the upstream, downstream, and information flow we experience in transportation networks.

OPTIMIZING TRANSPORATION NETWORKS

In our example with SunLove Soda, we applied lane consolidation to drive more efficiency and reduced cost. This is one level of consolidation but there are many others. In this section, we'll discuss the approaches commonly used to optimize transportation networks. In looking at the supply chain and the approach to creating effective and efficient networks, there are strategic approaches to consolidation and tactical approaches. Strategic approaches to optimizing the network are a one time, or a periodic approach to optimization where tactical approaches are made based on the context of the transportation execution that could be based on order volumes, surcharges, or other execution factors that drive specific load or route decisions.

STRATEGIC OPPORTUNITIES FOR TRANSPORTATON OPTIMIZATION

There are several ways we can make a network more optimized and the first factors are strategic, and we have one opportunity to decide and then we develop the network based on the decisions as both synergy and constraint. The core strategic decisions are:.

- Placement of Facilities – Where we place our facilities is a trade-off between the company's supply chain strategy (centralized, decentralized, distributed, etc.), the distances from manufacturing to suppliers and from the manufacturer to the customer markets, the cost of ownership of facilities, availability of labor, and other factors. Facility placement does consider transportation at a high level, but it is not the primary factor in making these decisions. Locations of market, production strategy (Just-In-Time versus Make-to-Stock, for instance), the amount of carried inventory and inventory levels, labor, access to major roads, ports, etc. and other factors will lead the organization to decide for their facility needs. Once defined, the transportation network uses these locations as constraints in the supply chain as the network must conform to the locations needed to be served and as synergy as effective placement of facilities, especially in a geographic sense will help to create opportunities for efficient network development if it results in supplier clustering (situations where the suppliers are located close to each other), and if there are opportunities like cross docking and other approaches to make transportation more efficient by keeping goods moving rather than being stored or at rest.

- Supplier Sourcing – A second strategic area are the decisions related to supplier sourcing. Supplier sourcing decisions are most often made based on the viability of the supplier, the material quality and ability to meet manufacturing specifications and the ability of the supplier to consistently deliver quality goods not rejected to the manufacturing facility. Consistency of supply and consistency of delivery of these goods are critical to an effective production environment.

Sourcing decisions should also be made based on the production environment, transportation network and ultimately transportation costs. For transportation needs, the best suppliers for Make-to-Stock (MTS), can be at almost any distance from the factory without causing challenges. This is because MTS does not require the speed and flexibility of JIT and will typically use slower modes, like rail or even inland river boats. Goods are moved in bulk and therefore deliveries are done when still a good amount of inventory be held. This reduces delivery risk and transportation costs due to the slower modes. It does result in increased costs of facilities like warehousing and high inventory carrying costs.

For the JIT environment, it's important that suppliers are relatively close to the factory and preferably within no more than five hours of the facility. This allows deliveries to be made daily with the carrier picking up and deliver in the same day resulting in the carrier's drivers being at home regularly. This speed is an important trait of JIT as it will often only hold a few days to maybe a week of inventory. JIT suppliers longer than a two or three days transit time will experience a break in the model and be required to hold extra inventory as safety stock. As most JIT environments are only the production facility, holding extra stock takes up valuable production space or causes the company to have an additional facility to manage the distance. We'll discuss this in more detail in Chapter 14: Transportation in Manufacturing.

- Using logistics facilities to manage speed and distance – A third consideration is a variation on facility placement. Here, we want to know what kind of facilities are in the logistics network that may affect our speed and flexibility in delivery. We'll use Figure 73 to illustrate this. The top

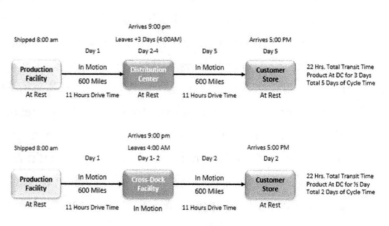

Figure 73. Use of Cross-Docking to Speed up Transportation

of the figure as based on an MTS based production and distribution mode. Moving goods

236

from the factory to a warehouse or distribution center allows a storage space for MTS goods made in bulk and sold over 90 days. In our illustration, we see the g oods are 600 miles from the distribution center which takes one day of transit. The goods are then stored in a distribution center and are ordered and picked three days after they arrive. In an MTS model, this could be a few days to months. Warehousing and distribution do allow goods to remain at rest. These goods will be regularly counted to ensure accurate inventory and will usually use a "First In / Last Out" inventory strategy so the oldest items are shipped before the newer ones that have come in. This means a warehouse or distribution center that carries 90 days of inventory will have the goods sitting at rest for 90 days before they are moved.

Compare this with the JIT model and we find a very different approach. Here, we have the goods leaving simultaneously but instead of a warehouse or distribution center, we apply a cross docking facility which provides a break-bulk sortation and consolidation capability and the goods spend about 6 to 8 hours there and then continue. This not only speeds up the transportation cycle time, it also allows for continue movement of goods. In this scenario, it takes about 11 hours of driving time to go 600 miles. In both instances, the driver moving the goods to the intermediate facility will have met their total daily driving requirements and will require a rest period.

By using the cross dock, we can move the goods toward their final location by sorting and combining the load with other loads moving in the same direction. When the goods are loaded after the 6 to 8 hours cross dock process, a new driver that has a fresh set of daily hours will take the load. This allows the load to move 22 hours in less than 30 hours of elapsed time. This is something that couldn't happen unless the goods were switched. So, the cross dock facility allows continuous movement with only a few hours of delay versus being received, stored, put-away and then picked, packed and shipped in the MTS model.

TACTICAL OPPORTUNITIES FOR TRANSPORTATION OPTIMIZATION

Besides the opportunities to strategically leverage facility placement and use to create a flexible and fast, or slower and more cost efficient network, there are several ongoing opportunities based on the situation, orders, loads, etc. that also help to driver efficiency and effectiveness in the transportation network. In this section, we'll explore each of these from macro to micro opportunities.

- Mode Selection – Within tactical execution, the first major decision and opportunity is the choice of the mode for the transportation. As we've seen, the average ton-mile cost of various transportation modes create opportunity for reduced cost of transportation. For instance, replacing truck transport with intermodal rail transport can have a significant impact on the cost of transportation when we look at truck ton-mile cost in the 17 – 19 cents per ton-mile compared to intermodal rail that would be 4 to 6 cents per ton- mile. The differences in cost can be startling and lead to significant transportation costs if the most effective mode is not chosen. Let's consider the following problem:

o Mosaic Grains is a large grain cooperative in Ames Iowa. They have a large contract with the government of Nigeria to deliver four deliveries of grain per year. Each delivery requires the movement of 24,000 tons of grain, or 48 million pounds of grain. The deliveries are scheduled at the beginning of each quarter with the first quarter delivery being 6,000 tons, the second quarter delivery is 8,000 tons, the third quarter delivery requiring 8,000 tons and 4th quarter delivery being 2,000. The goods must be at the Port of Galveston, TX, by January 10, April 10 July 9, and October 15 of this year. The company is look at different options for transportation because the last harvest of grain for the year ends on September 30th or October first and the CO-OP is concerned about load times to meet the port schedule. It takes about 6 hours to load 2,000 tons of grain on average because the co-op has an older delivery system slower than more modern systems. The company had an intern calculate rail and truck schedules for transportation to determine when the grain had to be loaded, based on the mode, to meet deadlines. The intern worked with their primary rail company and trucking company to do this. Figure 74 shows the preliminary scheduling from a pickup and delivery date, equipment availability and general weight constraints. Looking at this, the team determined that both truck and rail were feasible from a schedule perspective. The October third date would require the harvest operations to be done by the second of October. They is concern that if the date slips, they won't be able

		Truck				Rail				
	Execution	Pickup Date	Delivery Date	Equipment	Weight Capacity	Pickup Date	Delivery Date	Tons To Deliver	Equipment	Weight Capacity
	January	7-Jan	9-Jan	Tri-Axle Super Hopper	50,000	4-Jan	9-Jan	6,000	6,500 Cu Ft. Covered Hopper	286,000
	April	8-Apr	10-Apr			5-Apr	10-Apr	8,000		
	June	7-Jul	10-Jul			5-Jul	10-Jul	8,000		
	October	7-Oct	9-Oct			3-Oct	9-Oct	2,000		

Figure 74. Schedule Analysis of Grain Movement with Truck

to meet the October delivery deadline. The other lanes, however, appear to have no problem with running rail and since it will be the cheapest, John Birch, the co-op manager, asked the intern to go back and price rail for all four- quarters of delivery and to price truck just for the October delivery so they would have a carrier and a cost for a pickup on the 7th of October if they could not use rail. The intern put hypothetical orders into the planning portion of their TMS and then sent them to get quotes from rail for the January, April, June, and October loads.

238

In addition, the created an order for October for truck and sent it out to the TMS network to get the most competitive price. They felt this would be good enough for the planning cycle. Figure 75 shows the results of the rating cost by quarter.

The costs that result underscore the value of rail for moving large amounts of bulk items when flexibility and timing are not an issue. Similarly, the cost for the truck lane as a contingency enables the speed and flexibility of transportation but not the bulk movement as it will take eighty trucks to move 2,000 tons of grain versus 14 rail cars. The resulting cost, if required, is almost six times more expensive than rail. There's no question that the co-op manager will be watching the final harvest of the year intently to ensure all the grain is completed by the time the rail cars need to be loaded. A delay in schedule will be a very costly delay.

| Execution | Mileage Rate | Rail | | Equipment | Weight Capacity | Order Amount (Tons) | Number of Rail Cars | Rail Miles Per Car | Base Freight Rate | Fuel Surcharge | Other Fees / International Shipment | Total Order Cost | Cost / Rail Car |
		Pickup Date	Delivery Date										
January	1.78	4-Jan	9-Jan	6,500 Cu Ft. Covered Hopper	286,000	6,000	42	1,480	$110,645	$ 12,171	$ 3,319	$ 126,135	$3,003.22
April	1.78	5-Apr	10-Apr			8,000	56	1,480	$147,526	$ 16,228	$ 4,426	$ 168,180	$3,003.22
June	1.78	5-Jul	10-Jul			8,000	56	1,480	$147,526	$ 16,228	$ 4,426	$ 168,180	$3,003.22
October	1.78	3-Oct	9-Oct			2,000	14	1,480	$ 36,882	$ 4,057	$ 1,106	$ 42,045	$3,003.22

| Execution | Mileage Rate | Truck | | Equipment | Weight Capacity | Order Amount (Tons) | Number of Trucks | Miles Charged / Truck | Base Freight Rate | Fuel Surcharge | Border Surcharge | Total Order Cost | Cost / Truck |
		Pickup Date	Delivery Date										
January	$ 2.52			Tri-Axle Super Hopper	50,000								
April	$ 2.42												
June	$ 2.55												
October	$ 2.48	7-Oct	9-Oct			2,000	80	1,036	$205,542	$ 34,942	$ 10,277	$ 250,762	$3,134.52

Figure 75. Schedule Analysis of Grain Movement with Truck versus Rail

- Load Optimization – Another tactical opportunity is load optimization. Load optimization is accomplished in different ways and have varying amounts of value. In the SunLove Soda example, one way we accomplish load optimization is by combining various LTL loads into full truckloads. LTL to TL consolidation has the largest area of saving in load management. As we saw, we consolidated a lane that also required a load optimization by converting two LTL loads into one TL load. Here, it took both a lane structure and load structure change to complete this. But this isn't always the case. Besides the lane structure, there are also a few other ways we can look to convert LTL loads to TL loads as part of load optimization including:

  o Delivery Schedule Changes – The more we schedule deliveries of small loads to support JIT, for instance, the higher transportation costs become because the schedule is driven not by the goal to reduce transportation costs but to reduce inventory and carrying costs. To meet this desire and still enable load optimization using a model called a Milk Run which we'll discuss more in the Transportation in Manufacturing chapter.

A milk run is a lane used primarily in just-in-time (lean) manufacturing. It provides a single flat rate for a supplier to manufacturer inbound raw material lane. The price is "all-in" unless the carrier specifies a charge. If there is an additional surcharge it is most often a multi-stop surcharge for a milk run with multiple suppliers where the carrier charges for each additional stop after the first supplier. To illustrate this consolidation, let's start by looking at a customer being charged $350.00 per milk run and the daily milk run is delivering an LTL load that fills 45% of the trailer. If the receiver agrees to allow TL consolidation for as many of the five days as adjusted, we could go to a Monday, Wednesday, and Friday delivery to meet their needs where the Monday / Wednesday deliveries would be TL at $350 per run and an LTL delivery on Friday for $350.

While the Friday delivery is still sub-optimized from a load perspective, the resulting savings per week would be $700 by eliminating two days of runs. That would cause over $36,000 in annual savings.

o   <u>Multi-Vendor Consolidation</u> – Another method that leverages small loads that can be optimized into single TL loads involves multi-vendor consolidation. Multi-vendor consolidation occurs when multiple vendors need to deliver to the same place and the vendors are relatively close to each other geographically. This could be that they are less than an hour apart in location or that the lane construct is so one supplier is father away and the second supplier is part of the route used by the first supplier so a truck can stop along the way and add to the load. Regardless of the locations, we find that the following all must be true to enable this load consolidation:

- The loads, when combined, must be equal to a full truckload or less

- The locations must be part of the same lane

- The load schedules must be in sync, i.e. the must deliver on the same day

- The lane, including picking up the first load and the wait time to pick up the second load along with the total driving time must be less than the Hours of Service regulations which is 11 hours of driving and 14 hours of total operating time including any wait times or delays.

When the above are true and we consolidated the load, the driver's behaviors in the lane will change slightly. First, they will pick up the trailer from the first supplier who will have loaded the trailer before they arrive. They will typically carry an empty trailer from a yard not far from the supplier. The driver will check in at any required security gate and then pick up the trailer by talking with the shipping team at the factory.

The shipping team will direct the driver where to drop the empty trailer and which trailer in the yard to take with them. The driver will then drop the trailer in the spot specified and then hook up the partially full trailer and proceed on their route. We often call this pick up a "Drop and Hook". The driver will then proceed to the second supplier where they will check in at the security gate and then proceed to the factory. Once there, they will talk to the shipping team which will tell them which loading pay to back into. Once they are at the loading bay (loading door), they will then wait while the shipping team loads the trailer. It wasn't possible for them to preload the trailer because the trailer from the first supplier is used to load the second suppler. Once the load is complete, they will then proceed to the destination.

This load is often called a "Live-load" because the driver must wait while the trailer is loaded. We have a similar construct when a driver's full trailer only needs to be unloaded partially at a destination site. This is called a "Live Unload". When complete, the driver will then proceed to the destination and will likely perform another drop and hook with the factoring having an empty trailer that needs to be returned to the carrier.

By applying this technique, the shipments can be reduced in half due to the consolidation although there will be some additional surcharges for the multiple stops and, depending on distance, partial LTL fees for the first leg when the trailer is only partially full. Regardless, shippers that enable multi-vendor consolidation will typically experience savings of about 40% of the previous lane transportation costs so savings are significant.

- Route Optimization – Remember that a lane is a planning construct and the route is the actual driving directions used by the carrier to comply with any requirements in transiting the lane. Route Optimization is primarily about route compliance factors used to reduce the cost of a transportation route. compliance criteria are part of the transportation contract and require the driver to conform to certain rules when doing the lane route.

It's important to understand these requirements are set by the party paying for the transportation. Besides any contractual compliance requirements, various states may also have route compliance requirements especially based on the freight, transit in congested areas, and even environmental requirements. For the transportation contract between the shipper and receiver the most common carrier compliance areas are:

○ Avoid Tolls – Most transportation contracts will require that truckers avoid the use of toll roads even to the point of requiring them to take a longer route. The primary reason for this is cost. For instance, if a driver took the Pennsylvania Turnpike through Pennsylvania from the I-95 split in New Jersey at the beginning of the PA Turnpike all the way to the Ohio Border, it would cost a truck driver with a standard 18-wheel vehicle with five axels carrying between 35,000 and 40,000 (a standard dry van load) $150.40 for a distance of 356 miles, or a little over 42 cents per mile. If a passenger vehicle did the same route, it would cost the consumer about $36, or about 10 cents per mile. Interestingly, the PA turnpike is not one of the most expensive toll roads in the country. The top four most expensive toll roads and their cost per mile are [70]:

- The Chesapeake Expressway in Virginia which will cost a truck driver $1.05 per mile

- 17 Mile Driver (Monterrey Peninsula, California) which will cost a truck driver 54.4 cents per mile

- Fort Bend Parkway in Houston Texas will cost the driver 53.3 cents per mile

- Chicago Skyway (Gary Indiana through Chicago Metro) will cost the driver 51.2 cents per mile

Finally, let's look at the impact of tolls on a standard lane. I have a standard dry van (Box trailer) with forty-eight pallets weight 36,000 pounds. I'm going from Trenton, NJ (near the tolls road) to Zanesville, OH (about an hour into Ohio). The distance without tolls is 465 miles and using the toll road, the route would be 433 miles, or about 32 miles shorter. At a current dry van spot rate of 1.94 per mile, the 65 miles difference would be about $70.00.

---

[70] https://ezfreightfactoring.com/blog/expensive-toll-roads-united-states

However, using the shorter distance with the toll road would also incur the $150.4 toll charge which would increase the toll road lane cost by $80.04, or about 18 cents per mile. The quoted rate for the lane would be about $700 without tolls and $850.4 with tolls. Using tolls would increase the rate by 17.6% and the reduced mileage would not matter as the rating agency rated the base freight for both the same. While savings will vary, it will typically be 10 – 15% more expensive to use tolls, or, shippers could reduce their transportation spend by 10 – 15% if they avoid tolls.

o Interstate Use as a Priority – Another compliance area is the required use of interstate roads. It may sound counter-intuitive in that drivers would also use interstate roads, but the compliance rule is in place to ensure two things don't happen. The first is that freight rates are created based on interstate and four lane roads wherever possible. This means the rates are cheaper and the carrier then is motivated to ensure interstate roads are used to maximize their revenue. The second is time. Requiring interstate roads will typically mean that the speed per mile for the entire run is higher than if the driver used secondary roads. Sometimes, it can even be up to 50% higher depending on the lane and amount of traffic incurred on secondary roads.

o Avoid Congestion – This is an important one to ensure is in the transportation contract. The primary use of this compliance rule is to create routes that bypass areas of known high congestion sending the driver around, rather than through, these areas. If the driver is delivering to an area known for congestion, they won't avoid it but will typically have a few routes known to be quicker than others as part of the route map. Avoiding congestion will make a route longer, sometimes by dozens to hundreds of miles. Doing so, however, ensures consistency of transit times and helps ensure on-time delivery. It also can increase the driver's productive driving hours. For instance, a truck driver that picks up a load from Birmingham, AL with a delivery in Raleigh North Carolina with a route that goes through Atlanta, GA will have a 554 mile route taking them over I-20 out of Birmingham to the Atlanta Bypass of I-285 to I-85 through Charlotte, NC and then to Raleigh. As the driver approaches Atlanta on I-285 transferring to I-85 north (see inset right) they will find it will take them around the outer belt of Atlanta for about 46 miles. Before getting to I-285, the driver will typically go about 54 – 60 miles per hour. If the driver goes through Atlanta at the peak time, 4pm to 7pm, they will find their average speed to be about 28 miles versus about 50 miles per hour in the later evening or early morning. The transit time would be about

2 hours to get through Atlanta versus about an hour during times. If the driver average s 60 miles per hour for the other parts of the trip, including stops and breaks, they would arrive in 12 hours but would incur over 11 hours of driving time and might have to stop just short of Raleigh due to hours of service for driving time. Sitting in the "parking lot" of the Atlanta bypass system might cause the driver to lose a day. But if the driver avoided Atlanta all together, they would create a route from Birmingham, AL via I-59 to Chattanooga then via I-75 to Knoxville and then I-40 through Greensboro, NC to Raleigh. The distance for this route would be 616 miles. The driver, given the roads and general speed limit for them, would likely average about 62 miles, including stops and breaks, for the entire trip. This would require a transit time of just under ten hours which makes the trip a single day. This is not an unusual result when looking to avoid congestion.

Congestion not only happens around urban areas but in areas where there are major interstate connections between north south and / or east-west interstates. Figure 76 shows the Bureau of Labor and Statistics (BLS) list of the top 15 most congested roadways in the country[71]. For instance, we showed in the inset above the Atlanta GA between I-285 and I-85 north. In Cincinnati, the I-71 at I-75 is the convergence point of two major north south interstates. Compare that with the I-5 at I-90 interchange in Seattle Washington in the heart of the city. Avoiding congestion doesn't always save money but it always saves time. Given today's hours of service as set by the FMCSA, time is as precious as mileage. Reducing wait times on interstates increases the efficiency of routes and ultimately the driver's time.

Location
Atlanta, GA: I-285 at I-85 (North)
Chicago, IL: I-290 at I-90/I-94
Fort Lee, NJ: I-95 at SR 4
Louisville, KY: I-65 at I-64/I-71
Houston, TX: I-610 at US 290
Houston, TX: I-10 at I-45
Cincinnati, OH: I-71 at I-75
Houston, TX: I-45 at US 59
Los Angeles, CA: SR 60 at SR 57
Houston, TX: I-10 at US 59
Dallas, TX: I-45 at I-30
Atlanta, GA: I-75 at I-285 (North)
St. Louis, MO: I-70 at I-64 (West)
Seattle, WA: I-5 at I-90
Chicago, IL: I-90 at I-94 (North)
Austin, TX: I-35
Auburn, WA: SR 18 at SR 167
Los Angeles, CA: I-710 at I-105
Baton Rouge, LA: I-10 at I-110
Hartford, CT: I-84 at I-91
Houston, TX: I-45 at I-610 (North)
Seattle, WA: I-90 at I-405
Cincinnati, OH: I-75 at I-74
Indianapolis, IN: I-65 at I-70 (North)
Denver, CO: I-70 at I-25

Figure 76. Largest Areas of Congestion (US)

[71] https://www.bts.gov/bts-publications/freight-facts-and-figures/freight-facts-figures-2017-chapter-4-freight

Carrier Optimization – The last area we'll discuss in tactical optimization is carrier optimization. There are different ways we can apply optimizing our carriers and the general idea of this optimization approach is better performance and perhaps better incremental pricing. There are three factors we think about when we look at carriers: Performance, Volume/Price, and capacity. Let's break each of these down to understand the specific areas of opportunity:

- Performance – We use carriers on specific lanes and generally expect what good performance should be from them. Our balanced scorecard also helps us evaluate the carrier performance of the entire relationship and on-time performance is one of the most critical areas we'll evaluate. One way to optimize carriers for performance is by analyzing the carrier's available in your network and evaluating their performance for on- time pickup and delivery for all lanes and then analyzing their performance for each lane they run. Looking at this gives us insight into the consistency of the carrier's performance for delivery one of the most critical things we want as shippers. We can use the overall ranks of the carriers to determine which ones we might favor and use more often. We can also align the best carriers based on their individual lane performance. So, we may have a single carrier that has delivered on ten lanes. When we look at their performance, we find there are two lanes where they are consistently on-time and most effective.

  We can optimize that carrier by tending loads to them over those two lanes almost exclusively but not for lanes where their performance is lower. With modern TMS software, this is a straightforward activity because the system can be set to favor on-time delivery for lanes over other criteria. Evaluating overall on-time performance and lane on-time performance we can get a picture of our most effective carriers overall and by lane. Often this will help us to evaluate the 20% of the carriers we will have move 80% of our loads. For that 20%, we want to consider another element of carrier optimization: Volume and Price

- Volume / Price – These two variables go together in optimization, especially for carriers, because we can decide how we will allocate our carriers, and which will have preference for volume. Similarly, the prices we are charged for loads will also play a pivotal role in that decision. The expectation from the shipper will always be that the more volume provided to a carrier the better the rate should be. Carrier operations usually support this notion, but the volume needed for price- breaks will vary by the aggregated volume in the relationship but can also apply to lanes. Lanes that are popular and well-travelled are often the cheapest lanes because carriers can easily find back haul loads and other loads that fit into their transportation schedules.

Lanes that are more obscured, like Bozeman Montana to Little Rock Arkansas will require a higher volume to merit a better rate simply because of the lack of potential back hauls in both locations. If a shipper in this lane had significant back and forth traffic, i.e. there were load needs on both sides, then a high-volume lane like this would merit better rates because of the total volume and that that volume is spread between outbound and inbound loads. In terms of transportation performance and cost strategies, it is common to have one or two primary carriers that may have up to 80% of the total network volume to have larger price discounts on contracted rates. It is also common to have a few carriers that work specific lanes because of their performance or relative cost to performance for those lanes. Finally, a shipper will likely also have a broker relationship they use for obscure or other lanes and expediting. By using a single broker relationship, the shipper can continue to aggregate other volume to a single provider to get the most out of the relationships.

Transportation networks create the backbone of transportation for the shipper. Creating effective networks of lanes and routes that are efficient provide the shipper the greatest opportunity to manage transportation costs. When networks are not efficient, they result in poor delivery, in expending, and cost escalation. Planning the network to meet the needs of the company's goods movement and then translating that into effective transportation execution is key to manage transportation costs.

Using optimization techniques at both strategic and tactical levels are also key to managing transportation costs. Poor facilities strategies will lead to excessive transportation costs due to poor location, poor lane development, and even difficulty in finding carriers that can serve one-off lanes. Effective placement of facilities served by transportation is the best long-term strategy for keeping costs under control. Further, the tactical areas of optimization we have discussed can drive efficiency to a best practices level and help to ensure transportation costs as low as reasonable while ensuring the best carrier performance possible.

CHAPTER 13: TRANSPORTATION IN RETAIL

INTRODUCTION

The retail industry is a mass production environment of consumable, durable, and major end item products. The categories of products include:

<u>Consumables (Non-Durable)</u> – Consumables include all grocery and food items, household goods purchased in grocery or big-box retailers used to clean and maintain personal hygiene and the home, and all manners of items used for a short time (could be a day or as much as several months) and then discarded.

<u>Durables</u> – Durables are products that last three years or more when cared for and include items like automobiles and auto parts, home appliances, furniture, and more.

About 80-90% of consumer purchases are related to consumables.

Because of the varied volume requirements involved in consumer goods, retailers will often have very different supply chain structures and transportation needs for things like consumables compared to major end item purchases. The transportation networks are driven most often by consumer demand, especially the volume of demand, and the approach by the retailer to manage the stock available to consumers. With eCommerce, more changes have taken place in "brick and mortar" retail to be both competitive and cost efficient while maintain a local presence that supports brand and customer engagement. The Internet has been the major driver of changes in consumer buying since around the year 2000 and has been a challenge and opportunity for retailers.

In this chapter we will explore the logistics and transportation strategies various retailers use to plan, stock, and replenish goods sold within retail branch stores and the strategies and issues involved in eCommerce. The convergence of the two, eCommerce and ongoing store retail has created a new dynamic environment for retailers where managing the cost of inventory and transportation has been a critical element in maintaining profitability.

The foundation of the changes in eCommerce and traditional retailing can be represented by the concept of Omni-Channel Commerce. Omni-Channel Commerce retail is a technology platform that allows retailers to manage multiple channels (in-store, eCommerce, catalog orders, etc.) with integrated inventory and customer information enabling the customer to be recognized regardless of the channel they use to purchase goods while also allowing delivery flexibility to an approach that works best for them. Inside most corporations today, companies use a technology called Enterprise Requirements Planning (ERP) to manage the assets, financials, human resources and, where applicable, production and inventory management. Omni-Channel Commerce has become a key system for retailers and some B2B companies, so it equates Omni-Channel management as the "ERP of the Outside Firm". It should be a surprise that both the ERP and Omni-Channel platforms have deep integration between each other enabling data, orders, and other information to flow through them seamlessly. While not all retail companies have or use Omni-Channel Commerce platforms, they still deal with the same issues and therefore have the same basic issues likely with more limitations. We will use the Omni-Channel platform as a foundation of discussion on transportation in retail because many of the consumer buying and delivery choices are adjudicated and made in the platform and the routed to be processed and transported.

OMNI-CHANNEL COMMERCE: A SHORT HISTORY

What does it take to allow a customer to purchase goods by walking in the store, on their smart phone, at home on their computer, or even on the phone? What about the consumer that walks into a store and finds the product is out of stock? Traditionally, they would leave very unsatisfied and the company might lose a customer. What about the person that wants to buy something at 5:00 am and then wants to pick up the item later when commuting to work? Can we do that? Then, there's the ideas of "last mile delivery" or the notion that consumers could buy potentially anything, and have it delivered the same day by pulling from regional warehouses? How can this be done?

The answer to the question in all these instances is a technology platform that came to market initially around 2005 that has evolved to be Omni-Channel Commerce. An Omni-Channel Commerce (OCC) platform allows companies to unify their view of the customer and their ability to accept orders from any channel they provide to consumers and, in return, fulfill those orders to any channel the company has created to deliver goods. The technology and development of these capabilities are more complex than most realize and managing the complexity of a modern consumer supply chain needs a platform like this much like a manufacturing company needs an ERP.

THE TECHNOLOGY BEHIND OMNI-CHANNEL COMMERCE

Early attempts by retailers to respond to the Internet began in the late 1990s. By then companies like Amazon.com, Datek.com and others were creating new channels of commerce with a dedicated online channel. Datek.com, for instance, was one of the first online trading platforms that allowed investors to buy and sell stocks online without a broker or other registered representative. Amazon, who started as a book seller, was focused on discounted books for customers. Back then, Amazon charged for shipping and it typically took five days to a week to get the delivery. Some retailers were working toward development an Internet channel.

At the time B2B Integration was still in early development, and much of the retail technology infrastructure was immature beyond point of sales systems that provided daily sales and retail inventory systems centrally managed at the corporate level. Companies were not as interested in creating a single way for customer to access the selling channels (in-store, phone and catalog sales, and the new "online") as they were creating a channel for the Internet. Companies created "multi-channel" commerce.

This meant that companies could accept orders in the store, catalog sales, and Internet channel but they would have to fulfill them from the same channel. Further, customers might use multiple channels, but the company wouldn't know it because each channel was independent and the data for customer and inventory was not integrated.

In the late 1990's the first Internet protocols drove eCommerce. They were rudimentary but as they would evolve, they would lead to another new technology that would become critical to all computing platforms in the late first decade of 2000, Web Services. Web Services are set of protocols that enable computer applications to work seamlessly with the Internet, work seamlessly between system to system integration, and to simplify and create more powerful applications that would leverage the Internet and the Cloud.

Around 2001, the first B2B Integration platforms came on the market. These platforms enabled companies to integrate internal systems together but more important, they enabled multi- enterprise integration which allowed companies to drive system to system integration internal or external to the company.

As Web Services and B2B Integration improved, so did the tools by which applications were built. Between around 1998 and 2004, several new startups developed applications that could do new things with commerce and business including:

- <u>Distributed Order Management</u> – One of the first applications that looked to conquer lack of visibility of client and inventory data was a company called Yantra spun out of Infosys. The company developed integration and process flows as a "tool kit" that could be built to each client's needs to unify inventory across their enterprise and their stores and that could keep up with basic customer information across channels. One of the first early cross-channel initiatives was done by Yantra (Later Sterling Commerce) and IBM for Circuit City. Using these techniques, Yantra created a "buy-online / pickup- in-store" capability for online customers wishing to pick up their goods at a local store rather than wait for shipping. The service was very popular initially and Circuit City identified for two years in their annual report that fact this method, customers buying online and then pick up in a store based on their zip code, yielded a much higher order total than those using online only or those going to the store. This opened new possibilities for retailers and their use of local stores create value for consumer. One of the most interesting aspects of this technology was the ability for an order to come in with many order lines. These orders could be broken apart and sourced for fulfillment separately where the customer might want to pick things up while having other shipped. The order kept its integrity making order tracking simple and channel specific.

- <u>Guided Selling and Integrated CRM</u> – Another significant technology involved in cross- channel and later Omni-Channel was the concept of guided selling, customer integration, and order experience. This technology enabled much deeper integration of customer information around selling channels enabling customers to create accounts on retail websites which created a master CRM account for the total retailer. This means that any purchase made through any channel could be tracked, and, if a problem existed, the customer could use any channel of customer support (in-store, over the phone, through the website, etc.) to resolve the issues regardless of what channel they used to buy. In addition, guided selling allows retailers to move beyond single product selling to complex configuration based selling. For instance, A large retailer used the system for its custom blinds business allowing customers in-store, or online, to look at different samples of blinds and curtains and tailor their choices to meet their needs. Since not all combinations of blinds, curtains, rod sizes, etc. work with each other, the system was configured to guide the customer through the selling product and "highlight" or "grey out" choices that were compatible and incompatible to ensure that when the customer was done, everything would work together. Similarly, large electronics retailers would use this to help customers configure home theatre systems choosing televisions, electronic devices, speakers, and even furniture using guided selling. In one instance, the company even integrated its customer installation services and would schedule the service installation date two days after all the components the customer ordered were delivered. Sometimes, this even meant committing televisions from manufacturers directly rather than through their existing inventory.

These two technologies dramatically reduced the complexity of integration of online commerce with other channels and with coordinating and ensuring inventory availability, shipping time, and much more.

- <u>Data Synchronization</u> – Another aspect of the solution came through a small provider that pioneered data synchronization of order, customer, and inventory data called TR2. The power of this system included a data cleansing engine that could normalize data not only within the company but across companies that need to work with the same data, formats, etc.

Between 2004 and 2006, an integration software company Sterling Commerce, when an AT&T Company, purchased all three of these companies along with one of the first cloud-based TMS systems, and, along with its core B2B Platform created an entire technology portfolio stack that could integrate any companies, create the cross and Omni-Channel capabilities, and drive data normalization faster than any other company. Sterling Commerce had been a pioneer in Electronic Data Integration (EDI), Services Oriented Architectures which ultimately lead to Web Services platforms, and in large file movement over secure channels often needed to transfer data between branches and home offices and between clients.

They marketed the solution as a cross-channel platform and could unify any known selling channel at the time while enabling buy-online / pick up in-store (or Click and Collect), direct ship to the store, drop ship from the manufacturer directly to the home, or retail shipping to the home. By 2010, Sterling Commerce was sold to IBM and became part of the IBM software group. IBM officially launched the "Omni-Channel" Commerce platform integrated with several other IBM software capabilities in 2011.

Today, Omni-Channel Commerce has been implemented by most big-box retailers, larger retailers, and large electronics and specialty stores. IBM and Manhattan Associates have the largest market share for Omni-Channel Commerce today. Omni-Channel Commerce has also added new delivery capabilities that include ship from store which was an innovation developed by Pitney Bowes Logistics Software Group and a company called Pierbridge which created one of the first multi-carrier ratting systems for parcel. Smart Lockers were introduced around 2012 and, today, same day delivery is being integrated and becoming more popular in the market.

For many retailers seeking to differentiate with their customers, OCC has not become "table stakes" and the core platform they use. While the platform is very effective, managing order and inventory flow in modern retail requires much more than just technology. These platforms provide good visibility, reporting and data capabilities to help companies understand their order flow and needs.

How Do OCC Platforms Affect Transportation?

OCC platforms enable multi-channel commerce for both order and delivery. Because of this, inbound transportation and transportation approaches for customer delivery change significantly with the ability of Omni-Channel to optimize delivery channels to also optimize inventory. To understand this, we need to look at the two aspects of commerce involved in retail: B2B (Business-to-Business) commerce and transportation and B2C (Business to Consumer) commerce and transportation.

B2B COMMERCE AND TRANSPORTATION

In a retail environment, initial ordering and replenishment of goods, or merchandising, are the primary processes that drive transportation. Several considerations are involved in determining the most effective method of transportation for a specific retail situation including:

- Value of Goods – The higher the value of goods the more expensive it is to hold them in retail stores. For major items, like appliances, large TVs and furniture, the local store may only have one or two in stock, if that, and rely on regional distribution, or even consumer drop ship, the deliver the items.

- Seasonality – How often major sections of the store, or the store itself, must be "reset" is another are of understanding needed in retail B2B replenishment strategies. For some retail segments, like the fashion industry, the store will reset goods at least six times (winter, spring, summer, fall, back-to-school and Christmas). There are also "seasons within seasons" today that will require a partial reset. For most industries that are heavily seasonal, orders are taken at least three to six months before they need delivery and are sent in bulk, usually on container ships from oversees. Once goods are in the store, the retailer will find it will need to order items beyond their original plan because of sales velocity. These goods will also come from overseas but will use air transport due to the time criticality of ensuring they do not go out of stock.

- Sales Predictability – Grocery stores, big-box retailers, home improvement stores and similar typically have a large number of SKUs (Stock Keeping Units); individual products) that are sold with strong predictability. Sales for the majority of products can be planned annually. Once the planning is completed, regular replenishment orders are provided based on the annual plan. There is a variation to this called Collaborative Planning, Forecasting, and Replenishment (CPFR) that we will discuss later in the chapter.

- Replenishment Volume – For some retailers, replenishment occurs between the supplier and a national company-owned distribution network. Companies will typically order in large quantities and receive these goods by rail to reduce transportation costs. Once received, they become part of a replenishment cycle that could be every other week, monthly or longer. The main central distribution center will often feed regional and district level distribution centers that then feed the individual branch stores. In other models, replenishment is done with much smaller orders rapidly moved from the supplier through a cross docking system that can move replenished goods to branch stores in as little as 24 hours.

B2B RETAIL PLANNING USING CPFR

There are many approaches to merchandising in retail. Depending on the level of technology and the approach by the retailer, planning can relatively straight forward exercise looking at the previous year's sales, adding a growth factor and then planning the next year's sales from this. Modern software solutions have created technology enable planning called Sales and Operations Planning (S&OP) which can look not only at historical data, but seasonality, volume analysis for trends and anomalies, and current actual consumer demand.

This creates a much more holistic planning approach that can be evaluated throughout the year with the ability to adjust the plan to increase or decrease ordering of items to ensure no out of stock conditions but also no significant inventory overages.

Besides S&OP systems, big-box retailers, grocers and many other large retailers use version of a planning technique called Collaborative Planning, Forecasting and Replenishment (CPFR) (Figure 77). CPFR is a highly data centric approach that leverages the capabilities of S&OP but also breaks down the planning down to specific business units, or categories. Category Management defines a specific set of SKUs tied to specific shelves or areas of a store. Buyers are assigned categories to buy so a planning business unit has a buyer that will specifically work to plan, buy, and replenish categories in a store. In CPFR, however, the buyers do not do this alone or even internally. Buyers will oversee category planning processes by bringing all the major suppliers with them. Then, they will typically have the largest vendor in the category take charge and work with the other vendors to develop Planograms of the shelves to create the standardized shelf placement of each

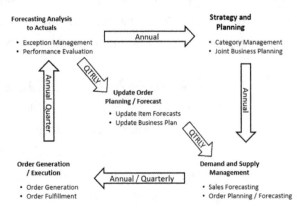

Figure 77. Collaborative Planning, Forecasting and Replenishment

vendor primarily based on their sales performance in the store. Planograms are both visual examples of the shelves and also an SKU distribution method that shows how all products in a specific area will be organized. Seasonal planograms may be added to show promotional events or other activities that deviate from the standard planograms. When complete, the buyer and the vendor team have created a plan for all supplier products, with shelf-space and promotional activities that the buyer will, when they approve, use to ensure the inventory on the shelf at the beginning of the year matches the category plan and then replenishes orders based on the planogram and category management inventory and sales levels throughout the year.

When completed, the output of the CPFR process is added into the S&OP planning engine. Store sales are then reported back to the supplier's corporate headquarters and are evaluated against the S&OP and category management plans. If sales of specific products are blow plan, the S&OP system may adjust the replenishment orders down, subject to the agreement by the buyer. Similarly, if sales are up, the system may increase replenishment orders. It's important to understand these systems do not work off short term immediate data but the planning engines consider historical sales, sales over an 8 – 12 week period, consumer indicators and more. Trending data, then, is finally evaluated against the category plan.

As replenishment orders are created, they are fulfilled through transportation. The frequency of this will have a lot to do with the distribution strategy of the company and could include low frequency, high replenishment volume orders to large warehouses and distribution centers. It can also be done through short "fill in" replenishment orders that yield just a few pallets from a supplier at a time. In the latter case, companies are choosing a vendor based fulfillment approach where the vendor becomes responsible for the fill in based fulfillment.

Retail companies have different approaches to replenishment style based on the retail business, the nature of the inventory, acceptable or standardized practices for that retail business, sales volume and more. In looking at replenishment strategies, we pay attention closely to three factors that drive these decisions more than others and they are:

- Lean versus Non-lean Practices – Over the last twenty years, lean practices have not only influenced manufacturing but also retail businesses. Retail businesses, like manufacturers, learned that "just-in-time" approaches to production and replenishment yielded significant savings in inventory. One retailer that uses large distribution with rail might hold an annual inventory of $1B with about $250M in annual transportation costs. Another, peer retailer, has a lean approach where they use cross docking facilities to pass through inventory on the way to fulfillment in district distributions. The district facilities have high turn replenishment items and the cross dock facilities from the regional distribution fill in lower turn items and replenish district facilities. This method has a much higher rate of velocity keeping inventory down but driving transportation up because of the number of replenishment trips and using truck transportation as the primary means. This retailer carries about $350M in inventory and has a $370M transportation cost. Interestingly, the second retailer has lower overall logistics costs:

- o Company A has a carrying cost of about $250M due to the large inventory. When adding their transportation costs, their logistics operating costs are about $500M per year.

- o Company B has a carrying cost of about $75M because of the smaller inventory and with the $370M in transportation costs their operating logistics costs are actually $60M less at $445M.

- Sales Velocity at the Item Level – Some retailers move expensive goods in overall small numbers. Big-box retailers and grocers have a high volume of sales of smaller priced items. While any retailer can apply lean principles, high velocity of sales of lower priced items drivers a much faster replenishment cycle

- Industry Practices – Often, a segment of an industry will adopt a "best practice" across the industry after competitors have innovated and shown the value it can provide. This is true when

B2B RETAIL REPLENISHMENT USING VMI

The last area of B2B retail is related to replenishment using a technique called Vendor Managed Inventory (VMI). Like CPFR, VMI is technique that has developed over time and is based on creating collaborative ordering and delivery of replenishment orders to reduce overall costs to the retailer and supplier. VMI has ultimately created a "just-in-time" approach to B2B replenishment. In the early 2000's, big-box retailers needed to reduce their inventory carrying costs further because of the ongoing price squeezing on retail commodity goods lead to lower and lower profit margins. Walmart as one pioneer of this capability and developed a VMI system that used a portal called "Retail Link" to allow suppliers to download all of their sales and inventory orders. By making the sales and inventory levels transparent to the suppliers, they then required the suppliers to keep ownership of the inventory when it was on the store shelves until sold. By doing this, Walmart and others reduced inventory holding costs but also the cost of the actual inventory. The savings related to this is calculated by the previous cost of the inventory multiplied by the corporations "cost of funds" or borrowing rate. It led to hundreds of millions in savings.

Initially, the suppliers as a group were not excited about this idea. As they worked with their customers, they found that the transparency of the sales and inventory data allowed them a much better planning cycle and a much better forecasting window. The suppliers took a mass market "just-in-time" approach to making and shipping goods.

They found they reduced their overall inventory levels due to increased predictability, and they by delivering goods into the retailer's distribution chain, they applied consolidation and other transportation techniques to reduce transportation costs. It became a win for both the retailer and the supplier.

While this is good background and information, the question to explore is "How does this change the approach to transportation". Figure 78 shows a diagram that discussed the data flow and information exchange in VMI along with how it triggers orders and shipping. Remember, this is one way this can be done. There are many variations. The numbers in the diagram are number 0 – 9. The process does:

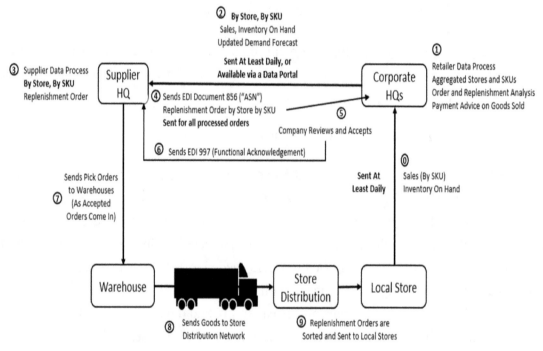

Figure 78. VMI System, Data and Process Flows

o Step 0 – Every day customers buy goods from a local store. As the goods are checked out, the transaction is stored in a file at the local store. Periodically, no less than once per day at a prescribed time, the file is closed and is compared to the previous day's store inventory. Item quantities by SKU in the sales file are subtracted to the store inventory creating a new quantity-on hand for every SKU in the store. This data is stored in a separate inventory file. When complete, the sales and inventory files are sent to the company corporate headquarters for further processing.

o Step 1: When the company receives the files from all the stores in the system, it then creates a master file of all sold SKUs, the quantities, and the amount that needs to be paid to the supplier for the sales. Remember, until this point, the suppliers have consigned their

256

inventory and so have not be paid. Besides determining the invoice to be paid, the processing also creates a supplier by supplier file that breakdowns all sales by store and SKU along with all the end of day quantities on hand. The company also trends the sales across the entire system, especially for those using CPFR, and provides any updated forecasts of sales.

- Step 2: Once all processing is complete, the company then sends this data electronically via EDI to the supplier, or a retailer may have portals that suppliers can log into to view the data and also download directly into their ERP or order systems.

- Step 3: When the supplier receives the file, it triggers processing on its side. This includes breaking down the data and running it through its ERP or order management system. This process evaluates the sales, item quantity-on-hand, and forecast and then processes this data to determine which SKUs, by store, have triggered a Reorder Point in the system so the company needs to send a replenishment of that item. It then aggregates all the replenishment items into orders by store and SKU. A typical replenishment order from a major consumer goods suppler might contain 10,000 – 15,000 replenishment items in various quantities.

- Step 4: When complete, the master replenishment orders is translated into an EDI Document 856, or "EDI 856" which is an Advanced Ship Notice message. The Advanced Ship Notice message has become the standard way in the industry to communicate impending orders. Before this, the company would send a purchase order (EDI 850), which would require an acknowledgement from the retailer (EDI 855). This would then generate the ASN (EDI 856) which explain the shipment. The first steps have generally been discontinued because the EDI 856 contains everything the company needs to know.

- Step 5: When the supplier sends the EDI 856, the data is received and compared to the retailer's ERP or order management system to determine if there are significant discrepancies like large quantities for replenishment when the items on hand are not low, etc. If it finds these, it will send back a modified EDI 856 with the corrections. The supplier will then use this. This is actually very rare because the systems are integrated and in sync and almost always show the same results.

- Step 6: When the retailer has reviewed and agreed to the replenishment order, the retailer will send an EDI 997 (Functional Acknowledgement) which is a small message. In the industry today, this message would be equated to a "head nod", or simply "OK".

- o Step 7: With the OK received, the supplier than sends pick and ship orders to various warehouses tied to different parts of the store distribution network based on geography. If the retailer has a national network with a single point of entry then all orders are pointed there. In advanced VMI environments, many retails have replaced traditional distribution points with cross docking points that allow for intake of all replenishment goods in a single area with the goods sorted and sent to regional cross docking or district distribution centers to speed up the cycle time for delivery.

- o Step 8: Once picked and staged, trucks take the goods to the intake point of the store distribution system. The time elapsed to this point could be as little as 8 – 12 hours or as much as a few days depending on how often the retailer wants replenishment deliveries to the local stores.

- o Step 9: When the goods are received into the store distribution network, the process is completed by delivering the goods through the store distribution network to the local store where it is received and stocked.

In the example in Figure 78, we are replenishing to local stores as part of their "brick and mortar" store network. The same process can be applied to companies that fulfill online sales through centralized distribution centers with all the steps being the same except step 7 where the supplier will more likely deliver directly the fulfillment distribution centers.

While most people understand the concepts of B2B and B2C, retailers are generally categorized as only B2C. The B2B component of order and replenishment enables strong centralized processing, transparent data flow between customer and supplier, a heavy use of EDI to enable systems, rather than people, to share and process data electronically, much improved inventory management and lower inventory levels and carrying costs, and using transportation consolidation and other transportation techniques to optimize transportation costs.

As we will see next, the B2C side of retail isn't quite as seamless or efficient today because of the myriad of buying and delivery channels available to consumers. Using an OCC platform, it can be optimized and well managed and coordinated to help driver better inventory and transportation performance.

B2C OMNI-CHANNEL ORDERING AND DELIVERY

The area of greatest chaos and uncertainty for retailers today is specific to serving customers in the channels they prefer, in the way they prefer, with the timing they prefer, and at a competitive price. Today, traditional retailers are expected to receive customers in-store, via the Internet and mobile networks, as a phone order, and even as an in-store kiosk order that will be delivered via a separate channel. The coordination to do this is immense and involves understanding inventory across the entire store and distribution network and sometimes all the way to the suppliers manufacturing schedules. It also means that the company must recognize and be able to identify a specific customer and their order history and even value to the company regardless of the channel they use knowing they may use many channels. Previously, the OCC platform was built to do this to help the retailer tame the complexity that has become the typical B2C environment. In this section, we'll discuss how the retailer and the OCC platform do this, so it helps optimize inventory, manage goods flow efficiently and new techniques that also help to optimize some of the transportation methods used.

As we have seen, retailers use B2B techniques for their supplier ordering and replenishment. Once goods are in the retail system, they are then ordered and shipped in several ways. The Omni-Channel platform helps the company optimize the most effective ways to deliver to customers, based on their preferences, while also helping to manage and balance inventory and current and future transportation costs. This is done via integrating the OCC to the retail store systems, customer order management systems (which Omni-Channel can also provide or integrate with an existing solution), and inventory systems across the retailer and supplier networks. The algorithms and approaches that yield results are relatively complex and are not something we need to discuss in any length. Rather, we will look at different customer buying styles and preferences for delivery approaches to help understand the information flow and the goods flow in the B2C retail side. Although there are many channels, we can generally categorize them as either "in-store" sales, or "electronic channel" sales. For our purposes, we will consider phone sales as an electronic approach. Given this, customers will "enter" the company either by walking into a store or entering electronically. We don't need to go deeper than that other than to say electronic orders can be domestic or international based orders. The shipping and transportation related to international orders is much more complex than domestic.

In terms of fulfillment, Omni-Channels flexibility and ability to analyze and help optimize channels bears much more discussion. Similarly, we can simplify this because many of the delivery channels have different levels of customer flexibility and choice, but all customer fulfillment can be broken down into four types of fulfillment:

1. <u>Customer In-Store</u> – The most basic fulfillment would be character as "buy here, take it home". We often forget this model is still the most dominant model in retail, eCommerce today, in its various electronic forms is still around 10% of all retail sales. It's important not to discount the value of the store today and in some segments, like grocery, this will be the case for a long time. Retail stores are stocked by the B2B approach to transportation in retail.

2. <u>Ship to Customer</u> – In this form, the customer will order through an electronic channel and have the ordered shipped directly to them. Where it is shipped is part of the Omni-Channel flexibility. Shipments today can be sent to a consumer's home, work, or other locations like electronic lockers. The Omni-Channel processes are the same, but the destination points vary. The most common way this is done. The most common transportation method for this order is via parcel shipping as most orders will be for items under 70 pounds. Secondarily, for items over 70 pounds, companies will use route based LTL deliveries for deliver items to consumer's homes.

3. <u>Courier or Local Route Delivery</u> – This form of delivery is newer and in development. A common term used here is "Same Day" or "Final Mile" delivery. Courier and local deliveries can be done by contracts with transportation providers, depending on the goods and the frequency and volume of deliveries. For instance, a major home improvement retailer recently signed a contract with a large transportation company to begin delivery appliances and other LTL goods to homes. This is a departure for both the retailer and the transportation company, and both represent new opportunities. Another way this delivery is being done today is via the "sharing economy". Uber and Lyft drivers, for instances, can sign up with companies to deliver goods as they pick up and deliver passengers. Amazon has launched Amazon Flex which partners with individual to create local and regional delivery networks for a minimum investment[72]. This non- traditional approach to transportation is focused on this area of delivery.

4. <u>Hybrid Models</u> – This last category is not specifically seen and acknowledge by consumers beyond their ability to fulfill goods between channels. This category requires the OCC platform to develop specific algorithms to manage the hybrid approaches. The most common approaches in this category are:

---

[72] https://money.cnn.com/2018/06/28/technology/amazon-delivery-partners/index.html

a. <u>Buy-online / Pick up In-store</u> – Also known as "Click and Collect" sometimes, this approach allows a customer to buy through an electronic channel and pick up the goods in the in-store channel. To do this, the platform is provided the zip code of the customers, usually when they log in or at the order checkout point. It looks at the zip code and maps stores within that zip codes and ones within a specific mile range, usually up to 10 miles away. It then checks the on-hand stock for each store to determine if there is enough shelf stock to pull the item without fear of the electronic ordered customer getting an out of stock condition. The amount of on hand can vary but it's usually no less than five items. It then determines the store closest to the customer and sets the delivery location as that store. When checking out, it provides the consumer with the pickup location and the store sends a notification to the customer, usually via text, when the order is ready to pick up. The customer usually then has a few days to pick it up before the order is cancelled. This method does not require additional transportation beyond having the goods in the store. It is usually seen as a convenience option when the customer wants the goods more immediately than shipping will yield. It is an efficient model that considers inventory availability and the convenience of the customer going to a service decks, and sometimes an electronic locker, to pick up their goods bypassing the traditional shopping and checkout process.

b. <u>Ship from Store</u> – The second hybrid model is generally unknown to the customer but is done to drive efficiency of inventory across branch stores and eCommerce fulfillment centers. Today, most electronic orders are filled through a distribution channel linked to a strong parcel shipping capability. Orders are picked, packed, and shipped from a central or reginal distribution center where the parcel packing, pricing, and shipping happen at the facility. For a company like Amazon who ships dominantly from its distribution centers via parcel, the transportation costs are high for parcel. For instance, in the Q2, 2018, shipping costs were about $6B on sales of $52B. This makes shipping about 11.3% of revenue very high compared to most industry standards of 5 – 6%. Amazon is very efficient, and most speculate parcel cost average is about $3.25 - $3.50. For traditional retailers without the same volume and synergy, the costs are more.

One way to offset the parcel costs for traditional retailers is through a method called "zone skipping". Parcel companies primary cost calculations are based on the dimensions of the box and the weight of the box. Boxes with larger dimensions that weight less, are charged more due to the dimensions rather than weight. Parcels that are heavier than expected for the dimension of the box are charged additional fees for the weight. In addition, parcel companies break their domestic and international delivery networks into zones. The more zones between where the product is entered into the parcel system and the zone in which it is delivered, the higher the price. Here, zone skipping is a shipping method where the parcel enters the system in the same parcel zone as the delivery thus eliminating multiple zones and reducing the price of the parcel. Zone skipping can also involve consolidating eCommerce orders from a central fulfillment center by their delivery zones and then sending the parcels as consolidated freight to an intake parcel center in the final zone. In our case, the zone skipping involved in retail has multiple layers of value:

i.   Underperforming Stores – One value of retail store zone skipping is that the Omni-Channel algorithm will target stores in the parcel delivery zone of the customer underperforming either or for the specific SKUs that need to be shipped. If this is not shipped out of the store, it will likely not be sold in the store and must be returned, processed, and sold on the secondary market. By having a zone skipping algorithm, the Omni-Channel platform can take orders from customers that want shipping to their location and instead of sending the order to a central fulfillment center, it sends the order to an underperforming store. The store then takes the item off the shelf, packages it and puts a parcel label on it. Later that day the parcel carrier picks it up and it is transported within the same zone reducing the cost of the parcel by anywhere from 10%- 30%.

ii. Total Shipping Costs – By using zone skipping with underperforming stores, the company can reduce the cost of its parcels shipping as discussed above but also reduces the end of life cost of the good shipped. Because it has been sold rather than left on the shelf, there will be no need to send it back to a central distribution point when the good is not longer to be in the inventory. This eliminates an unwanted shipping event. In addition, that good will not be liquidated through third Party channels so the company will get the value of the sale rather than pennies on the dollar.

c. <u>Drop Ship</u> – Drop ship is a hybrid model where the order is received by the retailer but fulfilled directly by the supplier bypassing the retailer's distribution network by shipping directly to the customer. This is a powerful tool for certain retailers with items that may be larger (appliances, TVs, furniture, etc.) and more expensive. The company can have one item on the display floor and then when the customer buys it, it is shipped to them directly from the supplier. This reduced inventory costs and B2B shipping costs and is typically as fast as other deliveries.

To bring this all together, consider Figure 79. While the system can handle high complexity in terms of its algorithms, business rules, etc. the buying and delivery approaches are actually rather straight forward. Similarly, the customer may choose fulfillment via a store, either as a customer in the store, or dropping by to pick up the order, or via a shipment to a location that works for them (home, work, intelligent lockers, and more). Time doesn't affect shipping options just shipping methods. For instance, if we add same day delivery as an option, all we are doing is speeding up the "Ship to Location" option. Similarly, ship from store, which is an optimizing technique for the company, still ends up in a shipment to location paradigm.

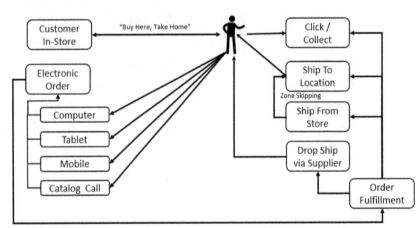

Figure 79. Summary of Omni-Channel Commerce B2C Order and Fulfillment Approaches

One of the most critical things to remember when working with retail companies and their transportation needs is that fact that they use both a B2B transportation model and an B2C transportation model. The B2B model, for many retailers, now operates more as a just-in-time model than a traditional bulk model. Similarly, the B2C model is dominated by the B2B side of store replenishment and the technology of eCommerce and OCC to enable many consumer choices for buying and receiving goods.

CHAPTER 14: TRANSPORTATION IN MANUFACTURING

INTRODUCTION

Manufacturing is one of the most diverse industries in the world. When we think about manufacturing, we think about production plants with raw materials coming in on one side and finished goods on the other. Strictly speaking this is correct. The challenge is that raw material and finished good, and the sales of these products, and the manufacturing style, create high diversity in the manufacturing process and its attributes. Because of this, the characteristics of manufacturing and ultimately the approach to transportation is based on these factors:

Kinds of Raw Materials – Raw materials are a general phrase to denote the inputs into a manufacturing process. Virginal raw materials come from materials taken from mining, logging, farming, oil production, and other natural methods of extracting or growing materials within the Earth. Components are another form of raw material that have had some processing done from their raw materials. Components are pieces of bigger products and can include things like the plastic housing of an MRI machine, a molded fender shell for a car, a cut piece of steel used to create something else when combined with other materials and much more. Another kind of potential raw material is a sub-assembly. A sub-assembly is typically made from component raw materials and other materials to create an item then incorporated into the final product. Aerospace, automotive, shipbuilding, Appliances, and many more other kinds of products use this method to build the final finished goods.

Approach to Sales – The approach to sales will often influence the transportation needed for the manufacture. For instance, how we manage raw materials and finished goods from a mode and transportation network perspective for mass market retail goods like housewares, clothing, etc. differs greatly from selling ten airplanes to a major airline and that differs from buying a car or farm machinery. Selling mass goods versus durable goods creates different needs for manufacturing, distribution, and transportation. Who the customer is and how they are sold has a major impact on how we create and distribute products.

Manufacturing Style – The manufacturing style is a specific philosophy, set of processes, metrics and expected outcomes based on the goods produced at one, the timing of those goods for replenishment, and how the manufacturing facilities are placed in the supply chain. The author argues that, in today's market, there are four typical manufacturing styles that exist that drive inventory needs, production processes, especially the production done at once, and the upstream and downstream transportation networks. Three of these are specific to the goods and selling channels and the fourth is a hybrid model that takes advantage of a concept of Postponement. The styles are:

o Make-to-Stock – The MTS model is a mass production model that takes very large amounts of raw materials, applies very large production runs characterized by work-in-process inventory, and results in many finished goods usually stored in warehouses until ordered by customers. This is the most traditional method of manufacturing and is very effective (especially when using CPFR and VMI) at producing goods for the masses. It is an inventory heavy model and using techniques with retailers like CPFR and VMI allow the company to have more accurate forecasting and better velocity on delivering finished goods which helps to incrementally reduce inventory at all levels. Transportation modes then to be more related to rail, ship and other slower, bulk-driven modes because of raw material and finished goods involved. For consumer goods especially, intermodal rail is a transportation approach that can help the company with finished goods over long distances with rail and short, final mile distances with truck. In MTS, manufacturing of goods takes place ahead of the knowledge of actual demand which can create out of stock or stock overage situations with large number of out of stock or large amounts of excess inventory if not managed well. In the case of MTS, proximity to suppliers and customers are typically at longer distances and buying habits of buying in very large volume.

o Make-to-Order – Make-to-Order is commonly called "lean", or "just-in-time" manufacturing. With Enterprise Requirement Planning systems (ERP) and lean Management and Continuous Improvement principles introduces by men like Dr. Joseph Juran who pioneered the Pareto principle to manufacturing and inventory leading to ABC management of inventory, Dr. W. Edwards Deming, who helped re-build Japanese manufacturing based on statistical analysis and continuous improvement pioneering Total Quality Management, and many techniques that would become to be known as "Six Sigma", Walter Shewhart who also worked with statistical quality control and created the "Plan-Do-Check-Act" method of continuous quality improvement. We can also go back to Henry Ford and the inventory of the production line in the early 1900's and Kiichiro Toyoda who, along with other pioneers developed the Toyota Production System in a post-WWII Japan. Make-to-Order is characterized by small lot productions, when compared to MTS, with low inventory levels of raw and finished goods.

Often the safety stock involved in raw materials is as low as one or two days and as much as five or six days for most production environments. This low level of inventory creates high efficiency and relies heavily on transportation as "rolling inventory" to meet ongoing production requirements. Lean bases its production runs on an initial production schedule that could go out six months to a year and then updates that schedule based on actual market results typically at a monthly level and then within a few days of actual production. This dynamism requires fast and flexible transportation and Make-to-Order is very truck transportation centric. Since the early to mid-1990s, transportation methods have been invented to enable the lean model to flourish. In a JIT model, transportation, rather than inventory management, is key to the model's success. Because of this, proximity between suppliers and the assembler is a critical factor and the father away a supplier is from the factory, the higher the potential risk of failing in this rapid and constant transportation model.

- o Build-to-Order – Build-to-order is the domain of very large expensive systems and products that include aircraft, spacecraft, high end medical equipment, special use construction and excavating equipment, etc. The typical sales cycle of a build-to-order product could be measured in months to years. For instance, a major airline will plan for integrating new aircraft on a schedule that meets regulatory needs and practical needs for updating existing models of airplanes to newer versions, purchasing new aircraft to meet specific route or customer needs, etc. Similarly, space systems, like satellites and space vehicles may be planned for up to a decade before they are finally ordered. The cost of these is high as is the complexity of most of its products. In this style of manufacturing no production is begun until a firm receives an order from a customer. The company will then plan for the raw material, transportation of the material, production of the item and shipment to its destination as a single "program" and will coordinate and sequence raw material throughout the lifecycle of production as needed. These are often small lots of production that could be as small as one item or up to a dozen at a time. The production itself is cell based with a product being organized by system and sections then produced in coordination to create the final product. Inventory levels are low as the inventory is almost immediately used when it arrives because of the planning and sequencing of the project. From a raw material perspective, transportation may be in bulk if it warrants it but more often will be via truck or similar method. Finished goods are transported in many ways including building the item on the site of its use, transportation using alternative methods, like the US Space Shuttle being transported on top of a Boeing 747, and similar. Like Make to Stock, proximity is not major concern in BTO as materials are procured after the order is received, o <u>Leagile (Postponement)</u> – Leagile isn't so much a production model as it is a hybrid of production and distribution. In Leagile, the production component produces a base product and configuration choices, like colors, styles, and components, are produced but left out of the final product. The product is then sent into distribution. As orders are received, they include the specific features and configuration requirements. Associates then "pick" the item and the associated configuration parts and finish the assembly of the product to a given customer's specifications. Dell, among others, pioneered this technique with laptop computers creating a very strong ability to meet customer specialization desires without increasing the cost of production. Inventory levels are related to finished goods and depend on the style of production. This is also true of transportation. Since most of these orders are configured when ordered, transportation is often via parcel to the consumer, or truck to a branch location or home.

Table 16 summarizes these styles and their impact to inventory and transportation. As seen from the table, we focus on the style of manufacturing and its approaches or impact to demand, how production works and then inventory and transportation.

Manufacturing Style	Description	Approach to Demand	Manufacturing Characteristics	Approach to Inventory	Approach to Transportation
Make to Stock	Mass production for mass consumption	Historical Forecasting leading to very large production forecasts	Large production runs often of 10,000 to 100,000s per day	Large Raw, WIP (Work in Process) and Finished Goods Inventory	Primarily Bulk Modes for Raw Material and Bulk or Truck for finished goods
Make to Order	Also Called "Lean", or "Just-in-Time" Manufacturing	Demand forecasts based on historical and actual recent demand	Smaller production lots tied to planned and immediate demand	"Just in Time" raw material delivery, low WIP, small lot finished goods	Lean Logistics that include trucks using different methods to meet lot production needs
Build to Order	Similar to Make to Order but Production Sequence tied to receiving an order	Demand Forecasting through the sales cycle and expected closed orders	Manufacturing doesn't start until an order is received	Raw material is not procured until an order is received	Small quantities (but may be large items) shipped via the most effective mode
Leagile	A kind of postponement where optional product features (color, accessories, etc.) are installed at the distribution point before delivery rather than at the factor	Could be any of the previous three but most likely based on Lean and smaller lot production	Orders are configured with customer preferences when orders come in	Inventory along with installable components stored in distribution centers	Outbound nature so could include truck transportation to customer distribution or parcel direct ship to customer

Table 16. Manufacturing Styles and their Impact on the Supply Chain

TRANSPORTATION AND THE MANUFACTURING MODEL

We will look at Make to Stock and Make-To-Order to contrast the approaches to transportation as the other models will use either technique depending on the product and the market.

• Make-to-Stock (MTS) – The first area we will review is how transportation works in a Make-to-Stock model. As we have seen, most MTS production models are inventory heavy and will typically require the manufacturer to have

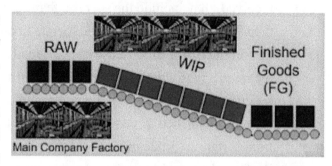

Figure 80. Make to Stock Manufacturing Model

warehousing capabilities to store raw materials and finished goods. We will often breakdown the transportation strategies between the upstream, supplier network, and downstream, distribution network. In large scale MTS operations, raw materials are sent by rail to keep the costs of transportation down. This is necessary due to the large raw material and the long production lots produced. Figure 80 represents a traditional Make-to-Stock production sequence. This depicts a large production run with a continuous flow of raw material transformed into finished goods. Inventory costs are high, and work-in-process makes up a large amount of short-term inventory because of the length of production runs. Quality control is typically implemented upon inspecting the raw material, checks at different stages of production and at the finished goods level.

Because of the business and its inventory, manufacturers will work to use slower and less costly forms of transportation to transport the bulk items for both raw and finished goods. Depending on the business, unit-trains may get the lowest cost possible for transportation of goods like grains, steel, oil, and other raw materials. Wherever the manufacturer can use unit, mixed, or intermodal rail, they gain a cost efficiency needed to offset the inventory carrying costs. Finished goods may also be transported by intermodal or unit rail to warehouses and distribution centers that receive 10,000's of items at a time.

Coordination is related specifically to production to forecast requirements rather than to any other demand sensing or other demand factors. Overall, transportation is a method used to move bulk good and rail, ship and similar are the favored methods.

Even if trucking is used due to need, the company will ship full TL loads over long distances between manufacturing and distribution. Transportation flexibility is not a premium in this manufacturing beyond on- time scheduling and an occasional need to expedite.

- Make-to-Order (MTO) – The Make-to-Order and other lean models act differently from the MTS model. With MTO, there are different relationships and levels of production that enables high specialization in production with methods that enable high quality of goods. To do this, the Original Equipment Manufacturer (OEM) becomes specialized in assembly of the final product and the creation of the most critical components. For instance, in the Automotive Industry, OEM manufactures (Toyota, GM, Ford, Honda, etc.) manufacturer their own engines and chassis (the steel shell in which everything else is connected) as these leads to customer satisfaction. For all other assemblies the OEM uses the next level of production, the Tier 2. In Tier 2 production, the company's assembly major assemblies like transmissions, bumpers, the center console of the car, the body parts, etc. The assemblies comprise components which the Tier II manufacturers look to Tier III manufacturing to produce.

Components are the parts that create the sub-assemblies like the tire rims and the rubber wheels that, when assembled become tire assemblies, the radio, instrument packages, and glove box components along with the molded center console that, when brought together by the Tier 1 becomes the entire dash of the car. Appliances, medical equipment, and farm equipment, and much more are built this way with multiple tiers of manufacturing. The final Tier of manufacturing is often Tier 3 which provides all the raw material, rubber, metal, steel, etc. that are used in the tiers of assembly.

By creating this environment, companies can flow the OEM's production schedule to all three Tiers to create visibility into the final production levels. Each Tier, OEM to Tier 1, Tier 1 to Tier 2, and Tier 2 to Tier 3, then manages their own production to meet the OEM schedule and pass on their buying requirements to the next level to ensure they have the raw materials needed to meet their production requirements for the OEM.

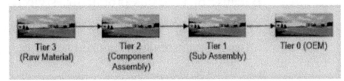

Figure 81. Example of Tiered Relationships (Make to Order)

An example of one relationship is shown in Figure 81. For each OEM, there will be several Tier I's and for each Tier I there may be 10 – 50 Tier 2 suppliers and so on through Tier 3. Most buying of parts and materials are driven by a five-day production schedule that may change week to week although planning for production and buying at a draft level are typically done on a 30-day cycle with committed orders as short as three days before production. This yields a production style where the inputs are raw materials and the outputs are finished goods (Figure 82). Because the goods are effectively specialized and

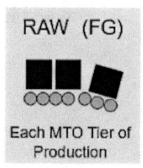

RAW (FG)

Each MTO Tier of Production

Figure 82. Make to Order

the previous level provides the goods needed to continue to build the full assembly, quality control happens on a very frequent basis over short production runs. Raw materials are inspected upon receipt and sometimes, this means a full engineering test of components like motors, pneumatics and many other components before release and shipment to the next level. Because of the speed and flexibility needed in this model, transportation plays a pivotal role in making the entire system work across tiers. This model requires very frequent, fast, and flexible transportation on the inbound side and the preferred mode is trucking for most of these applications. Because trucking has a general limitation of 10 hours of driving, for planning, this model is strong when production facilities between tiers is not over 400 miles apart. Remember, this is between each Tier so an entire Tier 0 to Tier 3 distance could be as spread out as 1,200 miles with 400 miles between each Tier. More practically, however, tiers are clustered between Tier 0 and Tier 1 with the Tier 1 being as little at 15 – 45 minutes apart creating a regular shuttle service between the facilities to keep the Tier 0 from having too much inventory on any day. Other items. Quality occurs at multiple states of production and then there is a full quality inspection of every finished good. The increased value of quality comes from every manufacturing output's being, effectively, a finished good. Because of this, this production style typically has more focus on quality checks and defect management than a traditional MTS model. This virtually eliminates all work-in-process inventory and focused solely on quality of raw and finished goods at each level of production.

Tier 1 and Tier 2 are usually within 400 miles of each other or less and may also have similar clustering. Sometimes, Tier 1 to Tier 2 or Tier 2 to Tier 3 may be much farther apart creating stress on the just-in-time model. In these cases, the transportation model must adjust much to the distance to still meet regular deadlines.

This can be done through line-haul (long distance) lanes to an extent but if the lane is over two or three days at most, it breaks the model and other adjustments need to be made to drive the MTO back to efficiency. In the next session we will discuss the specific transportation strategies used in MTS to enable the efficiency and effectiveness of the model.

TRANSPORTATION IN A MAKE-TO-STOCK (MTS) MODEL

As we look at our strategies, the easiest way we can stratify the model and strategy we need is based on the timing and flexibility. The JIT model requires high speed and flexibility to succeed. Most often, its load sizes are small when compared to a MTS model. We'll discuss the MTO transportation strategies in a moment, but lets first start with how we manage transportation most effectively in a MTS model. We've already discussed that much of the Make-to-Stock (MTS) model is based on bulk movement of goods. This fits well with the mass production model as the movement of bulk goods is often down by slower approaches to transportation in the supply chain, and therefore lower cost, than other models. We'll center our discussion around rail as a bulk mover of inbound raw materials and outbound distribution.

Remember that MTS companies are often involved in VMI requiring them to have a faster and more flexible channel for customer delivery. This doesn't negate the use of rail in MTS and depending on the configuration of the downstream distribution rail may still be used in the early stages of the downstream network.

As we've learned, the rail mode gives us a few options in how we want to move our goods (Table 17). One of the major factors for consideration is a rail siding at the factory facility. If rail is not accommodated at the facility, then straight rail becomes infeasible because trains must pick up the cars in straight rail from the facility requiring them to have rail access. If the facility does have straight rail capabilities, at both the supplier and destination plant, then the shipper can choose the best service based on the volume of

Service Type	Sub-Service	Description	Cost Per Ton-Mile	Requires Rail at Facility?
Straight Rail	Unit Train	100 cars going from one origination point to one destination	.02 - .03	Yes
	Mixed Train	Less than 100 cars or going from multiple points to multiple points	.04 - .05	Yes
Intermodal Rail	Unit Intermodal	200 containers in a single train double-stacked (rare)	.03 - .04	No
	Mixed Intermodal	1 to many containers less than 200 to be shipped	.05 - .07	No
	LCL Container	Less than a full 20 foot shipping container (special service)	varies	No

Table 17. Rail Operations for Freight Transport

the shipment. If the supplier can load 100 cars and go from their locations directly to the factory locations, then a unit-train is an option.

271

The unit-train is the most economical form of rail available, but it must have only one origin and one destination.

If a shipper has less than 100 cars that can sometimes be negotiated as unit rail provided, they meet all other factors. If less than 100 cars are needed, typically under 30, then a mixed train becomes the service to use. A mixed train comprises cars from many origination points going to many destination points. The shipper pays a charge for each car from the point of origin to destination. Schedules for unit-trains may often be shorter than mixed trains primarily due the need to classify, or switch the train, throughout its journey in a mixed train situation. A unit-train can bypass that part of the rail infrastructure as its going from one place to only one destination.

If rail is not available, or if the company is shipping downstream to consumer goods markets and must use containers, then intermodal rail is the right answer. There is a unit rail in intermodal, but it is used only by the largest shippers because it requires 200 containers, in a double stack form that creates a 100-car unit-train of 200 containers. This may occur in a port from an international shipment to a large distribution center served by rail or something similar, but intermodal also provides extensive business with mixed trains.

For smaller orders and other uses Intermodal can also provide Less than Container full, or LCL intermodal shipments. LCL operations are often provided by freight forwarders or 3PLs. They allow customers to ship goods that would not normally fill a 20-foot container by combining the items with other shippers until they get a full container. These services are primarily done through individual shipments to a warehouse where goods undergo break-bulk to stage and load them in containers going to similar places. When they arrive, they are again taken into break-bulk and then sorted to be delivered to the destination.

Rail quotes are provided by contacting the rail company in the region one uses for shipping. Scheduling rail is initially best done via phone unless the company has a sophisticated TMS that can rate rail without contacting the rail company. When contacting the rail company to set up a shipment, there are several things that go into the cost and schedule of the shipment, including:

- Point of Origin – If it is not intermodal, the point of origin for the rail pick up will matter. One consideration for the pickup, which assumes you have a rail operation capable at your facility, is whether the class I railroad will pick up the freight or will a Class II or Class III do the job. This is not a major consideration for the shipper, but the class I railroad will work through another rail company if that territory is served by them. The rail companies will have access to each other's schedules, but it may have an adjustment on pick up days or something similar.

- Point of Destination – Distance is the primary concern although if the shipment is going out of the class I's territory, it will also have to be rated by the partner on the other side of the Mississippi (regardless of the direction you're going). It requires handing the shipment over to a carrier that works in the destination region of the country. Via a transshipment location, like an Intermodal rail yard or similar. This is a common practice in rail.

- Tariffs – Tariffs are the "rate card" of rail. It describes every charge, every service, and every option the shipper will have. The rating is done by taking the order and determine the rates, surcharges, and other services and then, combining it all together to give you a price.

- Pickup and Delivery Schedules – Each freight lane in rail and every freight and Intermodal Yard has a cutoff time that must be met for the shipment to be accepted on the train. This is primarily for mixed shipments although unit rail has a similar cutoff because the mainline rail schedule and missing it could cause the shipment to be delayed. Some lanes run daily, some less, as infrequently as weekly, or even monthly. Shipper must conform to pick up and delivery days that meet the rail schedule requirements.

We'll discuss intermodal rail more in the section on MTO. In a MTS model, rail can play a vital role in moving large amount of goods often required from this production model, and do so at a cost cheap in comparison to most other options. Adding a few cents to the unit cost, or fractions of a penny on small commercial items makes rail a strong choice to keep and maintain low costs to meet consumer demands.

TRANSPORTATION IN A MAKE TO ORDER (MTO / JIT) MODEL

The MTO model requires very specific and unique approaches to transportation. Some of these methods go against the traditional teaching of transportation, especially related to trucking where full trucks, long distances, and well-travelled lanes create the best synergies. As we will find, in the MTO model, short runs of less than full trucks is one of the most efficient methods of transportation and long distances may actually put stress on the system because of the increased risk of on-time delivery and that smaller load size, regardless of distance is a top preference for delivering just-in-time loads. In just-in-time, we have specific strategies to ensure efficient transportation at the lowest possible cost.

Throughout this chapter we will introduce transportation strategies that enable rapid replenishment of production materials. The driving factor in the strategy is the distance, or proximity, between the inbound supplier and the factory. The father away we get, the higher the risk that we will break the JIT model by exceeding our ability to adjust our production planning and have transportation that can respond to that change. Typically, we look at a three day window for this. In order words, we want to be able to change the production schedule within three days of actual production and be able to have the right materials delivered on the production day. This suggests that transportation that takes longer than three days, from the day of the order, can break the flexibility we need in a JIT model.

These transportation strategies build off each other based on distance. For explanation purposes, we have created specific names of these strategies. In industry, these names are generically used for different strategies. For instance, a "milk run" is any replenishment route where the load can be delivered in the same day as it is ordered. It also denotes the use and return of "dunnage" (see inset) In this chapter, when we talk about milk runs, we will have specific names for specific strategies as follows:

- "Standard Milk Run – The most generic form of the strategy involving one supplier to one factor

- "Consolidated Milk Run – A scenario where we can combine multiple suppliers into a single route based milk run.

Similarly, in dealing with longer distances, we will introduce Line-Haul strategies. We use Line Haul as a generic term for any long distance route, typically over 1,000 miles but it can be less. While we will discuss the line haul as a method of delivery in JIT, we will also discuss how the Line Haul must be managed differently as distances get further. This will include the following terms:

- Line Haul – Any long distance route taking more than one driving day. This can include a single supplier or a consolidation situation. Timing is critical in this kind of line haul because there is an expectation that the driver is delivering against JIT requirements.

- Line Haul with an Intermediate Facility – This is a longer distance line that terminates in intermediate facility based on the operational strategy of the company. The Line Haul could terminate in a warehouse where the delivery time is most likely less frequent with larger loads that are then, separately, sent to the factory using a milk run that ships smaller amounts daily. In this case, time is not as critical. It could also be that the Line Haul terminates in a Cross Docking facility which would have a bit more time pressure to meet schedules so the loads

---

What is Dunnage?

Dunnage is a term that is used in general for any materials, pallets, or other containers that need to be returned to the supplier for re-use. Reusable totes, pallets, and other pre-made containers can be built to protect products are of unusual shapes or are delicate or they can be used to be more environmentally friendly and reduce costs over time.

Dunnage must be returned to suppliers which creates a transportation movement. If the milk run doesn't provide for a backhaul for dunnage return then carrier will propose an approach to returning dunnage and the cost to do so. Sometimes dunnage can be consolidated and instead of returned every day could be returned as little as once per week depending on customer needs.

could be consolidated with others and delivered on time.

- Intermodal Line Haul – In this scenario, we usually use either Truck Trailers or Containers and have them shipped via intermodal rail over longer distances to an intermediate facility; most likely a warehouse or distribution center. We do this to reduce the cost of long distance trucking, but this requires that the delivery is less frequent and that there is a milk run from the warehouse to the factory on a regular basis.

Transportation with Suppliers < 500 Miles Round Trip Distance

- <u>The milk run</u> – The milk run is so named from the home delivery milk routes popular in the 1950's and 1960's. Dairies would take orders the day before for a delivery the next morning. 99% of these orders were received by the delivery "milk man" when he delivered the milk and took them back to the home office for processing at the end of the shift. There are several characterizes of a transportation milk run including:

  o The distance between the supplier and destination is less than 200 miles.

  o The company uses reusable <u>dunnage</u> (empty trucks, pallets, etc.) that needs to be returned to re-fill for future deliveries.

  o Producing one Truck Load or less of required delivered goods per day. This is not a hard and fast rule. Some suppliers will use milk runs even if they are running twenty trucks a day. Companies with one truckload or less are the most efficient in terms of optimization of load size and equipment, consistent pickup and delivery times, 4and very strong on- time delivery capabilities. The basic milk run is often between one supplier and one destination (buyer). It would involve close to or at a truckload and would be picked up once per day and delivered within 60 minutes of being needed. This would allow the buyer, the next Tier of manufacturing, to have enough for one days of production which could be in the factor. This way, the next Tier holds effectively no excess inventory. The downside is that if the delivery is late, it shuts down the plant. Even with this, this milk run is used extensively in the MTO model. Figure 83 shows a simple depiction of this strategy. A daily milk run would be run five days per week for each week of a month.

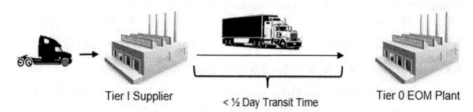

Tier I Supplier   < ½ Day Transit Time   Tier 0 EOM Plant

Figure 83. Single Supplier "Straight" Milk Run

Changes to the quantity of goods, provided they do not change the single truck configuration, are irrelevant to the transportation company because they most the same truck all the time. Many transportation companies that specialize in milk run transportation services only use the 53-foot dry van trailer, or a similar flat trailer for their runs regardless of order size. In this model a 53-foot trailer could carry five pallets or fifty and it wouldn't matter.

Most transportation companies that accept milk runs as a contract lane fix price the lane cost per run. This "all-in" price covers the pickup, delivery, and return of dunnage for one milk run. The flat rate also absorbs any surcharges, like equipment surcharges or fuel surcharges, unless it the surcharge is explicitly stated to be an allowable surcharge. Turning to the diagram, we see that with a milk run the transportation company arrives at the supplier at the pickup time specified. The plant will have completed production and loaded the trailer enabling the driver to check in at the entry gate, proceed to the dock area, check in with the shipping and dispatching team, review and complete paperwork, inspect the load, and then pick up the trailer and leave. This model is very efficient and often takes 15 to 30 minutes maximum from gate to exit.

The driver then proceeds to the destination the plant of the next Tier up. In our case we are showing the Tier I supplier to the Tier 0 assembly plant. At the assembly plant, the driver will perform a "drop and hook" operation to deliver the goods and then hook an empty trailer, or trailer filled with dunnage and leave.

From a transportation service level and supply chain delivery perspective, we are focused on the time the driver gets to the security gate at the supplier until the goods are delivered. Planning the timing of the lane is important to ensure the right service level. There will always be one piece of information provided and known: Time of Delivery. We will always know when we must have the goods at the next plant. Given this, we can back plan from that time to determine the pickup time. As an example:

o We need to determine the pickup time for a load that is a milk run between Crown Electronics and their customer Carleton Stereo Products. The required delivery time each day for delivery is 10:30 am. The company's policy is to allow for 15 minutes of flexibility on either side of the time. That's nice when needed but we will plan for the exact time as it will provided the most consistency in the delivery. To determine the pickup time, we can apply a very simple formula of:

Pickup Time = Delivery Time (military time) – Yard Time – Transit Time

NOTE: *Pick up time must assume the time it will take to get from their plant security gate to the plant dock for unloading.*

Yard Time *– yard time is the total elapsed time from the first check in at the security gate until the final release at the exit after the load has been pick up. Yard Time is expressed in minutes.*

Transit Time *– Transit time is the time required to complete the route from the time the driver has left the supplier to the gate of the destination plant with at least 90% confidence.*

With Crown and Carleton, the yard time at Crown Electronics averages 20 minutes and the transit time between the plants is 2 hours, or 120 minutes. We apply the formula above and get:

Pick up Time =

10:30 am, or 10:30 hrs – 15 minutes = 10:15 hrs – 2 hrs = 08:15 hrs, or **08:15 am**

In a just-in-time environment the milk run in any form is the most preferred approach to transportation. It has high reliability, expediting is rarely needed unless there is a production or supply problem, and the flat rate approach makes it easy to budget, plan, and manage.

- The consolidated milk run – The consolidated milk run uses the same construct as the milk run but uses a route approach to enable consolidation of multiple suppliers into one milk run lane. In addition, the previous characteristics defined in the milk run section, additional conditions must be met to consolidate.

- Total Volume Requirements – The primary goal of a consolidated milk runs is to combine multiple suppliers, all of whom cannot fill up a trailer on their own, to become part of the same lane that, when combined, equals a truckload, or a larger load than would be sent on their own.

- Distance and Drive Time - The inbound lane distance between the first supplier and subsequent suppliers to the final destination plant cannot exceed the legal driving limit based on hours of service for truck drivers. The current limit would have a consolidated milk run be no longer than driven, assuming traffic, congestion, etc., within an 11 hour period. The current estimate most used is around 600 miles total one way.

- Total yard time - The total yard time for all suppliers in the lane when combined cannot exceed four hours practically.

- Total Cycle Time – The cycle time combines the number of hours from the distance and drive time analysis plus the total time in hours of the total yard time. These two variables cannot exceed 14 hours under any circumstances and if the total is 14 hours, are encouraged to determine there is 100% confidence in both numbers ever being exceeded. Since the answer to this question can never be 100% (we're in transportation here folks! Noting is 100% guaranteed!), the real standard combines no more than 13 hours between yard time and total transit time. This should de-risk the plan sufficiently and if there is some other risk in addition, use 12 hours as the standard.

- Dunnage Return – In a consolidated milk run lane, dunnage return is most often considered as a separate transportation movement and is planned and executed as a separate lane; usually at a discount. Dunnage is more complex in a consolidated lane. Some suppliers may not use dunnage while others only use it. Some suppliers might go a week without returns while others may need it more often. Usually the carrier will work with the manufacturer involved in planning the milk run to develop an economical lane provided they provide the carrier flexibility to do so. Each supplier will typically be charged for return of dunnage which may be offset by the cost per unit of the product to the manufacturer.

The consolidated milk run works very similar to the single supplier, or "Straight" milk run. At the first pick up time, the driver arrives at the first supplier in the run. They check in at the security gate and then pick up the trailer which has been preloaded with the pallets in the back of the trailer. The truck then proceeds to the next supplier, checks in at the security gate, then waits at the loading dock while the goods are physically loaded in the trailer they brought. This process differs from the "drop and hook", or "drop and go" in that the driver must wait. When loading, this is a live-load. If the driver was dropping off a partial load, it would be called a live unload.

Because of the live load, the yard time for each supplier after the first will vary and will usually be higher than the first supplier. This process is continued until the last supplier loads their pallets in the truck and the truck proceeds to the next Tier manufacturing gate. We discussed how to determine the pickup time of the first supplier by knowing the delivery time, yard time, and transit time. We can apply this same idea to a multi-stop, or consolidated milk run. This can be expressed as a formula but is better as a function. The formula, which gives us some continuity from the first milk run formula would look like:

Supplier	Distance to OEM Plant	Distance to Crown	Distance to Fuse	Distance to Rodgers	Pallet's / Yard Time per Order	Weight per Order (lbs.)
Crown Electronics	110 Miles / 1 hr., 50 min.	N/A	135 Miles 2 hrs., 15 min.	110 Miles 1 hr., 50 min.	15 / 20 min.	7, 500
Fuse Batteries	78 Miles 90 min.	135 Miles 2 hrs., 15 min.	N/A	81 Miles 95 min.	26 / 60 min.	10,400
Rodger's Packaging	22 Miles 25 min.	110 Miles 1 hr., 50 min.	81 Miles 95 min.	N/A	9 / 10 min	2,700

Table 18. Distances, Transit Times, Load Size, Yard Time and Weight by Supplier

Besides Crown Electronics, Carleton Stereo also have two other suppliers. Carleton has increased the frequency of deliveries to keep their inventory space to a minimum. Because the order quantities will drop by 80%, they want to have all three suppliers (Crown Electronics, Rodgers Packaging Company, and Fuse Batteries Inc.) to be a part of a consolidated milk run. Carleton Stereo analyzed the load requirements of each supplier based on the data in Table 18.

This number had to be less than the maximum pallet count of the largest trailer available and the weight has to be less than the maximum weight allowed in the trailer. For our purposes, the largest trailer available is a 53 foot trailer with a maximum load capacity of fifty-two pallets double stacked with dimensions of 48 inches long x 40 inches wide by 48 inches tall, and a maximum weight capacity of 40,000 pounds for the entire load.

When analyzing our suppliers, we have a total pallet count of fifty pallets below the maximum of fifty-two pallets and a total weight of 20,600 pounds well below the 40,000 pounds of freight capacity. In analyzing the load this load will cube out, i.e. meet the maximum pallet count before it weighs out, i.e. exceeds the weight of the trailer with excess pallet capacity. Regardless, we find that all pallets will fit in the truck and meet weight requirements so we can make this a consolidated milk run.

The next question was which supplier would be the first suppler. To do this, they then looked at the locations of the suppliers and found that farthest to closest, Crown Electronics was the farthest away at 102 miles and two hours of transit time Fuse Batteries was next at 78 miles and ninety minutes of transit time. The distance between Crown and Fuse Batteries is 135 miles with a transit time of 2 hours and 15 minutes. Rodgers Packing is 22 miles with a transit time of 25 minutes to the manufacturing plant and 81 miles between Fuse and Rodgers with a transit time of 95 minutes.

Next, we look at distributing freight in the truck. For Crown, they are shipping fifteen pallets of goods and it will take about 20 minutes to load. Fuse is delivering twenty- six pallets of goods and it will take about 60 minutes to load due to fragility and volume. Rodgers is sending nine pallets of goods which takes about 10 minutes to load. Rodgers is fast because they have no security gate.

One of the most common ways to de-risk these lanes is by starting at the farthest supplier away from the factory. If we are farther away from the factory and encounter a delay, we can provide notice earlier than if our last leg was at the same distance. So, a problem with the truck or hitting congestion that happen farther away can be reported earlier in the run and dock schedules can be adjusted. Figure 84 shows the results of consolidating the lane from the farthest supplier. Each individual distance from the plant is listed along with the total mileage for the milk run. When computing it, the milk run is 238 miles and the original routes of all three was 210 miles.

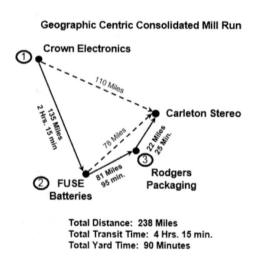

Figure 84. Geographically Centric Consolidated Milk Run

280

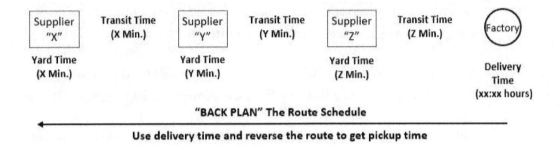

Figure 84. Geographically Centric Consolidated Milk Run

On the surface this may seem less efficient because the new route is longer than the old route. Remember, however, the milk run will operate one lane and one truck whereas the others required three lanes and three trucks. This reduces the cost of the entire network by between 60 and 70%. In terms of yard time, the combined time in this configuration for yard time is Crown

(20 min.) + Fuse (60 min.) + Rodgers (10 min) = 90 minutes.

To determine the pickup time, we apply a back-planning approach (see diagram below) that starts at the destination and then reverses the course by subtracting the various delivery and transit times of each supplier in reverse order.

Based on a three-supplier milk run, we would use the following:

Delivery Time (military time) – Yard Time - Transit Time

= Pickup Time (Supplier 3)

= Pickup Time (Supplier 3) – Yard Time – Transit Time (To Supplier 2)

= Pickup Time (Supplier 2) – Yard Time – Transit Time (To Supplier 1)

= Pickup Time (Supplier 1)

= Milk Run Pickup (Supplier 1) (Start Time)

As we see, there is the flexibility to have specific variables for each supplier's yard time and transit time which allows us to take into the time of a live load of many pallets, local traffic congestion, etc. We apply the formula above and get each supplier's pick-up time:

Delivery Time (OEM Plant) 13:30 hours – yard time (10 min.) – Transit time (25 minutes) = **Rodger's Packaging Pick up Time = 12:55 hours or 12:55 pm**

Delivery Time (Rogers) 1255 hours – yard time (20 min.) – Transit time (1 hr. 50 min.) = **Crown Electronics Pick up Time = 10:45 hours or 10:45 am.**

Delivery Time (Crown) 1045 hours – yard time (20 min) – Transit time (2 hours and 15 minutes = **Fuse Battery Pick up Time = 08:10 hours, or 8:10 am.**

If the company has a Transportation Management System, the system can do the planning we just completed using its route software for planning and for optimization.

In a just-in-time environment the milk run in any form is the most preferred approach to transportation. It has high reliability, expediting is rarely needed unless there is a production or supply problem, and the flat rate approach makes it easy to budget, plan, and manage. At the beginning of the section, we identified these strategies for lanes under 500 miles total distance. This would create close to a 12 – 14 hour day for the driver but would keep them below the hours of service. We are also estimating the average speed at 45 miles per hour rather than a normal sixty or higher for interstate driving because of the routes. Speed and time variables vary by situation so use the 500 miles as a rule of thumb.

Transportation with Suppliers > 500 Miles to 1,000 Miles Round Trip Distance

What happens if we go beyond 500 miles? We strain the standard milk run and its ability to have the driver complete the entire lane in a day. Would we do this? Absolutely. The different would be that the driver would make the deliveries in day one and then return back, likely returning dunnage, to home base in day two. This is best done when we can adjust the delivery schedule to twice per week. If it is required daily, then we'd need three drivers, one for Monday and Wednesday, one for Tuesday and Thursday, and one for Friday. The third driver would not return until Saturday which might require an additional surcharge, but often does not.

Because milk runs are typically same day, to maybe a second day they are popular with drivers. The pay is a little less than a traditional OTR driver but the hours are very advantageous getting the driver home every night usually or they are overnight only two nights out of the week.

Part of the assumptions we will make at this distance is that we will see more use of the US interstate system for transit. Because of this, we will likely see speeds that average around 55 miles per hour blended between long transit runs and using secondary roads for picking up and delivering goods. This increase the effective range of the truck making this feasible for a two day run. The milk run concepts will act the same, but the lane doesn't yield a daily run without the potential of more complexity and issues. Better, this distance is very good for twice per week deliveries where possible.

One of the other major factors in this distance when using a milk run strategy is that the dunnage, anything from an empty trailer to reusable totes, are returned as part of the backhaul of the lane. That keeps the milk run elements, especially the return of dunnage, in place. If dunnage cannot be returned, we would see this more as a line-haul because we must create a separate movement, as a primary haul, to get the dunnage back to the supplier.

Multi-supplier milk run consolidation also works at this distance with the lane typically moving backward on the back haul to deliver dunnage to the last supplier first and then proceeding until the final delivery of the trailer and dunnage to the first supplier.

Transportation with Suppliers > 1,000 Miles to 1,800 Miles One-way Trip Distance

As we get beyond 1,000 miles of round-trip distance, we stretch the just-in-time model to larger loads and less frequency. It is not unusual to have long distance runs from supplier to plant delivered once per week with one-way distances over 1,000 to 2,000 miles. Most OTR, or TL long distance driver's average between 2,000 and 2,500 miles per week. Because of

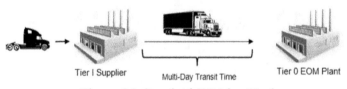

Tier I Supplier   Multi-Day Transit Time   Tier 0 EOM Plant

Figure 86. Standard JIT Line Haul

this, it is possible to have two deliveries per week at up to 2,000 miles one way.

This will consist of two line-hauls done by two drivers. This would be done as a straight line-haul lane that would provide an inbound lane for delivery. These lanes are straight forward line-hauls as depicted in Figure 86. As a line-haul, the carrier would dispatch a truck, so it allows them to meet the pickup time. This could be any driver based on schedule and availability. The driver shows up at the Tier 1 supplier, picks up the trailer and then proceeds over a few days to the OEM plant. They drop off the trailer and pick up an empty if available and if required. If they do pick up a trailer for return, it is returned to a local freight yard of the carrier rather than returned to the supplier who a few days away. Once received, the carrier then will accept the trailer and dispatch a trailer near a freight yard close to the supplier if they need one for loading. This method is called "trailer pooling" and makes the return and receipt of trailers much more efficient. Again, it's important to keep the following in mind when choosing this strategy:

- Because it is a line-haul, it must contain multiple days of production capability or the lane will become very costly

- If the transit time exceeds three days, JIT buyers may be challenged to meet actual production number meaning the plant will likely carry safety stock to ensure it has enough to produce

- Dunnage is generally returned as a separate back haul or new line-haul

- Trailer return is typically done with a carrier pooling technique

Transportation with Suppliers > 1,800 Miles One-way Trip Distance

Lanes beyond 1,800 miles break down the just-in-time model and its inherent efficiencies. The issue is order cycle time to delivery. Most JIT operations lock in their production schedule within three days of production. This means that production volume changes can occur up to three days before production. Last minute production changes change supplier order quantities either up or down depending on the change. If an order can be communicated to a downstream supplier by the morning of the third day before production, order changes can be accommodated. This is part of the flexibility of the milk run which can typically run daily, or every other day as the lane time is flexible enough to do this.

A three-day line-haul makes it possible if the pickup is in the afternoon and the order can be conveyed before they load the trailer. Beyond that, the order and the load are set and the supplier cannot accommodate a change when the order has left. Any lane longer than three does risks either having less material than needed or more material than they expected. Because of this, buyers must have a regular level of safety stock available that is at least four days of stock if not more. Further, they make incremental order changes to subsequent orders to get the stock back to the levels it needs to be.

This can create an <u>Accordion Effect</u> in the supply chain where the buy is constantly trying to either catch up or draw down stock to acceptable levels. Provided the change is only periodic, say a few times per month, this is manageable. If the production schedule changes with any regularity it becomes difficult to manage. When this happens, we need to either accept this, which happens, or we need to create compensating mechanism to better manage long distance lanes. This can be done in two different ways, but both require a facility between the supplier and the plant which will increase costs. The two methods are:

- <u>Employ Relay Terminals to swap out drivers</u> – Relay terminals for line-haul are becoming more popular as hours of service have become limited. This is usually done at the carrier level because it is an inefficient method for carriers unless the timing is precise enough to keep all the drivers in motion and being paid. Usually, relays are used more when one driver hits their total weekly service hours and a fresh, or one with enough hours left, can pick up the load and deliver it. Here, it would involve a "relay race" type of structure where a driver would hand off a load at the end of their daily hours of service to another driver etc. to enable total hours driven in a 24 hour than normally achieved by one driver. If the company has its own private fleet and can allow drivers to operate in zones strategic to the lanes, i.e. this is possible but still generally inefficient unless there is equal traffic going between the supplier and the destination plant so backhauls can be employed at the relay point to allow drivers to have loads both ways. This method is rarely, if ever employed simply because of the coordination and impact on drivers.

- Use cross docking at within one day's drive of the factory - cross docking allows us to sort and rearrange freight or simply pass it through as part of load transportation. In some ways, this is similar to the first option but here we mix in many drivers going to many places. A carrier or 3PL would have a cross docking facility within a day's drive of the factory. A driver on a three plus day run can encounter the cross dock around the end of day two. The load can immediately be passed through and loaded on a truck that will be bound for the manufacturing facility. This reduces the total cycle time from three or four days to two to three days. This is also possible but rarely done because it requires close coordination, it may incur additional charges because of the timing involved, it will include fees for the load transfers etc. and it doesn't solve the majority of the problem.

- Remove the distance through a local facility with daily milk runs – The most effective way to manage a long distance lane outside of the ordering window is to have those suppliers deliver to a local warehouse and then have the warehouse load trucks for daily milk runs to resolve the lack of flexibility issue. This comes at the cost of an additional facility, touching the freight at least twice, including loading trucks for the milk run, and paying for the local milk run. The warehouse could be owned by the manufacturing facility that receives the goods or it could be a third Party provider. The challenge is that the cost of the line-haul, which could be from $1,500 - $4,000 or more depending on distance, whether there is a cross-border involved, etc. and the added cost of the facility and the milk run.

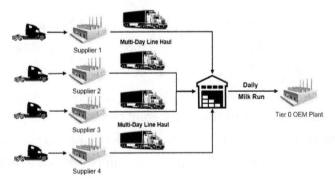

Figure 87. Using a Warehouse to Manage the Accordion Effect for Line Hauls over 1,800 Miles

285

What would this look like in practice? Let's look at an example that keeps the line-haul, has a frequency of a once per week delivery, and then uses a local warehouse to receive the goods and loads a truck for a milk run. First, as we are delivering one truck per week, the milk runs will be 1/5 (20%) of a truck. This means it can be consolidated with other loads or combined with other loads in the warehouse also line-hauls.

Let's continue our assumptions to keep things simple by saying we have four suppliers like this, all of whom need only 1/5 of a truck per day. All four suppliers could be combined into one milk run with no additional stops. Let's look at this the four-supplier perspective to see what happens to both cost and delivery. To simplify, we'll assume all four suppliers have the same distance and rate and therefore all four suppliers have the same line-haul cost. For our purposes we'll assume $4,500 cost per line with one delivery per week (which could be all on the same day or staggered to enable optimized staff in the warehouse. The milk run for one consolidated truck from the warehouse would cost $450 for the run and it would cost $150 to load the truck for a total cost of $500 per milk run. In addition, there is a storage cost for keeping the freight in the warehouse about $400 per week for all suppliers, or $100 per supplier (they got a good deal on that one).

When adding them up, the weekly costs would be:

- 4 lanes at $4,500 per lane = $18,000.

- One daily milk run that includes one consolidated truck, 5 times per week for ($500 * 5) = $2,500.

- Storage and Warehouse Fees of 4 * $100 per week or $ 400 per week.

- Total Cost per Week = $20,900.00 or $83,600 per month.

These are expensive lanes to begin with and with the added cost, they have become very expensive. What sticks out the most is the $18,000 of line-haul costs per week. That is effectively what it would have cost without this method, so the challenge is that we have added $2,900 per week to enable flexibility. This is a good thing from a production perspective because it allow us to keep the plants relatively empty of excess stock and it removes the accordion effect from the plant buyers to the warehouse. The warehouse can manage to specific stock levels and run replenishment based on actual inventory metrics with a little safety stock.

This take the pressure of the milk run, or plant side, and leaves a weekly line-haul for the supplier but at a cost to the unit price of the components or assemblies being shipped. If we employ this strategy, we want to reduce the cost much and we will look primarily at the mode of the line-haul to find cost improvements.

When we think about mode and just-in-time manufacturing, we almost always think about truck for its speed and flexibility. With our line-hauls over 1,800 miles, we can solve the transit time issues by using a warehouse and setting up a local milk run. That provides the speed and flexibility. Because of this, do we need the same flexibility and speed using truck for the line- haul? Not really. We need efficiency and strong on-time delivery weekly, or longer if we go to a shipping every other week approach. In our case, we're running one truck per week from four suppliers.

Truck makes sense for this, but the line-haul costs are high. Straight rail, traditional rail using large freight cars like box cars, could be an option provided the supplier and the warehouse both have rail access. Here they do not. This doesn't mean we can't use rail. Instead of straight rail we could consider intermodal rail as an option to reduce costs. The intermodal rail will change our mode and lane configuration from truck to rail. We will need a shuttle service to get goods from the factories to the intermodal yards and from the destination intermodal yards to the warehouse. For this example, we will do this once per week.

Figure 88 shows how this would work. Like the other approaches, we need a truck that can provide short distance shuttle service (each supplier has an Intermodal Yard within 100 miles of their location). The shuttle service must have a pickup time that allows the truck to travel to the intermodal rail yard before their contractual cutoff time for receipt of the trailer to ensure it will be posted on the train. In our case, the cutoff time is 8:00 pm on the shipment day. We also must understand what days this schedule runs. Sometimes, the supplier may only ship two or three times per week. Major lanes may be daily. We'll say ours are daily. Again, for simplicity, the transit times from each supplier to their individual intermodal yards is 90 minutes. Therefore, to meet the 8:00 pm

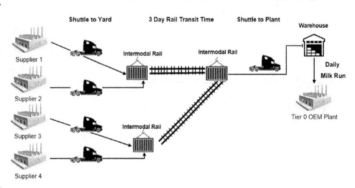

Figure 88. Using Mode Changes to Reduce Freight Cost

(20:00 hours) cutoff time of each location, the truck must pick up the load by 18:30 hours, or 6:30 pm. As a supplier, this is a little too close to the deadline, so each set the pickup time at 6:00 PM (18:00 hours). Let's assume we schedule each supplier to ship their goods on Thursday of each week. When will the goods arrive at the Tier 0 manufacturing facility?

Rail publishes its transit schedules to enable shippers to know exactly the cutoff time for a specific shipment lane and the rail schedule times, along with station stop times, from the origin point (Our first Intermodal Yard) to the destination freight yard, or in our case, Intermodal Yard. Note that virtually any Intermodal Yard could be used for intake of our freight from suppliers. 15-8 shows two yards for intake for simplicity, but it be up to four yards depending on supplier locations.

The destination, however, will always be one yard and that's the yard closest to the destination plant. For planning, we can use a simple rule of thumb to understand the number of days it will take from when the supplier releases it until it arrives at the warehouse. It is:

Day 1: Freight Pick up and Shuttle to Intermodal Yard – Our first day is always the day we put the freight into the system before its cutoff time

Day 2 – Day 4: 3 Day Rail Transit Time – In our case, the rail schedule indicates it will be in the rail freight system in-transit for three days. This also means that at the end of that day, it will arrive at the destination freight yard or Intermodal Yard.

Day 5: Having received the freight the night before, the shuttle service will now go to the Intermodal Yard and check in, pick up the trailer, or container, and then deliver it to the warehouse based on the warehouse dock scheduling time.

The rail transit time in our example in Figure 88 is three days. From the above we see those three days do not mean the delivery is complete in three days. We add an additional two days for this. The first additional day is for finishing the load and transporting to the rail point. The second additional day is for having the load coordinated to be delivered. Again, companies with TMS integrated to rail will manage this process for the shipper. Equally, calling the rail yard with an order will enable the shipper to have the specifics on the freight movement.

How does this affect the overall transportation cost? By moving from truck to intermodal rail, we should see reduced total shipping cost because we've balanced the need for speed and flexibility through the milk run so we can reduce the speed and flexibility to enable the use of rail. The intermodal rail rate will be $1.10 per mile for our shipment so we see a reduction in rate. The distance isn't necessarily the same because rail and truck distances vary. In our case, we are charged for 2,200 miles.

Again, for simplicity, the truck rate of $4,500 was based on base on 2,000 miles at $2.00 per mile plus 12.5% fuel surcharge. There is also a shuttle service we can use on both ends with each costing $200. For the intermodal shipment, the costs are:

- Base Freight at 2,200 miles at $1.10 per mile = $2,420

- Fuel Surcharge at 12.5% = $303.00

- Shuttle Service from supplier to Intermodal Yard = $200

- Shuttle Service from Intermodal Yard to Warehouse = $200

- Total lane Cost (Per supplier) = $3,123.00

- Four Lanes at $3,123 once per week = $12,492

- One daily milk run that includes one consolidated truck, 5 times per week for ($500 * 5) = $2,500

- Storage and Warehouse Fees of 4 * $100 per week or $ 400 per week

- Total Cost per Week = $15, 392.00 or $61,568 per month

Now that we have both numbers (4 truck line-hauls and four intermodal rail loads) we can evaluate the potential savings:

4 Truck Line-haul Costs (4 Week Month):	$ 83,600
4 Intermodal Rail Loads (4 Week Month):	<u>$ 61,568</u>
Savings of Intermodal over Truck Line-haul:	**$ 22,032 or over 26% savings**

The milk run is the most efficient approach to moving goods in a JIT environment, especially when each supplier can be consolidated into a smaller number of routes. As we go past the logical limits of distance and time, we depart from the milk run strategy and must move to a line-haul strategy. While this necessitates changes, we can still make a line- haul work for up to about 1,800 miles in a 3 day ordering window.

After we get past 1,800 miles we are in danger of breaking the JIT model that drives inventory and operational efficiency. We've seen that using an intermediary facility, like a warehouse close to the factory that can provide suppliers at distance with an effective milk run can work, at a price. Adding an intermediate facility between the suppliers at distance and the destination manufacturing facility is valuable to operations and timing but increases costs that need to be offset. The best way to do this is to look to a mode switch. By having an intermediate facility in place, the move to slow down the supply chain between that facility and suppliers while maintaining a fast and flexible milk run between the warehouse and the plant. This enables us to look to rail (standard or intermodal) as way to reduce our lane costs to not only absorb the warehousing costs but to add cost savings.

We've covered most of the impact of the lean, or just-in-time model on transportation and need to cover one other category: Dunnage and Demurrage.

Managing Dunnage and Avoiding Demurrage in Equipment Return

When looking at the lean and JIT models that lead us to MTO manufacturing, we find that standardization of processes, equipment, production, inventory management and transportation all play a big role in driving the synergies and efficiencies into the system. Many companies will employee specialized equipment to pack and ship their goods to protect them and make it easy to get access to use them in production. These "reusable totes" help drive quality and efficiency and must be returned to the supplier that uses them for packing and shipping. In addition, the trailers, rail cars, intermodal containers and other similar equipment must be returned to the carrier within a reasonable time period. If they don't, they may charge the company for holding on to its equipment for too long.

Carriers of all kinds require their primary equipment back within a short time of the equipment being provided. This is true of truck trailers where the expectation is that the truck will be unloaded within an hour and ready for the trailer to be picked up by the carrier. Trucks not unloaded and available for pick up by the specified time are subject to demurrage (di-mur-age) charges. Carriers that charge demurrage charges for trucking typically charge by the hour and the rates can be from $25 per hour to $200 or more per hour or, in rail and maritime, by the day. At the same times, deliveries get backed up and not all deliveries are needed immediately. Some of this can be negotiated but generally, the carriers need their equipment back. Similarly, drivers hate waiting because many companies don't pay them when they wait, only when driving.

So, we have two needs. The first is to get the dunnage back to the supplier. The second is to ensure we have the equipment back to the carrier within the negotiated time or we'll be charged for demurrage. Depending on the transportation strategy, some techniques used help eliminate the issue. In other instances, the issue becomes a problem. We'll look at this issue from the two core strategies we use: The milk run and its consolidated cousin and line- haul and its variants.

- Milk Run and consolidated milk run – The approach to a milk run, a daily or several times per weeks shipment from suppliers relatively close to the factor creates efficiency for the MTO model and it also helps us set up for dunnage return and to avoid demurrage costs. When a truck arrives with a milk run shipment, they will check in with the delivery, park it at the dock or at a designated space and then drop and hook the load to pick up an empty trailer, or if dunnage is used, a trailer filled with dunnage for the supplier. The truck can complete the round trip of the milk run and drop off both the trailer and the dunnage to the supplier so they can almost immediately use the trailer and dunnage to load the trailer for the next day, although more likely the third day out because they will have what they need for the next day. This creates a very simple and "round trip" process for both the shipper and receiver and the carrier. Sometimes, the carrier terminal is close enough or the delivery time is later in the afternoon, so it doesn't make sense to return to the supplier that day.

There, the driver can park the trailer in the carrier's yard and then pick it up in the morning and return it when they arrive for their daily milk run pick up. Either way, this creates a closed loop system where the only time there could be demurrage is if the empties aren't ready when the shipments arrive.

Consolidated milk runs can happen in a similar way but also may be more complex; especially if the total transit time exceeds five hours one way. The only real variation between a single milk runs and consolidated milk runs are the number of stops involved. Each stop, however, has a supplier that may use a different tote and each supplier will also have a different quantity of pallets they ship. The dunnage needs to be returned to the supplier for both the right equipment and the right number of pieces of equipment. As there is only one truck involved mostly, returning the trailer, i.e. picking up an empty still applies to avoid demurrage.

The bigger challenge with a consolidated milk run is the return of dunnage. It is not effective to bring a full truck of dunnage to a first supplier and then have them load their pallets in the front of the truck and then leave the dunnage in to be returned. This creates a large time drain at all supplier facilities as they work to manipulate the load by unloading their dunnage, loading their load and then re-loading the dunnage for the next supplier. Because of this, a drop and hook at the destination with a single trailer return to the first supplier is not a good method. Most of the time, a multi-supplier consolidated milk run needs to have a backhaul to return the dunnage in reverse order of the milk run. The destination plant can load the dunnage into the trailer with the first supplier in the front, the second supplier in the middle and so on until the last supplier in the milk run is loaded in the back of the truck.

When the driver arrives at the designation and performs a drop and hook, they then reverse their route and go back to the suppliers in reverse order (supplier 3 to supplier 2 to supplier 1 where they do a live unload of dunnage). Even this is not efficient, but it does work and the value of the milk run and the savings make this a feasible approach.

- Line-haul – When we encounter a line-haul, we lose the ability to make dunnage return part of the standard route. This is because the distance is so great that to return the trailer and one load of dunnage would make the lane cost very expensive. So, how is this handed? The most common ways are trailer pooling and dunnage return loads. Trailer Pooling allows us to use a local return of a trailer equal a full return to the supplier. Carriers need their trailers everywhere and every day the trailers are moving, being dispatched, checked in, etc. So, when a line-haul is finished, IF the driver doesn't need the empty trailer for their next run, then they return the trailer to the local carrier terminal. There, the trailer is checked in and the driver is released to his next route. Once the trailer is checked in at the local terminal, this information becomes available to all freight terminals. The terminal that serves the supplier will get an acknowledgement of return and will then authorize a dispatch of an empty trailer to the supplier. This approach is very common because of the large number of long-distance lanes and the velocity of shipping on any day in the US.

Dunnage is a different matter. For long distance suppliers that use dunnage in reusable totes or pallets, the challenge gets that equipment back to the supplier so it can be reused. As we mentioned earlier, many reusable totes and pallets are relatively small and purpose built and most will conform to the 40"x 48" standard pallet dimensions unless it is impossible. Because of this, many totes are specially built pallets moldings that fit the product to the pallet to increase its security and to keep things from moving into each other and there's more. When unloaded, this pallet may be as short as four to six inches in height. You could stack twenty of these pallets on top of each other and still not be at the top of most dry vans. Assuming even double stacking a trailer with, say, forty-eight pallets for a standard load, the dunnage load could accommodate around nineteen full loads before it fills a truck with dunnage. For a weekly line-haul, this would be about 19 weeks of loads. So, when we need to return dunnage to the long distance supplier, we can do so on a much less frequent basis. Even on a once per quarter, or 12 week period, the company is only paying for four additional routes per year out of the twenty-four it will run. This is still 25% more loads than otherwise.

The question that companies consider is does the cost of the four loads outweigh the value of the reusable equipment. Sometimes the answer is yes but the company has no choice and therefore must absorb the cost or pass it on. Other times, the company ends the reusable totes due to the cost and return to traditional materials. Companies that do this often also add a pallet switching service that refreshes pallets, send broken ones to be fixed and recycles those at the end of their usable life.

SUMMARY

MTS is an important model in global commerce. Mass production has been tuned, optimized, and driven by a bulk model of large production that can efficiently manage large volumes of inventory and offset these costs with transportation planning and execution using slower modes of the supply chain where possible to keep costs low. Where needed, they also have a modern platform of technology and networks that allow them to marry the slow bulk modes with the fast and flexible VMI trucking environment. Those brands that master that trade-off will outperform the market year after year.

Lean / JIT Manufacturing have created a world of fast supply chains and demand-oriented production for demand-oriented consumption. Companies whose business model supports this can create optimized and highly efficient systems to produce and deliver product the lowest possible cost with some of the best quality to in the world. To do this, these companies rely on an expertly coordinated flow of goods constantly shifting and changing. Transportation strategies that enable low volume order and delivery on a frequent basis create an efficient use of inventory and space. It comes at the cost of transportation as a trade-off to inventory. Companies that can manage the many variations of suppliers, lanes, consolidation opportunities and mixing modes where possible will own the most efficient supply chains in the world and will have a major competitive advantage.

LIST OF FIGURES

LIST OF TABLES

INDEX

TABLE OF ABBREVIATIONS

ABC	(80/20 Approach to Inventory)
ACH	Automated Cash Handling
AEO	Authorized Economic Operator
AES	Automated Export System
AREMA	American Railway Engineering and Maintenance-of-Way Association
ATS	Automated Targeting System
B&O	Baltimore and Ohio
BCR	Benefit Cost Ratio
BLS	Bureau of Labor and Statistics
BNSF	Burlington Northern Santa Fe
CAB	Civil Aeronautics Board
CBOE	Chicago Board of Exchange
CBP	Customs Bureau Protection
CDL	Class A Driver's License
CIF	Cost Insurance and Freight
CFR	Cost and Freight
CFR	Code of Federal Regulations
CIA	Central Intelligence Agency
COFC	Container on Flat Car
COO	Chief Operating Officer
CPFR	Collaborative Planning, Forecasting, and Replenishment
CPM	Certification Project Manager
CPT	Carriage Paid To
CSCMP	Council on Supply Chain Management Professionals
CSX	CSX Railroad
CRM	Customer Relationship Management
CTK	Cargo Ton Kilometer
DAT	Delivery at Terminal
DAP	Delivery at Place
DDP	Delivery Duty Paid
DHS	Dept. of Homeland Security
DOD	Department of Defense
DOT	Department of Transportation
DWT	Dead weight tonnage
EDI	Electronic Data Interchange
ELD	Electronic Logging Devices
EPA	Environmental Protection Agency
ERP	Enterprise Requirements Planning
EXIM	Export-Import Bank

FAA	Federal Aviation Administration
FAK	Freight of All Kinds
FAS	Free Along Ship
FBI	Federal Bureau of Investigation
FCA	Free Carrier
FDR	Franklin Delano Roosevelt
FEIN	Federal identification number
FEMA	Federal Emergency Management Agency
FMC	Federal Maritime Commission
FMCSA	Federal Motor Carrier Safety Administration
FOB	Free on Board
FRA	Federal Railroad Administration
FTC	Federal Trade Commission
FTK	Freight Ton per Kilometer
FTL	Full Truck Load
GAAP	Generally Acceptable Account Practices
GDP	Gross Domestic Product
GHG	Green House Gas
GMDSS	Global Marine Distress Safety System
GSP	Global Safety Plan
GVWR	Gross Vehicle Weight Rating
Hazmat	Hazardous Material
ICAO	International Civil Aviation Organization
ICC	Interstate Commerce Commission
IDIQ	Indefinite Quantity
IFTA	International Fuel Tax Agreement
IMO	International Maritime Organization
INS	Immigration and Naturalization Services
IRP	International Registration Plan
IRR	Internal Rate of Return
IPO	Initial Public Offering
IT	Information Technology
JIT	Just-In-Time
LAC	Less than air cargo
LCK	Rickenbacker Airport
LCL	Less than Container
LCV	Longer Combination Vehicles
LGC	Livingston Grain CO-OP
LLP	Lead Logistics Providers
LNG	Liquid natural gas
LOC	Latter of Credit

LTC	Less Than Container	SEO	Search Engine Optimization
LTL	Less than load	SKU	Stock Keeping Units
LST	Landing Ship, Tank	SOLAS	Safety of Life at Sea
NAICS	North American Industry Classification System	STB	Surface Transportation Board
		STAT	STAT Trade Times (Airline Statistics Web Site)
NMFTC	National Motor Freight Transportation Commission	STCC	Standard Transportation Commodity Code
MARAD	Maritime Administration		
MEL	Minimum Equipment List	TBO	Time Between Overhaul
MP&L	Materials Planning and Logistics	TEU	Twenty Foot Equivalent Unit
MTO	Make-to-Order	TL	Truckload
MTS	Make-to-Stock	TMS	Transportation Management System
NEPA	National Environmental Policy Act	TOFC	Trailers on Flat Car
NMFTA	National Motor Freight Transportation Association	TPC	Train Performance Calculator
		TSA	Transportation Security Administration
NS	Norfolk Southern	TSP	Transportation Service Providers
NSA	National Security Agency	UP	Union Pacific Railroad
NTS	National Targeting System	UPS	United Parcel Service
NTSB	National Transportation Safety Board	US	United States
OCC	Omni-Channel Commerce	VLOC	Very Large Ocean Carriers
OEM	Original Equipment Manufacturer	VMI	Vendor Managed Inventory
OOIDA	Owner-Operator Independent Driver's Association		
OSRA	Ocean Shipping Reform Act		
OTR	Over the Road		
PASI	Pre-Application Statement of Intent		
PAX	Wide-Body Passenger Airlines		
PHMA	Pipeline and Hazardous Material Administration		
PHMSA	Pipeline and Hazardous Materials Safety Administration		
PIC	Person in Charge		
PRB	Powder River Basin		
PTC	Positive Train Control		
PUD	Pickup and Delivery Terminal		
PUP	Truck Trailer between 26 and 29 feet in length		
RFID	Radio Frequency Identification Device		
RFP	Request for Proposal		
RFQ	Request for Quote		
ROI	Return on Investment		
S&OP	Sales and Operations Planning		
SARTS	Search and Rescue Transponders		
SAS	Safety Assurance System		

Printed in the USA
CPSIA information can be obtained
at www.ICGtesting.com
LVHW072121211123
764347LV00040B/1019